Sustainable Development
and
Mining
in **Sierra Leone**

Sustainable Development

and

Mining

in Sierra Leone

Priscilla Schwartz

PNEUMA SPRINGS PUBLISHING UK

First Published 2006
Published by Pneuma Springs Publishing

Sustainable Development and Mining in Sierra Leone
Copyright © 2006   Priscilla Schwartz
ISBN10: 1-905809-05-0
ISBN13: 978-1-905809-05-9

Cover design, editing and typesetting by:
Pneuma Springs Publishing

A Subsidiary of Pneuma Springs Ltd.
230 Lower Road, Belvedere Kent, DA17 6DE.
E: admin@pneumasprings.co.uk
W: www.pneumasprings.co.uk

A catalogue record for this book is available from the British Library.

To my husband and children; Schlomo, Nathanaella and Sharon

ABSTRACT

The conflicts between pursuing mining activities to foster economic development and protecting the environment in which such activities take place is a recurring dilemma for mineral reliant countries like Sierra Leone. The concept of sustainable development was designed on the international platform to ameliorate such dilemmas. The concept functions as an arbiter to reconcile biases between developmental goals and environmental objectives, by advocating an integration of one in the other. This book presents sustainable development as valuable recipe, by which mining ventures could be pursued as an economic imperative (to meet the needs of present and future generations), while protecting the environment and its components in the pursuit of such developments.

The book begins with an introduction into mining in Sierra Leone. It illustrates the international breeding of sustainable development in environmental protection (as oppose to economic development), and emphasise the importance of sustainability principles for sound legal and policy guidance at the national level. It also establishes the applicability of the concept to mineral resource developments generally. Mineral-specific laws and other legal controls in Sierra Leone are then examined as a case study; their sustainability content is ascertained and their capacity as a legal regime to direct or achieve sustainable mining in that country is explored. Finally, aspects of implementation of sustainable development in Sierra Leone's mining and its domestic implications are examined.

This work shows that despite the definitional questions, sustainable development has direct and primary relevance for environmental protection in the economic exploitation of natural resources. It identifies a legal character in the concept beyond legislative processes, and a flexibility in its principles that allows for their interpretation within legal rules to enhance environmental protection at the national level. It also illustrates the link between effective implementation and ensuring sustainable mining.

TABLES OF CONTENTS

ACKNOWLEDGMENTS

I thank God for having kept me under his watchful guidance and for imbibing me with the wisdom and understanding needed to achieve this project.

I would like to acknowledge my debt and profound gratitude to Professor Malgosia Fitzmaurice of Queen Mary, University of London for giving me initial direction on the research topic of "Sustainable Development". She also gave me constant motivation to reach limits of research capability I did not believe was possible and was always supportive of my efforts. This project could not have been completed on schedule without her.

I am especially beholden and extremely indebted to my husband Schlomo Schwartz and daughters Nathanaella and Sharon for their sacrifices, dedication and love, which cannot be expressed in words. They have being very understanding of my desire to embark on this research in the United Kingdom and Sierra Leone and never once made me feel guilty for being away from them in order to fulfil my ambition. Schlomo's love, understanding and sole support in meeting all my needs and financial commitments on this project has been invaluable, not to mention his important and constructive comments upon some of the ideas that I was developing on the project. I am eternally grateful.

My thanks and appreciation also go to my mother Mrs. Patience Fofana and my in-laws Isaac and Pircha Schwartz for their support and care over my daughters, without which I would not have been able to confront my research exigencies and accomplish this task.

I would like to thank Justice N. Matturrie-Jones, Solicitor General Tunde E. Cole, Valesius V. Thomas, Professor Victor Strasser-King (USL) and Andrew Keilli who gave me important reflections upon my chapters on the Laws of Sierra Leone. I would also like to acknowledge the assistance of officials of the Law Officers' Department, officials of the Mininstries of Mines, Environment, Health, Development, Planning and Forestry, the representatives of mining companies and NGOs. Without their support I would not have been able to access important documents or obtain in-depth insight into various issues dealt with in this work.

The views expressed in this book are entirely mine and do not represent views of the Government of Sierra Leone.

LIST OF ABBREVIATIONS

ARMD/SL- Annual Report of Mines Department Sierra Leone

ADF- Agricultural Development Funds

ASEAN- Association of Southeast Asian Nations

ADMS- Alluvial Diamond Mining Scheme

BSC- Bethlehem Steel Corporation

BYIL- British Yearbook of International Law

BP- British Petroleum Minerals International

BSL- Bank of Sierra Leone

BSLER- Bank of Sierra Leone Economic Review

BIC- Bank Information Center USA

CAO- Compliance Advisory Ombudsman

CBA- Cost- Benefit Analysis

CBAN- Community Biodiversity Action Network

CBD- Convention on Biological Diversity

CCF- Chief Conservator of Forests

CCSL- Conservation Society Sierra Leone

CHECSIL-Council for Human Ecology Sierra Leone

CEL- Commission on Environmental Law

CDF- Community Development Funds

CDAP- Community Development Action Plan

CITES- Convention on International Trade in Endangered Species of Wild Fauna and Flora

CIMRD- Commonwealth Institute Mineral Resource Department

CR- Corporate Responsibility

CSD- Commission on Sustainable Development

CSO- Central Selling Office

CPU- Central Planning Unit

CUP- Cambridge University Press,

DACDF- Diamond Area Community Development Fund

DoM- Director of Mines

DDoM- Deputy Director of Mines

DoE- Director of Environment

DAA- Development Assistance Agencies

DO- District Officer

DWRD- Department of Water Resource Development

DG- Director General

DELCO- the Sierra Leone Development Company

DCSL- Diamond Corporation Sierra Leone

DSPWP- Diamond Sector Policy Workshop Paper

DGS- Director of Geological Surveys

EAMP- Environmental Assessment of Mining Projects

EB- Environmental Board

EC- European Community

ECDP- Environmental Community Development Plan

ED- Environmental Department

EHSG- Environmental Health and Safety Guidelines

EIA- Environmental Impact Assessment

EIAP- Environmental Impact Assessment Procedures

EIR- Extractive Industry Review

ELQ- Environmental Law Quarterly

EMP- Environmental Management Plan

EMR- Environmental Monitoring Report

EMS- Environmental Management System

EPA- Environmental Protection Act

EPL- Environmental Policy and Law

ES- Environmental Statement

ESCAP- Economic and Social Commission for Asia and the Pacific

ESIA- Environmental Social Impact Assessment

EU- European Union

Eur Envt'l LR – European Environmental Law Review

Eur LR- European Law Review

FIELD- Foundation for International Environmental Law and Development

FAO- Food and Agricultural Organisation

FBC- Fourah Bay College

GATT- General Agreement on Tariffs and Trade

GNP- Gross National Product

GOSL- Government of Sierra Leone

GVWC- Guma Valley Water Company

GEF- Global Environmental Facility

GDO - Government Diamond Office

GGDO- Government Gold and Diamond Office

GSD- Geological Survey Division

GIR- Gross International Reserves

GNI- Gross National Income

HRLJ -Human Rights Law Journal

ICED-International Covenant on Environment and Development (Draft Covenant)

ICMM- International Council for Mining Metals

IMBO- Institute of Marine-Biology & Oceanography

IBP-International Best Practice

IPVS- International Private Voluntary Standards

IBA-International Bar Association

ICEL-International Council of Environmental Law

ICJ-International Court of Justice

ICCPR- International Covenant on Civil and Political Rights

ICESCR-International Covenant on Economic, Social and Cultural Rights

ICLQ- International Comparative Law Quarterly

IFC- International Finance Corporation

ILA- International Law Association

ILA-TEEL- ILA Transnational Enforcement of Environmental Law (Committee)

ILC- International Law Commission

ILM- International Legal Materials

IMF- International Monetary Fund

ISO- International Standards Organisation

ITLOS- International Tribunal for the Law of the Sea

IUCN- International Union for Conservation of Nature

ICS- Institute of Commonwealth Studies

JEL-Journal of Environmental Law

KHL- Koidu Holdings Limited

KPCS Kimberley Process Certification Scheme

KPML- Koidu Kimberlite Project Mining Lease (Modification and Ratification) Act 2002

LDC- Least Developed Country

LSM- Lead Sector Ministry

MAI-Multilateral Agreement on Investments

MAFFS- Ministry of Agriculture, Forestry and Food Sufficiency

MAB- Minerals Advisory Board

MDEP- Ministry of Development and Economic Planning

MDBs- Multilateral Development Banks

MEAs- Multilateral Environmental Agreements

MIGA- Multilateral Investment Guarantee Agency

MLHCPE- Ministry of Lands, Housing, Country Planning and the Environment

MMSD- Mining Minerals and Sustainable Development

MNCs- Multinational Corporations

MNEs- Multinational Enterprises

MOX- Mixed Oxide

MoM- Ministry of Mines

MPA- Model Petroleum Agreement

MPSL- Mineral Potential of Sierra Leone

NDMC- National Diamond Mining Company (SL) Ltd

NMJM- National Movement for Just Mining SL Ltd

NAAEC- North American Agreement on Environmental Cooperation

NAFTA- North American Free Trade Area

NBP- National Biodiversity Plan

NEAP/SL- National Environmental Action Plan of Sierra Leone

NEB- National Environmental Board

NEC-National Environmental Council

NEF- National Environmental Fund

NEP- National Environmental Policy

NEPA- National Environmental Protection Act 1969 (US)

NIEO- New International Economic Order

NGOs- Non- Governmental Organisations

NRC- Nords Resources Corporation

OAU- Organisation of Africa Unity (African Union)

OECD- Organisation for Economic Co-operation and Development

OPIC- Oversees Private Investment Corporation

OUP- Oxford University Press

OTI-Office of Transition Initiatives

PAC- Partnership Africa Canada

PCDP- Public Consultation Disclosure Plan

PCEC-Project Classification Evaluation Criteria

PDA- Peace Diamond Alliance

PEPA- Petroleum Exploration and Production Act

POI- Plan Of Implementation

PRU- Petroleum Resource Unit

PRSP- Poverty Reduction Strategy Paper

PPGC-Pittsburgh Plate Glass Company

PSPMS- Policy Support Planning for the Mining Sector (Report of)

PMMC- Precious Minerals & Metals Company (SL) Ltd

PRPDP-Progress Report on Diamond Policy and Development Program

RSO- Reserve Settlement Officer

SIEROMCO- Sierra Leone Ore and Metal Company

SLST- Sierra Leone Select Trust

SALWACO- Sierra Leone Water Company

SCM- Small-Scale Mining

SNR- Strict Nature Reserve

SRA- Sierra Rutile Agreement (Ratification) Act 2002

SRL- Sierra Rutile Limited

SL.Env.IB - Sierra Leone Environmental Bulletin

SLDPS- Sierra Leone Diamond Policy study

SACEP- South Asia Co-operative Environmental Programme

TCPA-Town and Country Planning Act

TNE-Transnational Enterprises

UDHR- Universal Declaration of Human Rights

UN- United Nations

UNIDO- United Nations Industrial Development Organization

UNCTAD- United Nations Commission for Trade and Development

UNCED- United Nations Conference on Environment and Development

UNCHE- United Nations Conference on Human Environment

UNCLOS- United Nations Convention on Law of the Sea

UNDP- United Nations Development Programme

UNECE- United Nations Economic Commission for Europe

UNESC- United Nations Economic and Social Council

UNEP- United Nations Environmental Programme

UNYB- United Nations Yearbook

UNRFNRE- United Nations Revolving Fund for Natural Resources

Exploration

UNFCCC - United Nations Framework Convention for Climate Change

US/NEPA- United States National Environmental Protection Agency

USAID- United States Assistance for International Development

USD- United States Dollars

VIs- Voluntary Initiatives

WBCSD- World Business Council for Sustainable Development

WCA- Wild Life Conservation Act 1978

WCED- World Commission on Environment and Development (Brundtland Report)

WCN- World Charter for Nature

WCS- World Conservation Strategy

WCB- Wildlife Conservation Branch

WCU- World Conservation Union (IUCN)

WCPA- World Council for Protected Areas

WSSD- World Summit on Sustainable Development

WTO –World Trade Organisation

WDR- World Development Report

YB Int Env L- Yearbook of International Environmental Law

INTRODUCTION

(i) General Overview

Mineral resource development in Sierra Leone is inextricably linked with issues ranging from political choices, international influences, economic imperatives, social and environmental concerns. Underlying these linkages is an apparent conflict between pursuing mineral exploitation on the one hand, so as to accelerate economic development in the country, and to afford protection of environments in which mining activities are undertaken. The general pattern of resolving the apparent conflict has been an economic bias in favour of the pursuit of uncontrolled and largely exploitative mineral development ventures, at the expense of the natural and community environment. Sierra Leone had paid little or no attention to protecting its natural, social and cultural environment throughout over seven decades of mining activities. The result is one of environmental degradation, over-exploitation of renewable and non-renewable resources alike, and a pollution of poverty. Such consequences contradict the objectives of the pursued economic development, and have left decision makers in untold dilemma as to how to address this fundamental conflict.

The concept of sustainable development was designed on the international platform to ameliorate such dilemma that is often pervasive in third world mineral rich countries like Sierra Leone, and provides guidance on resolving economic and environmental conflicts. Emerging as an arbiter between the pursuit of economic development and environmental protection, 'sustainable development' effects to reconcile the differences between these two distinct and separate ideologies, by advocating an integration of one in the other. The concept should inform and direct economic and environmental goals at a cross-disciplinary level, based on two important realisations: First, that any development strategy, plan, programme or activity (including mining related ones) must recognise the importance of the environment and the functions it performs in present and future societal developments.

Second, that the formulation and application of environmental policies, laws, rules and precepts should consider economic and social developmental perspectives. As a concept therefore, sustainable development presents a valuable prescript by which development activities (especially mining), could be pursued as an economic imperative to meet the needs of present and future generations, while respecting and maintaining the integrity and quality of the environment and protecting its components in the conduct of such activities.

It is this defining character of sustainable development in international law[1] that has inspired the writer to examine the concept in detail to establish its value for regulating development activities for environmental and social sustainability.

Chapter one presents a background introduction into mining in Sierra Leone. Chapters two and three examine the evolution of the concept of sustainable development from its international orientation, and reveal its primary relevance and purpose for environmental protection in the economic exploitation of natural resources. Relevant principles of the concept that are deemed fundamental for legal and policy guidance in effecting sustainable *activities* (as opposed to economic development agendas) will be examined. The methods by which these principles can be implemented at the national level will also be illustrated. In order to establish the value of the concept for environmental protection in natural resource exploitation, chapters 4 to 6 would specifically apply sustainable development in international law to mining, using Sierra Leone's mining industry as a case study. A cross-section of the country's laws will be examined for relevant sustainability principles and the context in which their formulation, interpretation and application would afford sustainable mining ventures in that country will be established. Chapter 7 will investigate the efforts at implementing sustainability objectives within legal and policy dictates to regulate mining in Sierra Leone and chapter 8 presents the conclusion.

(ii) The Purpose of this Book

The aim of this work is to analyse the concept of sustainable development in international law (including its principles) and impress its importance for sound legal and policy guidance in protection of mining environment in Sierra Leone. It is an international consensus that 'poverty and environmental degradation are closely interrelated'.[2] Therefore it has been recommended that environmental protection in developing countries must be viewed as an integral part of development processes.[3]

The concept of sustainable development was to impress this interrelationship and integration and was further to be promoted at the national level by *inter*

[1] That is, the regulation of development activities for social and environmental sustainability.

[2] See the Preamble to Resolution 44/228: UNCED (GA Res.44/228; 1989).

[3] *Report of the WSSD* (Johannesburg, South Africa,26 August t- 4 September 2002) Cf. UN Doc A/ CONF. 199/L6 (2 September 2002), paras. 163

alia, enacting and enforcing clear and effective laws that support sustainable development.[4]

Upon this premise, and recognising the constraints in applying general international environmental obligations to control mining in Sierra Leone,[5] the concept of sustainable development is considered as providing a better alternative for integrating environmental issues into development processes and ensuring environmental protection. Through its elements and principles the concept effects to impose some constraints on developers and development processes, including those who regulate them, in order to ensure the proper utilisation and management of environmental resources and overall protection of development environments. The principles advocated by the doctrine are flexible, practicable and more compatible with local application and my aim is to show that it is more convenient to adopt, implement or interpret these objectives within legal and policy precepts, to foster environmental protection at the national level.

Sierra Leone's mining industry is thus selected as a case study to examine the influence of the concept on selected laws and agreements, and how they can enhance the mining environment for the benefit of present and future generations.

This book appreciates that the concept of sustainable development embraces more than just maintaining the balance between economic development and environmental protection, but informs a wider agenda.[6] But this wider dimension which encompasses sustainable development of societies, does not fall within the scope of this work. Further discounted is a specific discourse on the application of general international environmental law in regulating or controlling mining in Sierra Leone. However, applicable conventions will be alluded to where necessary, though the primary purpose is to present the values in the principles of sustainable development for regulation of development activities.

Overall, the thematic emphasis in this work is on the environmental dimension of sustainable development, which for purposes of this book is considered to include both the natural, social and cultural environment, based on the interrelationships and interaction that exist between people and

---

[4] WSSD *(ibid).*

[5] The writer is aware of the limitations in applying international law generally in Sierra Leone, since in spite of Sierra Leone's accession or signatory capacity to a host of international environmental conventions, principles and customs (multilateral and regional), it has ratified very few of these and even so, still remains to effect their application through the required implementing legislation.

[6] For an insight into some of these issues see Agenda 21, Programme of Action for Sustainable Development; *Report of the* UNCED, 1 (1992) A/CONF. 151/26/Rev. 1, (1992) 31 *ILM* 874; see also WCED, *Our Common Future,* OUP, Oxford, 1987 (Brundtland Report); Some of the diverse developmental objectives relate to international trade, financial transfers, population control, poverty eradication, food security, economic growth *etc. etc.*

other environmental materials, components and beings during conduct of development activities. Throughout this work therefore, wherever the terms 'natural' and 'social' are omitted, these should be implied in the term 'environment'. Also references to 'sustainable development' must be understood in the context of its formulation and orientation in international law, and in relation to some defined set of principles relevant for guiding development activities to sustainability.

(iii) Why the Choice of the Mining Industry in Sierra Leone

Sierra Leone is a developing low-income country, considered to be the poorest and least developed country in the world according to the World Bank development and economic indicators.[7] But the country is stated to have impressive minerals potential and has persistently sought development through the conduct of mining operations for over 70 years.[8] Evidently, the reliance on mining has not brought about the desired objective but it has, and continues to wrought severe environmental degradation and adverse social consequences.[9] Mining however still remains on the top of the country's development agenda, and therefore, the 'environment in development' paradigm of sustainable development becomes very vital to mining in Sierra Leone, if it is to be sustained over time, to fulfil the needs of the present and future members of the country, within a sound and healthy environment.

(iv) Methodology

As this thesis is predominantly a legal research with aspects of it grounded in theoretical as well as practical analysis, the methodology used is based on documentary research (of texts and internet resources), undertaking field trips and conducting interviews. In respect of the former, academic works, international agreements, 'soft law' instruments and reports relating to

---

[7]World Bank: *World Development Report* (2003), OUP, and Oxford New York p. 236 ff. At date of writing, the country sustains on a GNI of 0.7% out of billions of dollars and GDP of only 3.1% growth. With a population of 5.1 million and a life expectancy of 39 years, 68.0% of the total population lives below poverty line, and 76.0 % of that figure live in rural Sierra Leone, where most mining activities take place. 74.5 % of the country's population lives below the international poverty line on less than $2 (USD) a day and only an estimated 43.6% of the highest 10% of the total population share the benefits of income of the country.

[8]GOSL: *Mineral Potential of Sierra Leone* GSD Freetown, December 2000 (MPSL).

[9]Some of these impacts are highlighted in chapter 1. It should be noted that no individual or corporate entity has been found legally culpable for environmental damage since the commencement of mining in the country in the 1930s. Equally, no arm of government has accepted responsibility for environmental damage consequent upon development policies, nor has there been any judicial determination on the subject. At the moment, present generation has little to show from the wealth that has been amassed from mining and they are deprived of the natural resources that form the immediate alternative to improving their basic quality of life. In the circumstances, future generations have no chance in the contest unless the legal rules and principles that regulate the industry become reoriented in the values of sustainable development.

environmental protection and sustainable development have been analysed in order to establish a practical meaning and purpose of sustainable development in international law, including an appreciable legal context within which it can be enabled to regulate development activities. Also analysed are academic works, official study papers and Reports of GOSL and mining companies relating to economic, social, development and environment issues surrounding mining in Sierra Leone. The revelations uncovered in these, justify and stress the relevance of sustainable development for mining in Sierra Leone. A cross-section of legislations and mining agreements have also been examined to establish their sustainability content including their capacity to effect environmentally sound mining pursuant to the principles of sustainable development in international law.

Visits were made to the rutile and Bauxite mining areas in Gbangbama and Mokanji in Moyamba district in south-western Sierra Leone. Visits were also made to some diamond mining areas in Kono district- Tongo-field, Nimikoro; in Kenema District- Bama and Konta, all in the east and south-eastern province; and Baoma in Bo district, southern Sierra Leone, in order to obtain a personal appraisal of some of the appalling visual effects of mining activities. In addition, individual interviews were conducted with various government officials of the departments of Mines, Environment, Forestry, Planning, Health and some members of the NEPB, all of who are involved with the formulation of policies, decision-making and/or the implementation of the various legislations examined in this work. The interviews enabled the writer to establish the link between effective domestic implementation of the concept of sustainable development and ensuring sustainable mining. Further interviews were held individually, with mineral right holders, representatives and consultants of SRL and KHL, other private entities, representatives of civil groups and NGOs, local chiefs and some miners in the mining communities visited. The information obtained from this exercise enabled the writer to ascertain the extent of national implementation of the relevant sustainability principles and objectives that are represented within the policies and legal mandates analysed in this work.[10]

---

[10]Note also that some of the interviewees wished to remain anonymous.

1 EXTRA-LEGAL FACTORS OF MINING IN SIERRA LEONE

1:1 Introduction

The environmental revolution of the last four decades has had the strongest influence on natural resource exploitation calling to question mining activities in most parts of the world including Sierra Leone. Exploitation of minerals in this country is driven by a variety of factors, but has been championed primarily by the imperative of pursuing economic goals, a choice which puts into sharp focus concerns over social and environmental objectives. While mineral resource development is essentially a multi-dimensional and a multi purpose issue involving *inter alia* economic, political, international and other national policy demands, understanding its social and environmental impacts, must always be the imperative. They help to clarify the link between mining and poor (or sustained) growth and development.

This overview attempts to describe extra-legal aspects of mining in Sierra Leone. The aim is to provide an insight into some of the incidents of mining in this country, in the pursuit of economic development. But the ultimate purpose is to stress the negligible place that social and environmental concerns held throughout decades of mining activities. It is hoped that this background will cause to better appreciate the value and primary relevance of sustainable development for environmental protection in the economic exploitation of natural resources, as canvassed by this book.[1]

1:2 Sierra Leone's Terrain and Minerals Potential

Sierra Leone is situated on the west coast of Africa, bordering the Atlantic Ocean between Guinea and Liberia to the North and North-east and South-

---

[1] The legal regime and institutions regulating the country's mining industry for environmentally and socially sustainable mining practices will be dealt with in subsequent chapters.

east respectively, with an estimated population of 5.4 million.[2] It encompasses a total area of 71,740 sq. km of which, 120sq.km is water and 71,620sq.km of land.[3] The country is tropical with dry, windy hammattan and rainy seasons. Rainfall along the coast can reach to 459cm (195 inches) making it one of the wettest along coastal western Africa.[4] Generally, the geography and land systems of mining regions are believed to reflect similar characteristics in many ways. For the most part, they are alluvial plains interspersed with low hill ranges, streams and river basins, coastal mangrove swamp and secondary forest.[5] Land use in the country is estimated at 6.7% arable, 0.78% of permanent crops and other at 92.46%,[6] which includes substantial minerals development ventures concentrated in the three provincial regions, outside the western area.[7]

Sierra Leone is endowed with substantial mineral resource wealth.[8] Its mineral potential was recognised between 1920s and 1960s.[9] Diamonds, Rutile, Gold, Bauxite, Iron ore, Platinum were most popular of minerals located and harvested,[10] and Petroleum exploration is underway.[11] Mineral deposits are not peculiar to any particular region, as they appear to have been located in all regions of the country - northern, southern, eastern and western.[12] While some regions are notable for one particular resource, others hold more than one.[13] Of the country's rich mineral resource base, only certain minerals have been attractive for immediate investment - heavy mineral sands, diamonds, gold, bauxite, iron ore and platinum.[14] Sierra Leone has long recognition for its capacity to develop these resources and made significant contribution to world marketing in these minerals, despite

---

[2]*Sierra Leone Ready for Business*, February, 2003, Mining Journal Ltd. 2003, (*SL Mining*) p.2.

[3]World Fact Book 2002- Sierra Leone, (available at <http://www.umsl.edu/services/govdocs/

[4]*Ibid*

[5]*SL Mining* (supra n. 2) p.2 see also, Cremer and Warner, *ECDP for SRL Report* No. 92040, July 1990.pp.8-9 .

[6]World Fact Book (supra n. 3)

[7]The total land area over which industrial mining rights are currently held in the country is estimated at 32,015.041 square miles (see "Industrial Mining Rights in Sierra Leone, (Status 2004) available at http://www.daco-sl.org/encyclopedia2004/). Established diamond fields alone cover almost 20,000 sq. km area (over one-quarter of the Country) *SL Mining* (supra n. 2) p.5.

[8]Wright L., (2002), Sierra Leone, *in Mining Annual Review* 2002: London, United Kingdom, Mining Journal Ltd. CD-ROM.

[9] Wurie A C., (DGS) "The Role of the Geological Surveys In Sierra Leone", DSPWP, March, 2003 Freetown pp.1-3.

[10]*Mineral Potential of Sierra Leone*; GSD, Freetown, December 2000 (*MPSL*); Other minerals that were explored over that period included Columbite, Corundum, Graphite, Ilmenite and Titaniferous Magnetite, Lignite, Molybdenite, Nepheline-Syenite, Cassiterite, Dimension Stone and Platinum. See also *ARMD/SL 1939/44* at the CIMRD, London.

[11]Wurie A C., (supra n. 9) p. 6. For a detailed exposition of the country's rich mineral potentials, see *MPSL* (supra n.10); *SL Mining* (supra n.2) pp.5-7.

[12]For a detailed exposition of the country's rich mineral potentials, see *MPSL* (supra n.10); *SL Mining* (supra n.2) pp.5-7

[13]*MPSL ibid.*

[14]D'Souza K. "Mining Investment Climate" in *SL Mining* (supra n.2) p.4.

its negligible size.[15] Minerals find their way into the international market mainly as, `raw`, `rough` or `unprocessed' products, with profound implications for mining in context of economic sustainability. But while issues relating to economic aspects of sustainable development do not fall within the purview of this thesis, relevant economic aspects of Sierra Leone's mining are discussed in this chapter.

1:3 The Place of Minerals in the Economy

1:3:1 1920s-1990s Developments

The major source of hard currency[16] in the period before the country's civil strife consisted of the mining and export of gold, diamond, bauxite, rutile and iron ore,[17] with estimates of between 70-80% contributions to the economy. Yet, the country holds a status of 'the least' developed country in the world.[18] The poor state of Sierra Leone's economy has been blamed on a decade of civil war, which halted all industrial mining.[19] But this sector had a chequered history of growth and decline even before the outbreak of the war in 1990. Its place in the economy ought therefore to be placed in context.

Organised mining in Sierra Leone began with the promulgation of the Mines and Minerals Ordinance in 1927. From 1930 until 1976, Iron ore was mined at Maramper by DELCO.[20] Apart from exports of Iron ore, almost 90 Km of railway was constructed to route these exports but none was sustained after Iron Ore mining ceased. In respect of Gold, only small alluvial operations were conducted by a number of companies until 1956. Revenue impact was negligible.

Industrial diamond mining commenced in 1930s,[21] with SLST granted the sole right to prospect for and mine diamonds in the country for 99 years, only relinquishing rights to all alluvial deposits outside its lease area in 1955.[22] This ushered in the ADMS in 1956, established for artisanal and

---

[15]See Cleeve E.A., *Multinational Enterprises in Development: Mining Industry in Sierra Leone*, Avebury p.41; *MPSL* (supra n.10); Gilbert S., (De Beers Group London): "World Class Mining Majors and Their Role in the Future of the Diamond Industry in Sierra Leone", DSPWP, (DFID) March, 2003 Freetown; *SL Mining* (Supra n.2).

[16]All Dollar references are in USD

[17]*SL Mining* Ibid p.4

[18]The World Bank: *WDR, 2003*, OUP, p.236 ff.

[19]*SL Mining* (supra n. 2) p.4

[20]*Ibid* p.5

[21]*Ibid*

[22]Tani Pratt L.J., "The Contribution of the Diamond Industry to the Economy of Sierra Leone" DSPWP, (DFID) Freetown, March 2003. p.1

small-scale mining, to regulate *inter alia*, illicit mining.[23] A total of about 9,500sq miles, covering 69 chiefdoms in 6 districts had been declared for licensed mining by the end of 1961,[24] and by 1965, large numbers of the provincial population had abandoned farming and were panning the alluvial streams. SLST's output combined with ADMS yields in the early 1960s, ranged between 1 and 2 million carat of good quality diamonds,[25] which was marketed solely by DCSL of De Beers Group, until 1974.[26] It is believed that the prices paid for Sierra Leone's diamonds were far lower than those prevailing at the world level.[27] The GDO replaced DCSL, as the sole legal exporters of Sierra Leone's diamonds though in reality, GDO was managed by DICOR Ltd, again a De Beers subsidiary.[28] The 1970s saw the direct participation of GOSL in formal mining by the acquisition of 51% share value of a new company Diminco (NDMC), with SLST retaining 49% and management of the company.[29] It began to show signs of decline both in management and exports by the mid-1970s with a total export value decline from almost $44million in 1980 to $2million in 1988.[30]

PMMC, a private Sierra Leonean company took over control of NDMC including sale of its diamonds. Sale was conducted through the GGDO, which held the monopoly for buying and exporting diamonds and gold.[31] In 1988, oversees statistics recorded diamond exports from Sierra Leone at $200 million, while the official country record was $4 million.[32] The company ran huge debts from other companies including their associate companies, in exchange for percentage of interests in PMMC's 49% Share value. It was also subsidised by government of up to $10.8 million a year.[33] At the company's demise, the creditors,[34] the debtors (PMMC) and even the government were all claiming the 49% shares of NDMC[35]. By the end of 1990, official diamond production and trade showed considerable decline and had very little impact on government revenue or the conditioning of other sectors of the economy.

---

[23]*Ibid.*

[24]See *ARMD/SL* 1956-1965, CIMRD, London.

[25]*SL Mining* (supra n.2) p.5

[26]Tani-Pratt L.J., (supra n. 23); diamond sale prices were fixed by their London- based CSO.

[27]Cleeve (supra n. 15) p. 42

[28]Tani Pratt, (supra n. 23) p.2

[29]*Ibid* p.2

[30]Cleeve (supra n. 15) p.42; SLST managers reportedly, failed to order essential mining implements, and reduced other capital expenditures in preparation for their exit. SLST was taken over by BP, for a brief period, between 1980 and 1984

[31]*Ibid* p.48

[32]*Ibid* p.43

[33]*Ibid* p.49

[34]The figure of shareholders and creditors are estimated at 46 individuals and companies (Tani-Pratt, (supra n. 23) p.3 (citing Greenhalgh, 1985)

[35]Cleeve, (supra n. 15) p.49

Other detrimental influences on the diamond sector are identified as '... pervasive corruption... compounded with misguided policies'.[36]

The development of bauxite commenced in 1963, by SIEROMCO, to become the second most important export by mid 1980s.[37] In 1988, it earned $22 million in export revenue and was recorded as being on substantial increase.[38] Marketing of the product was exclusively external, conducted with the parent company by an agreement to sell all of SIEROMCO bauxite, and at a price that was acceptable to their principal.[39] Productivity rate subsequently declined in the late 1980s and negligible export was registered at mine closure in 1995.[40]

Rutile development met initial set backs at commencement in 1967.[41] However, since 1980, rutile has been exploited and exported by SRL,[42] and took over as the mainstay of the country's economy between the late 1980s and early 1990s.[43] Output in 1988 was 126,000 tons of natural Rutile, 42 tons of Ilmenite, and an operating profit of $9.3million in 1989.[44] But there was already a marked decline in total exports and revenue before operations ceased in 1995 with the outbreak of civil war.[45]

The period 1991-2000 marked the era of Sierra Leone's civil war, the last straw that halted all forms of industrial mining in the country. Diamonds still continued to be exploited and traded unofficially by the rebels who occupied the regions. There was no policy regarding environmental management, rehabilitation or investment in critical mine-related social issues throughout these mining years. It was not until 1988 and 1990s that mining policies referenced rehabilitation responsibilities and aimed at 'sustainable economic and social development of the communities'.[46] But the adverse social and environmental impacts still continued and remain pervasive.

---

[36] Amco-Robertson Mineral Services, in *SL Diamond Policy Study*; (DFID) January, 2002

[37] *SL Mining* (supra n. 2) p.5; SIEROMCO was a subsidiary of Alusuisse, an Italian based Company

[38] *BSL, Annual Report and Statement of Account*, (1980s) BSL Freetown.

[39] Nickson A., *The export of Bauxite from Sierra Leone, 1979*, (Commissioned Study for the CPU), MDEP, Freetown.

[40] *MPSL* (supra n.10) p.1

[41] *SL Mining* (supra n.2) p.5 Initial operations were by PPCC, and later by BSC (MNCs)

[42] *Ibid* SRL was a wholly owned by Nords Resources Corporation of United States

[43] *Ibid* In 1991/92, out of a world total of 92.8% minerals export, Rutile and Ilmenite exports was 50.4% accounting for $73.3 million

[44] Cleeve,(supra n 15) p.51

[45] *Ibid*

[46] See Sierra Leone Gazettes, No.43. of 30th July, 1998 and No.100, of 10 March, 1995 respectively; also Government Notice No.7, December 1988

1:3:2 Mining and Politics

The concern over people and their relationship to contemporary modes of production makes no development possible without a grasp of its political nature.[47] In the case of Sierra Leone, minerals development acquired a political context in colonial era, when ownership of the resources (and some form of control) was placed in the state. Also, the reliance on it for economic growth and development, including its direct interaction with whole communities, make mining a vehicle for enhancing political stability and national security.

Another political implication of Sierra Leone's mining is the structure of the land tenure system that entails in the provincial regions where most mining activities take place.[48] The need to protect the local subsistence farmers and their families, the need to improve security and scope for investments, the need to encourage and enhance Artisanal and Small-scale mining,[49] and the need to benefit mining communities while protecting their environments, all acquire political dimension one way or the other, requiring various politically competing choices.

A more recent political dimension of mining in Sierra Leone manifested in its civil conflict as rebels used proceeds from the country's diamonds to fuel the war. The presence of rebels in rich diamond areas aided by their international links for marketing diamonds in exchange for ammunitions, gave them power and political recognition. The legitimate GOSL was coerced by the 'international political community'[50] acting as 'moral guarantors',[51] into negotiating a peace deal under which the rebel leader, by an unprecedented gesture, was granted chairmanship of all mineral resources in the country and a status of Vice President.[52] This newly acquired dimension of minerals made the issue of 'Conflict Diamonds' a concern for the UN, intergovernmental organisations, NGOs and other vested interests, culminating in the KPCS, which currently regulates the country's diamond exports.[53] The implication of such efforts while indirect has beneficial

---

[47] Middleton & O'Keefe, Redefining *Sustainable Development*, Pluto Press London, 2001 p.16

[48] Varying customary rules in particular mining communities regulate land tenure and surface rents. Note also that different rules apply for artisanal mining depending on whether it is conducted within the ADMS area or not (see Kamara-Boie U., (DDM) "Mineral Rights, Ownership, Access and Exploitation", DSPWP, Freetown; March, 2003. For Customary tenure practices see Renner- Thomas A.R. D., *A Dual System of Land Tenure: the Sierra Leone Experience*, PhD Thesis (Laws Board of Studies) 1984 Ext.;

[49] Over 200,000 livelihoods depend on it; for estimates on the 'digger' population, see Tani-Pratt, (supra n. 22) p.9

[50] O'Flaherty M., "Sierra Leone's Peace process: The Role of the Human Rights Community" in *HRQ*, Vol. 26 No.1 February, 2004, p.33;

[51] See Peace Agreement between the Government of Sierra Leone and the RUF of Sierra Leone, Lomé, 7 July 1999, Art. XXXIV.

[52] *Ibid*

[53] For text of the KPCS, see http://kimberleyprocess.com

31

consequences in regulating the effects of war on the environment.

Finally, since the 1970s, 'the environment' has become a political issue especially in the third world as a result of both internal and external pressures, partly owing to an increasing awareness of the damage being done to the environment as a result of internal and externally initiated economic policies including mining. The GOSL therefore faces increasing political pressures for the social and environmental abuses of its mining partners.

1:3:3 The International Dimension

There is no area of international dominance than Sierra Leone's mining sector, primarily because of the predominance of foreign actors and ownerships, the structure of the industry and the manner in which the firms conducted their operations. As evidenced in the preceding discourses, industrial mining has largely been carried out over the years by MNEs, through concessionary agreements between the GOSL and the foreign parent companies through their locally incorporated subsidiaries.[54] Generally, these companies reportedly had very few links with the domestic economy,[55] exercised more externally concentrated control over mineral production and marketing (intermediate purchases and sale) by inhibiting free markets,[56] and pursued environmentally unfriendly practices.[57] Thus there is the need to secure from mining companies adequate levels of revenue, improved technological transfer, social and environmental responsibility.

Another aspect of international influence on Sierra Leone's mining is dominance of multilateral organisations (including the WTO), trans-national, inter-governmental and regional organisations, bilateral investment protection treaties, international financial institutions and NGOs. All these exact economic influences on mineral resource policies and operations in diverse ways, but are recently becoming increasingly important in advocating environmentally sound mining practices. Above all, the demands ushered in by the globalisation of resources, capital, labour, services and property, including its inherent dictate of liberalisation, deregulation and Transnational corporate dominance has further embellished the international

---

[54]Cleeve (supra n.15) p.103

[55]*BSLER* (1983) BSL, Freetown

[56]Cleeve (supra n.15) pp.24-25

[57]Such influences of MNCs increased efforts by the UN and the UNCTC to require regulation of MNEs in relation to LDCs development and cub sensational abuses of corporate power. (See Mulinchksy P.T., *Multinational Corporations and the Law*, Blackwell, Oxford 2003 p. 6)

influence on mining in Sierra Leone. The system is already predicted to have an adverse impact on the welfare of developing states and industries,[58] and non-trade policy goals such as social development and environmental protection are likely to be jeopardised.[59]

1:3:4 Highlights of Social and Environmental Impacts

(i) Social Aspects of Mining

The assessment of adverse social impacts resulting from mining projects has generally not been incorporated into national policies on mining, laws, agreements, concessions or licences over the years. It was assumed that such activities only have positive social impacts through *inter alia*, infrastructure, employment generation and the value addition between high wages and profits, all of which create an effect on income distribution. This linkage is deemed vital for economic activity and independent long-term regional development.[60] But what is missed from this linkage is the social costs such activities off-load on mining communities, the 'true cost' of which has largely been discounted throughout years of the country's mineral exploitation. For instance, where large-scale or industrial mining is applicable, elitism and class distinctions has been the norm, with own schools, health facilities, shops, transportation, recreation facilities to enhance mine life. The term 'income distribution' acquires a new translation in the existence of social groups who have gained disproportionately from mineral wealth, whilst being insulated from the harsh realities of environmental degradation.[61] On the other spectrum are rural mining communities including small farmers, fishermen, peasants and individuals who are cheated from the equitable distribution of natural resources and mineral wealth. Their culture is seriously undermined by such activities through deprivation of grazing, fishing and wood-cutting rights, and they are forced into unequal competition with powerful companies for environmental resources on which their livelihoods depend. Yet, they are made to bear the social and environmental costs of mining operations and agendas, usually exemplified in scarce natural resources, more polluted environment, health hazards and physical displacement.

---

[58] Mulinchksy P., *ibid* p.11

[59] French D., " The Role of the State and International Organisations in Reconciling Sustainable Development and Globalisation" in *International Law and Sustainable Development*: Schrijver N. & Weiss F. (Eds.) 2004 Koninklijke Brill NV., The Netherlands p.55

[60] Cleeve (supra n. 15) p.6

[61] The category includes company employees, mineral dealers, policy formulators, and rich chiefs who are far removed from the reality of mining hazards.

Most of the country's mining regions display appalling public health conditions. Poor mining methods usually allow for collections of stagnant water in abandoned excavated areas and contamination of water sources. Instances of improper use of mercury in gold mining result in contamination of water sources, exposing the communities to health hazards locally and down stream.[62] Communities interacting with these hazards are exposed to diseases such as malaria, diarrhoea and other water-borne diseases like schistosomiasis, which can be fatal to young children.[63] To compound these hazards, health care delivery systems in mining regions are reportedly, insufficient and inadequate to cope with the population and type of illnesses prevalent in mining areas.[64]

Also, the issue of in-migration into mining areas has profound social implications. First is the pull of men toward diamond rich areas for artisanal mining to amass quick wealth. But these are caught by the conspiracy of poverty and ignorance, and led into a system of 'virtual servitude'.[65]

Second, the congested and overcrowding living conditions in poorly constructed houses makes environmental sanitation deplorable. Inadequate provisions of infrastructures and facilities, such as housing and water supply further aggravate this.[66] Sanitation in mining villages is described as *'has been, and is still critical'*,[67] and so is availability and quality of water wells.[68]

Moreover, the creation of non-traditional employment opportunities has warranted changes in occupational patterns as teachers, dispensers and nurses in government service move into corporate employment or other loan-financed or subsistent small-scale mining ventures. Such population changes are predicted to have devastating consequences for most mining areas, particularly when mining ceases, as no alternative long-term service of employment (farming or industries) is being developed.[69] Local and cultural values of communities are also seriously being impaired by social vices like drug abuse, prostitution and child labour.[70]

Then there is the thorny issue of resettlement or relocation of individuals and

---

[62]*NEAP/SL Vol. 1*, 1995, MLHCPE February 1995 p.62

[63]Sipkins S., "Sierra Leone Mining and the Environment", (1995) p.2 available at www.american.edu/projects/mandala/Ted/leone.htm

[64]Bendu P.E., "Mining Sector Reactivation: Real Help and/or Real Impact" in *Enviroscope* Vol. 5 No.3 August 2002p. 7; see also Cremer & Warner (supra n.5) p.16

[65]USAID (OTI) "Sierra Leone Conflict Diamonds", PRPDP, March 30, 2001 p.5; also at www.usaid.gov/hum-response/oti

[66]See *NEAP/SL* (supra n. 62) p. 64; Cremer & Warner (Supra n.5) p.12

[67]Cremer & Warner, *ibid*, p.13; emphasis added

[68]Bendu E.P., (supra n.64) p.7; also, Creamer & Warner, *ibid*, p.16

[69]Cremer & Warner, *ibid* p.12

[70]Brima A., "Problems in the Mining Sector", DSPWP (DFID), March 2003 p.7

whole communities as and when mining needs demand. Over the years, this has been done in largely unplanned, uncoordinated and irresponsible manner bringing with it several social pitfalls. Communities are not consulted from the on set or in the resettlement process;[71] and where compensation is given, the targeted beneficiaries are under-cut with nowhere to seek redress. Also, villages are often relocated in places where basic community needs such as water, sanitation facilities or farmland are either absent or inadequate, with sub-soil often incapable of supporting plant growth due to methods of site clearing.[72] Sometimes, the grants of land to new settlers, while ignoring the customary land-rights of indigenous tribal groups, result in conflict over scarce resources. In other cited cases, villagers have been relocated in places where the immediate farmlands were unexpectedly flooded or cleared again for mining activities causing further intensification of already existing farmland shortages, extra economic and social hardships on villagers.[73] One reason for the pervasiveness of the forgoing social impacts has always been the exclusion of the affected masses in mining decision-making process and benefit sharing. Sierra Leone's mining has yet to discover and familiarise with this 'inclusion vision' that was misplaced in almost eight decades of mining history.

(ii) Environmental Impacts

The environmental impacts of mining in Sierra Leone is premised on the fact that in the past, more economic than environmental issues were emphasised in mining rights and agreements. No established mechanism existed to monitor either industrial, large scale or artisanal mining. Consequently, there were no efforts to protect the environment, mine the resources responsibly, reclaim or rehabilitate mined out areas.[74] Thus the most devastating effects of mining are borne by the physical and natural environment as all forms of mining activity have subjected it to systematic abuse and mismanagement. Today, five diamond chiefdoms in Kono district are described as 'patches of land, sandwiched in-between dug up areas'; while tropical virgin forests which once held rich flora and fauna, 'now abound in savannah with hard

---

[71]Sipkins S. (supra n. 63) p.3

[72]Creamer & Warner; (supra n.5) p13

[73]Ibid.

[74]NEAP/SL (supra n.62) p. 62 For instance, SRL and SIEROMCO held 520 sq. ml and 375 sq. ml of land respectively and had not surren-

dered any of these lands after prospecting (as required by their leases) for over 30 years (See Cleeve (supra n. 15) p.120). Note also the issue

of tensions emanating from landlessness caused by land 'hold-ups' tied to surface rent conditions or mine closure (Bendu E.P., (supra n. 64)

p.7

gravel top soil that is good for nothing'.[75] In the Tongo-Field and Pujehun diamond rich areas, streams and rivers which used to be protected habitat for fresh water animals and plants, and source of drinking water and are now muddy and yellow.[76] Originally, a wide variety of wildlife was present in what is now the Rutile lease area. Herbivores included deer, monkey, baboon chimpanzee, gorilla, bush- cow and wide variety of rodents. Among the predators were leopard, lion, bush-hog and fox. Reptile included lizard, snake, tortoise, crocodiles and alligators.[77] The proportion of the destruction of habitat or wildlife loss due to mining is not definite, though it could be said to account for a substantial part as efforts have never been made to protect, re-habituate or account for wild-life or species within mining lease areas.

Another investigation into diamond mining in south eastern Sierra Leone, reveal that in certain locations miners not only remove vegetation and economically valuable trees, but their activities also divert surface drainage, cause heavy siltation in river beds and creeks and effectively reduce coastal coral and fish population that feed and breed in it.[78] Also, toxic wastes in water sources contaminate marine life on which community life depend making them unfit for human consumption.[79] Dredging is also known to destroy bottom topography and biota especially of fish and suspension feeders.[80]

Rutile mining methods have also effected changes in the physical characteristics of the natural environment, such as vegetative cover, soil exposures, slopes and drainage depressions. Impoundment of streams by damming and other activities in the rutile catchments have also produced some changes in the run-off regime and water volume in streams.[81] Similarly ponds and cleared areas have formed impervious surfaces that have led to the rapid concentration of run-off incidence of floods.[82] The pH of water samples are said to be generally lower in ponds near mining activity than in ponds reaches not yet been mined, as a result of dredging activities and constant interruption of soil formations. It is also difficult to maintain the

---

[75]Brima A., (supra n.70) p.3

[76]Ibid

[77]Cremer & Warner (supra n.5) p.11

[78]Sipkins S., supra n. 63) p.2

[79]Ibid; see also NEAP/SL (supra n.62)

[80]Ndomahina E T., (IMBO) FBC, Freetown

[81]Cremer and Warner (supra n.5) pp. 25 & 26

[82]Ibid; see also Bendu E.P (supra n.64) p.7

level of natural fish populations.[83] While aquaculture is adopted for utilising flooded and degraded lands,[84] concerns have been expressed over this method especially in relation to environmental quality, contamination of culture products, water and measures for risk prevention.[85] Finally, Dam constructions in rutile mining limit fresh water supplies to the mangroves in SRL lease area and create deficits that eventually result in changes in the ecological balance especially modification of the hydrological regime. This will ultimately have direct adverse effects on the mangroves.[86] These negative social and environmental impacts do not only undermine peoples' health, their ability to earn their livelihood, but does bear a direct relationship with poverty.

1:4 Mining, Economic Growth and Economic Development

A common reaction to this sector is fiscal praises. For instance, one view alleges it to have operated in pre-war years, in a manner that contributed significantly to government revenue.[87] The sector's 'revenue generation' strength, including its multiplier effects on development, is described as 'ensur[ing] a big boost to socio economic development'[88]. On the other hand, evidence has been adduced in the forgoing discourse, of marked decline in all ventures, mismanagement of operations, revenue losses and overwhelming social and environmental abuses. Also, the basic development indicators of the 1989 WDR (preceding the 1991 civil war) reflected this downward spiral.[89] The decline in output has been blamed severally on the significant increase in unaccounted trade, depletion of resources, rural out migration, increased urban unemployment, inequality of income distribution and price inflation.[90] But to an insider, '...dependence on ...mining of [the country's] precious minerals has brought more than enough woes...'[91] Thus, some general observations ought to be made regarding the contribution of this sector, before any determination could be made regarding growth and development.

---

[83]Cremer & Warner (supra n.5) p.37

[84]SRL, *Implementation of the Environmental and Community Development Programme*, January 1992 p.50

[85]Bendu (supra n. 64) p.7.

[86]Cremer & Warner (supra n.5) p.29ff

[87]AMCO-Robertson (supra n.36)

[88]Bendu (supra n.64) p.7

[89]NEAP/SL The World Bank *WDR 1989*, OUP 1989; For example, it shows an average growth rate of 0.2%; whilst current account balance 1970 amounted to $20 million, by 1987 it had declined to $9million (before official transfers); and with GIR in 1970 at $39million, in 1987, it amounted to only to $ 6 million; pp. 164 & 198.

[90]Sipkins (supra n.63) p.1; Cleeve (supra n.15) p. 5

[91]Wurie A.C., (supra n.9) p.6

First, it was (and still is) an export-oriented sector of non-renewable, raw and unprocessed minerals with no value addition - an economically unfeasible condition. For economic sustainability, mineral rent-seeking must be converted into social and economic capital, which sustains itself through development of skills, frugality and investment habits if it is to survive physical depletion or fading market demands.[92] Second, mining contribution to government revenue has always been affected by various tax exemptions, often granted under concession agreements.[93] Further, because the companies involved were especially MNEs, they were accorded retention facilities that were used as avenue to transfer resources out of the country with implications for local sufficiency of foreign exchange, and problems of 'low multiplier' effect on the country's economy.[94] Under-declaration of exports and prices were also common.[95] Similarly computation of mineral rent, royalty, development aid etc. in particular cases, was related only to the quantity (not quality) of minerals shipped out based on tonnage.[96] This may not be unconnected with the early depletion of most of the rutile deposits and iron ore.

In terms of development of mining regions - commonly symbolised in roads, bridges, electricity, pipe-borne water, heath facilities, schools, shops etc - Sierra Leone's case has been described as 'unfortunate'. Most of these facilities were designed only to enhance efficient running of the mines, and feed the life-style of employees and their families.[97] Local communities benefit from such facilities is generally indirect, largely depending either on their proximity with the main body of the mines or its physical operating capacity, thus making mining less relevant to the socio-economic well-being of distant communities.[98]

Finally, environmental and social concerns found little relevance throughout the period commencing mining between 1920s and early 1990s. Concerns

---

[92]Walde T.W., "Natural Resources and Sustainable Development: From "Good Intentions" to "Good Consequences"" in Schrijver & Weiss (eds.)(2004) (Supra n.59) p .128

[93]See *BSLER*, 1986; For example SIEROMCO was granted a tax holiday which covered a period from start of operation in 1963 to 1971, while SRL only started paying income tax in 1987, since it started operation in 1972 (see Cleave E.A (supra n. 15) p.44)

[94]USAID (OTI) (supra n.65) p.14; the estimated impact of such facilities on the country's balance of payment ranged from a positive net impact $34 million to a negative impact of $51 million (see Cleeve (supra n. 15) p.124)

[95]See Nickson (supra n. 39) SIEROMCO is reported to have been engaged in under-declaration of both export prices and exports, causing an estimated loss to the country in foreign exchange, of $2.5million between January 1964 and April 1975.

[96]*Ibid*

[97]Cleeve (supra n.15) p.110; note also that mining companies were not the major source of employment (at p.125)

[98]*Ibid*

with foreign exchange contribution to public revenue and other direct economic benefits became paramount as companies were granted extensive rights to exploit natural resources, subject only to royalties and taxation. The economic boom attributed to mining often excluded external costs, in particular, the negative social and environmental effects of such actives including the appropriation of responsibility (financial or legal), whether on GOSL or the relevant companies to address them. It must be re-echoed that 'only if true costs and benefits are part of an actors decision-process, will market based competition help to encourage adaptation and innovation to reduce such costs and favour activities with less damage'.[99]

In light of the forgoing therefore, it is easy to reach the conclusion made by Cleeve on Sierra Leone's mining in the late 1980s, that 'by way of long term sustained development, nothing much has been done'.[100] More recently, there is a call for the government to promote social and environmental mitigating programmes;[101] and on mineral developers to bring sustainable development to the country as they generate returns to shareholders.[102]

1:5 Current Mining Trends

With the end of the war in 2002, the determination is once more focused on the development of the mining sector to boost the much needed, post conflict development initiatives. Presently, Rutile and the Kimberlite agreements are regulating the two operating industrial mines and there are also several mineral rights relating to diamond and gold mining,[103] including some exploration projects that are likely to transform into industrial and small-scale mining leases.[104] The Government is addressing mining related sustainable development issues in the context of an action plan developed for implementing the recently adopted mining policy.[105] Rights to search for, mine and dispose of minerals are acquired and held in the form of Licences which may either be for Prospecting (exclusive or non-exclusive),

---

[99] Wälde (supra n.92) p.135

[100] Cleeve (supra n. 15) p. 118

[101] Sipkins (supra n. 63) p.4

[102] D'Souza (supra n.14) p.4

[103] The numbers of current mining licenses in respect of diamonds are estimated at about three hundred and forty in total; (*Africa Research bulletin*, Issue: 15532, 2003).

[104] *SL Mining* (supra n.2)

[105] For policy version, see *Core Mineral Policy*, MMR, September 2003, Freetown; also at <http://www.minmines-sl.org/>. The World Bank has however, identified broad and discriminatory tax and duty exemptions within fiscal policies, raising fiscal sustainability concerns (see World Bank Document: ERRC for GOSL. 2003 (ERRC)

Exploration, Artisanal or Small-scale mining, or mining Lease.[106] Land tenure is determined by customary rules, while royalties, taxes, licenses, concessions and fees are regulated by the central government. Environmental and social issues have yet to take primacy in mining agenda.

Conclusion

The purpose of this chapter was to present some of the issues that dominated decades of mining in Sierra Leone (as it pursued economic development), while stressing the negligible place of social and environmental concerns. This overview sought to canvas the relevance of sustainable development for mining in that country. The exercise has unveiled how concerns with public and private sector agendas to reap economic benefits from mining over-shadowed the adverse environmental and social consequences of such activities. It illustrates how continued exploitation of mineral resources in the face of such misplaced emphasis generally leads to greater environmental, social and undoubtedly economic costs, defeating the goals of economic development. The underlying theme suggest that any meaningful assessment of Sierra Leone's mining must not be quick in emphasising the economic potential of such ventures over their attendant social, environmental and resource management parameters, as these must define the way resources are exploited. The pertinent principles that define these parameters are embedded in the concept of sustainable development and they are designed to instil these social and environmental considerations into development activities including mining, and direct them toward sustainability path, with positive economic consequences.

The next chapter is thus devoted to a discourse on the concept of sustainable development in international law, bringing out its primary relevance and value for sound legal and policy guidance for environmental protection, in the economic exploitation of natural resources. The methods by which sustainable development could be implemented at national level will also be explored.

---

[106] Industrial mining rights are secured through the MAB. (Kamara O.B Supra n.48)

2 SUSTAINABLE DEVELOPMENT IN INTERNATIONAL LAW

2:1 Introduction

The preceding chapter illustrated how exploitation of mineral resources amid misplaced *primary* emphasis on economic agendas, and in diminution of environmental objectives, generally leads to greater environmental, social and undoubtedly economic costs. It also showed how the sum of these costs effect to defeat goals of economic development. It was further suggested that the concept of sustainable development as espoused in international law, defines the parameters that could direct development activities (including mining), towards social and environmental sustainability, with positive economic consequences.

What then is 'sustainable development'? This phrase has popular currency and use in diverse areas-international, regional and national; through varied forms-treaties, decisions, declarations legislations, policies and statements; and different dimensions - social, environmental, economics and development. As its employments are varied, so are its meanings, objectives and concerns. It therefore, must certainly have a valuable purpose, which in this book, is to hold a balance between exploitative economic *activities* (in the name of development) and protection of the environment within (and outside) which such activities take place. This chapter therefore seeks to unravel the relevance and value of this international concept in addressing the conflicts between environmental goals and development activities, but with particular bias toward the regulation and management of natural resource for environmental protection[1]. It will show that despite the definitional questions, sustainable development has direct and primary relevance for environmental protection in the economic exploitation of natural resources.

The chapter is in two parts: Part A will describe the evolution of the concept

---

[1]Note that emphasis is placed on the environmental dimension of sustainable development; (see introductory overview supra p. 22, A (ii))

of sustainable development[2], stressing its international environmental orientation. It then presents an analysis of the concept relating to its formulation, definition and meaning, but does not purport to add to the web of definitions on the subject. It will however, identify a workable interpretation of the term and suggest a practical meaning that will be employed in this work. This part also explores the legal aspects of the concept so as to ascertain its true legal character on the international arena. It identifies a legal character in the concept beyond legislative processes, and a flexibility that allows for their interpretation within legal rules to enhance environmental protection at the global or domestic level. Some pertinent developments on the concept since its international inception are also explored, further embellishing its importance. Part B examines the context in which sustainable development can be implemented at national level. It will show that national implementation represents an important and necessary means of applying sustainable development in order to protect domestic development environments.

PART A

2:2 Review of Evolution, Definition and Legal Aspects of the Concept Of Sustainable Development

The Concept of 'sustainable development' is rooted in the ideology of introducing change in the way natural resources were exploited in production processes for economic purposes. There existed a long-standing conflict between developers and conservationist, both respectively promoting their ideologies. Developers chanted exploitation of natural resources for economic development while conservationists advocated environmental protection in order to preserve and maintain the resilience of nature. The bias was often in favour of the developmental imperative, which sold often on its economic ticket, with little or no difference to the environmental degradation caused by such activities.

The 1972 UN Conference on the Human Environment (Stockholm), was the green light that signaled environmental attention on the international platform. It was convened, to consider the need for common principles to inspire and guide the peoples of the world in the preservation and

---

[2]Note that 'sustainable development' as employed in this work, may sometimes be used in reference to some relevant elements and principles embedded in the concept. These are identified and dealt with in chapter 3.

enhancement of the human environment[3]. Fundamental amongst such principles, was the recognition of the sovereign rights of states to exploit their own resources pursuant to their own environmental policies[4]. In such exploitation however, they were required to guard against future exhaustion of 'non-renewable resources' and safeguard the natural resources of the earth through careful planning and management, for the benefit of present and future generations[5].

These prescriptions certainly demand change in the way natural resources were exploited, and a more rational management thereof. To achieve this change, states were directed to 'adopt an integrated and co-ordinated approach to their development planning, so as to ensure that development is compatible with the need to protect and improve the environment'[6]. It was the Stockholm Declaration that sought for the first time to limit the right of states to exploit their natural resources, especially those that are non-renewable, in an unhindered manner[7]. UNEP was constituted in sequence as the world's first environmental agency.[8] Stockholm had identified a common outlook and link between resource exploitation for development and environmental protection; a link that was subsequently adopted in the World Conservation Strategy. The strategy gave birth to the phrase 'sustainable development', and maintained that, 'for development to be sustainable, it must take account of social and ecological factors, as well as economic ones'[9].

This was the contextual background within which the Brundtland Report[10] was presented to the international community, popularising the phrase 'sustainable development', and proposing both an official definition and suggested dimensions of the concept. It was later adopted at the UNCED[11], by an overwhelming consensus of nations through the Rio Declaration[12] and Agenda 21[13]. UNCED and the Rio Declaration, it has been suggested, gave

---

[3]Stockholm Declaration on the Human Environment adopted June 16, 1972, UN Doc. A/CONF 48/141 Rev. 1 at 3 (1973), 11 *ILM* 1416 (1972) (Stockholm Declaration)

[4]*Ibid* Principle 21; Note that the exercise of 'sovereign right' is subject to respect for the environment of other States.

[5]*Ibid* Principles 5 & 2

[6]*Ibid.*, Principle 13

[7]Suebedi, S.P, "Sustainable Development *Perspectives in International Economic Law*" in Perspectives in International Economic Law, Asif H. Qureshi (Ed.), Kluwer Law International, London/ The Hague/ New York, 2002, pg. 265.

[8]UNEP was established by GA Res. 2997 (XXV11); 15 Dec. 1972

[9]*WCS* (1980), at <http://www.unep/wwf/iucn.nr>

[10]Brundtland Report: *WCED: Our Common Future*, OUP, Oxford, 1987; (hereinafter *WCED*)

[11]UNCED, Rio de Janeiro 1992.

[12]Rio Declaration on Environment and Development, June 13, 1992, adopted by the UNCED at Rio de Janeiro. UN Doc A/CONF. 151/26 (Vol.1) (1992) *ILM 874*, 1992 (Rio)

[13]Agenda 21 (approved by the UNCED at Rio de Janeiro) UN Doc A/CONF. 151/26 (Vols.1-111) reprinted in *Earth Summit '92, United Nations Conference on Environment and Development Rio De Janeiro*, Quarrie J. (Ed.), The Regency Press Corporation, London, (1992), pp. 46ff.

the principle of sustainable development 'credible international standing',[14] and anointed it formally for legal use within the corpus of international environmental law.[15] The principal merits of the concept are judged as twofold. First, it modifies the previously unqualified development concept in so far as development must possess both economic and ecological sustainability;[16] and second, it makes a state's management of its own domestic environment and resources a matter of international concern for the first time in a systematic way.[17]

2:3 Sustainable Development: Formulation, Definition and Meaning

2:3:1 Overcoming the scepticisms in the Rio formulation

The 3 non-binding instruments concluded at UNCED, provide no composite formal definition of the concept of sustainable development.[18] They are however popularly held to be significant for any meaningful elaboration of the concept because they establish objectives, set targets and standards. For Silveira, the instruments translate a 'common purpose' between environmental and developmental objectives.[19] Mrs. Brundtland explicitly refers to Rio, as the 'Declaration on legal principles for sustainable development';[20] and Sands, perceives it as providing basis for defining the concept and its application.[21] But other scholars have viewed with scepticism, the formulations that translate its meaning in the Rio Declaration.

The general concern is that the primary objective that symbolised the concept - addressing environmentally unfriendly exploitation of natural resources- is lost within the UNCED instrument. Pallmearts considers this a 'skillfully masked step backwards' from international environmental efforts,[22] while Fitzmaurice perceives it as subordinating environmental responsibility of

[14]Suebedi S.P., (supra n. 7) p.269

[15]Sands P., "UNCED and the Development of International Environmental Law", YBIEL, Vol. 3 (1992), Handl et al. (Eds.), Graham & Trotman/ Martinus Nijhoff, London/Dordrecht/ Boston (1992) p.17

[16]Lynton K. C., International Environmental Policy; second edition, Duke University Press, Durham London, 1990, p. 207

[17]Birnie & Boyle, International Law and the Environment, (second edition), OUP, (2002) pp.79-152

[18]These are: Rio Declaration (supra n.12); Agenda 21 (supra n.13); and the 'Non-Legally Binding Authoritative Statement of Principles for a Global Consensus on the Management Conservation and Sustainable Development of All Types of Forests' (Forest principles), UN Doc. A/Conf.151/26 (vol. III) (1992), 31, ILM 881(1992)

[19]Silveira M. P., "The Rio Process: Marriage of Environment and Development", in Sustainable Development and International Law; Lang, W. (Ed.), Graham &Trotman/ Martinus Nijhoff, London/Dordrecht/ Boston (1995) p.10.

[20]Brundtland G H., "Our Common Future and Ten years after Rio: How Far have We Come and Where Should We Be Going?" in Earth Summit 2002: A New Deal, Dodds F. (Ed.) Earthscan, London, 2000 p.255. On this point, see also UNGA Res. 47/190 and 191 (1992) and 48/190 (1993).

[21]Sands P., Principles of International Environmental Law, Cambridge (2003) p. 53

[22]Pallmearts M., "International Environmental Law from Stockholm to Rio: Back to the Future?" Reciel Vol. 1, No.3 (1992), p.256

states to the requirements of national development policies and the economy.[23] It is not surprising that this document, which holds the layered components of the concept of sustainable development, has been described as one of uneasy compromises, delicately balanced interest, and dimly discernible contradictions'.[24] These criticisms are primarily set in motion on two counts. First, that the addition of the phrase 'and development' in the formulation of Principle 2 of the Declaration (which hitherto was not reflected in Principle 21 of the Stockholm Declaration), effects to downgrade environmental policies. Second, that the placing of human beings at 'the center of concern for sustainable development' in Principle 1 of Rio, subjects the values of environmental materials, resources and animal species to human beings.

These emphases, it has been suggested, upsets the delicate balance struck at Stockholm between the sovereign use of natural resources and the duty of care for the environment.[25]

In my view, the addition of the phrase 'and developmental' to the sovereignty principle, does not detract from the duty to protect the environment, nor does it render environmental concerns subordinate to developmental concerns. The addition should be understood as an emphasis on sovereign right of states to exploit their own resources (as they so often do) through development policies; save that, as indicated by the conjunction 'and'', environmental policies are made a competing factor. Ideally, it allows for states to pursue their own 'brown' as well as their 'green' agenda.[26] It could even expand the scope of responsibility for environmental damage, to apply to national development policies as well as national environmental policies.[27] The addition thus, serves nothing more than a clarification purpose highlighting the distinction between environmental and developmental policies.

Similarly, upon careful semantic consideration, a positive environmental protection objective could be deduced from the placing of human beings at the 'center of concerns' for sustainable development. As an important part of environmental components, human beings possess greater capacity to affect

---

[23]Fitzmaurice M.A., *International Protection of the Environment*; Hague Academy of International Law, Martinus Nijhoff Publishers, Hague/ Boston/ London (2002) p.43

[24]Porras I., "The Rio Declaration: A New Basis for International Co-operation": *Reciel* Vol.1 No. 3 (1992) p. 246.

[25]Pallmearts M., (supra n. 22) p.257

[26]Layard A., "The legal Framework of Sustainable Development" in *Planning for a Sustainable Future*, Layard, Davondi & Batty ((Eds.)) Spon Press, London, 2001, p. 33.

[27]Sands P., (supra n.21) p. 55

the environment in either a positive or negative way by their activities, and depending on their perception of it.[28] As aptly put by Wälde, 'sustainable development values more to the modality and context of the production process and the role of human intelligence in it.'[29] Even though the ecosystem, living and non living species, flora and fauna of the environment may be capable of regenerating themselves, they can hardly manage their being and existence without interference, and independent from human endeavours.

It therefore becomes very important for human beings to understand this centrality in their relationship with the environment, and the responsibility (implied in 'center of concerns') imputed on them in achieving or enhancing sustainable development.

Equally, the phrase should not be understood as the environment serving only a beneficial purpose for human beings, but that in the extraction of environmental benefits, cognisance should be given to the effects of their activities on other environmental components. It is this attention and duty of care that exemplifies the integration of environmental concerns into development policies and projects, and the entitlement of human beings to a life in harmony with nature. Understanding this interrelationship is the first step to identifying the sustainable development *problematique*. The solution is to be found in the interpretations that define its primary relevance and purpose in regulating development activities for environmental protection.

2:3:2 Dealing with the Definitional Question

There is an apparent definitional problem that goes to the very core meaning of the concept of sustainable development,[30] and one that has received ample response from scholars. Given the omission to provide a formal composite definition of the concept in the UNCED instruments, the definition of the WCED has been generally accepted as a reference point. It defines sustainable development as 'development that meets the needs of the present without compromising the ability of the future generations to meet their own needs'[31]. To enhance clarity and analytical ease, the various views

---

[28]Note that conversely, degraded environments wrought severe consequences for humans.

[29]Wälde T. W., "Natural Resources and Sustainable Development: From "Good Intentions" to "Good Consequences"" in *International Law and Sustainable Development* Schrijver & Weiss (Eds.), 2004 Koninklijke Brill NV., The Netherlands p.125

[30]Handl G., "Sustainable Development: General Rules Versus Specific Obligations" in *Sustainable Development & International Law*, Lang W. (Ed.) 1995 (supra n.19) p.36

[31]WCED (supra n.10) p.43

on the definition and meaning of sustainable development are dissected into four categories. First, there are those who source the meaning of the concept from the Brundtland formulation.

These have generally either inferred a utilitarian perspective of the concept,[32] stressed its anthropocentricity,[33] or emphasise a development-orientated view of environmental resources.[34] Others have imputed in the concept, a conditioning of development activities to recognize environmental protection.[35] But in Jacobs view, 'sustainability' cannot be expressed in terms of 'total wealth'. Crucial to it is the degradation of environmental wealth, a meaning that must underline sustainable development.[36] Along this line, Shiva warns against the danger in upholding interpretations which suggests "sustaining not nature, but development itself," with disregard for the 'limits of nature' and the necessity of adhering to them.[37]

The second definitional category have used the elements and principles of sustainable development in the Rio declaration (or other international instruments), either as guide to discerning the true content of the concept, or as means of achieving it. For instance, in applying the concept in the *Gabcikovo Nagymaros case*, the ICJ defined the concept in terms of its sources.[38] In the court's view, sustainable development can be inferred from 'new norms and standards' that are "set forth in a great number of instruments'. These must be 'taken into consideration and …given proper weight, not only when States contemplate new *activities*, but also when continuing with *activities* began in the past'[39]. In other words, what the concept denotes at any

---

[32]Handl G., (supra n. 30) Sustainable development imposes restraints on developmental activities in so far as these would undermine the environmental basis for further development. For the ILA, the concept entails 'a rational system of resource management that can operate in so far as the resources on which it depends are not exhausted and the environment is not irreparably damaged' (ILA *Report of the Sixty-Sixth Conference* Buenos Aires, Argentina (1994) Crawford & Williams (Eds.), London 1994) p.128)

[33]IIED/WBCSD, *Breaking New Ground: Mining Minerals and Sustainable Development* (MMSD), Earthscan London/ Sterling, VA, 2002 Seen as holding multiple layers of meaning and flexibility of application to different development activities (executive summary); see also Boer B., "Implementation of International Sustainability Imperatives at the National Level" in *Sustainable Development and Good Governance*, Ginther, Denters & De Waart (Eds.) Martinus Nijhoff Publishers Dordrecht/Boston/London, 1995; sustainable development will vary according to political, economic and social contexts, including the particular economic activity to which it is applied (p. 104)

[34]Pearce, Markandya & Barbier: *Blueprint for Green Economy*, Earthscan, London 2000 Sustainable development implies an increase in 'development indicators'; 'capital accumulation' or 'welfare maximization' for improving human condition (p.33); (see also Pearce & Kerry, *Economics of Natural Resources and the Environment*, Harvester Weatsheaf, New York/London 1990, p. 24); Redclift M., *Sustainable Development: Exploring the Contradictions*, Routledge, London (1984) p.32-33).

[35]Shiva, V. "Resources"; in *The Development Dictionary*: Sachs W. (Ed.), Zed Books, London, (1992) - In its original context, sustainability "implies maintaining the integrity of nature's processes, cycles, and rhythms"; therefore production processes and markets should be reshaped in line with nature's logic of returns, not the logic of profits, capital accumulation and returns on investment. (p. 217)

[36]Jacobs, M. *The Green Economy: Environment, Sustainable Development and the Politics of the Future*, Pluto Press, London, 1991 p. 84.

[37]Shiva, V. (supra n. 35 above)

[38]*Gabcikovo- Nagymaros Project* (Hungary/Slovakia) 1997, *ICJ Reports* 15 September 1997, GL No. 92

[39]*Ibid* para.140 (emphasis added). This analysis defines the concept also as a process that is ongoing.

given time will depend on how it appreciates in any instrument, and identifies either as a rule or standard. But more significant, is its poignant relevance for regulating development activities.

The third category of views defining sustainable development, derive a meaning by focusing on the two-worded phrase itself. For these, the term has been assessed as 'vague' or 'theoretically obscure',[40] as lacking content, 'logically redundant' or 'basically flawed'.[41] But interestingly, others have identified within this 'broad vagueness', practical definitional values of the phrase.[42] Jacobs asserts that the concept does entail three 'core ideas', namely: a discussion of the operational objectives required to achieve sustainable development; the management of principles needed to generate more sustainable policies; and the articulation of policies and practices required to achieve sustainability. The collection of these features into a single phrase does not rob them of the substantive value that they each represent as components of making sustainable development 'meaningful' and operational in practice.[43]

The final category will draw a meaning from a blend of the previous three sources and employ a descriptive definitional method, which identifies 'sustainable development' as a process, or as a concept with an instrumental role in effecting change in development patterns. In one view sustainable development embodies 'the logical framework for change and for identifying best practice' in the conduct of development activities.[44] It is also said to imply a 'permanent process that requires emphasis on process issues for it to be achieved and maintained;[45] and as an ever continuous and ongoing process of change and adaptation.[46]

Regarding its instrumental role, Judge Weeramantry emphasises the capacity of the concept to direct sound processes, and for solving fundamental

---

[40]See Malanczuk P., (citing –Divers & Handmer) " Sustainable Development: Some critical Thoughts In The Light of The Rio Conference" in *Sustainable Development and Good Governance*, Ginther et.al.(Eds.) (1995)(supra n. 33) p.26; Lowe, V. "Sustainable Development and Unsustainable Arguments" in *International Law and Sustainable Development*, Boyle & Freestone (Eds.), OUP, oxford, 1999 pp 30-31.

[41]Beckerman W., "Sustainable Development: Is it a Useful Concept?" in *Environmental Values 3 (1994):* The White Horse Press, Cambridge, U.K.1994, p.205. For him 'sustainable development' mixes up together the technical characteristics of particular development path, Programme or project, with a moral injunction to pursue it (pp. 30-31)

[42]See Sands (supra n. 15) p. 26.

[43]Jacobs, M. "Sustainable Development as a Contested Concept" in *Fairness and Futurity*, Dobson A. (Ed.) p. 27

[44]*MMSD* (supra n. 33)

[45]Gaines S.E.,(Citing Howard Mann) "International Trade, Environmental Protection and Development as a Sustainable Development Triangle" *Receil Vol. 11. Issue 3, (2002)* p. 264.

[46]In this process, resource exploitation, investments, technology and institutional change relate in harmony to enhance current and future needs and aspirations. (Lindner W.H "Sustainable Development: Its Social Political and Economic Implications", in *Environmental Liability*, Graham & Trotman, London/ Dordrecht/ Boston 1991(IBA Series), p.6. See also WCED (supra n.10) p. 9

problems in international environmental and development law. Sustainable development expresses the need to reconcile development and environment, by steering a course between their needs, and harmonises them.[47] From this perspective, the WTO Appellate Body also used the concept as an aid to define the extent to which environmental objectives can be pursued within national and international trade policies.[48] This instrumental role, no doubt is likely to save 'normative anarchy', its significance resting on resolution of tensions and 'environmentally related disputes'.[49] It must also be pointed out that the identification of sustainable development with (directing or resolving) processes instils in it a decision-making component that must not be missed when discerning the meaning of the concept.[50]

2:3:3 Sourcing a Workable Interpretation and Practical Meaning

Clearly, perspectives on the definition and meaning of sustainable development continue to abound and this work holds little space for their inclusion. The profound variation in interpretations is in my view warranted by an apparent confusion over delimiting the scope of the concept to arrive at a practical meaning. Judging from the various definitions and interpretations of the concept earlier stated, one easily observes the reasoning to generally relate to one of two dimensions - that of socio-economic development on the one hand (including development activities), and environmental protection on the other. Evidently, all the Rio principles reflect some form of international consensus on general and specific objectives of sustainable development that are needed to balance the general interrelationships that exist between socio-economic development and international protection of the environment. One could similarly apply this observation to the recent ILA New Delhi Declaration,[51] which codifies broad, varying but related principles for sustainable development, without distinguishing between 'core and peripheral' ones,[52] otherwise than their *'relating'* to sustainable

---

[47]See Separate Opinion of Judge Weeramantry in the *Gabcikovo-Nagymaros Project* (Hungary v Slovakia) Case (1997), *ICJ Reports* 15 September 1997, GL No. 92 pp. 86-87.

[48]The *Shrimp Turtle Case* (WT/DS58): Report of the Appellate Body in WTO DSR 1998: Vol. VII, 1998, Cambridge p. 275ff.) See also Sands P. "International Courts and the Application of the Concept of 'Sustainable Development'" in *Max Planck Yearbook of United Nations Law*, Vol.3. (1999) 398; also in *Law and Development: Facing Complexities in the 21st Century* - Hatchard & Perry-Kasseris ((Eds.)), London Cavendish, 2003 pp 147- 157

[49]Judge Weeramantry (supra n. 47) p. 95

[50]*MMSD* (supra n. 31); such decisions may either advance all the goals or objectives identified by sustainable development- ('Win-win-win decisions); or result in gains and losses-('Trade-off' decisions'), or may seek to protect critical natural capital- ('No-go' decisions) p. 22

[51]ILA New Delhi Declaration Of Principles Of International Law Relating To Sustainable Development' (NDD), 2002, available at http://www.ila-hq.org and UN Doc.A/57/329

[52]Campins-Eritja M. & Gupta J., "The Role of "Sustainability Labelling" in the International Law of Sustainable Development" in *International Law and Sustainable Development*, Schrijver & Weiss (Eds.) 2004 (supra n. 29) p.258

development. It thus represents as concision of the Rio Declaration.

But the concept becomes less practical if embraced in that form without more. There must be a yardstick that delimits the scope of the concept (though not the content) so as to portray its practical implication. Achieving a practical (or meaningful) articulation of sustainable development rests on two factors, which must generally, always be discerned from the context in which the concept is employed. It cannot be defined in abstract. In other words at any usage of the term, one should primarily seek to determine its purpose or the goals it is meant to achieve. Accordingly the exercise would involve a determination of whether the concept is an articulation of international (regional or national) development policy, strategy or agenda on the one hand; or whether it is to inform or direct development *activities* (whether through ventures, projects, programmes or investment policies). In either case the interrelationships between the goals should not be missed or eroded, but can be compartmentalized to fit the particular preferred choice.[53] In the context of a wider development agenda, the environment becomes an indication factor for economic growth and development, and this category to my mind does best define the concept 'international law in the field of sustainable development'.[54] This branch of law is 'still emerging', and cannot be identified as distinct principles and rules which are 'independent and free-standing'.[55] In this context sustainable development may have relevance only in interpretation and development (as oppose to regulation) of varying fields of international law.

As regards the pursuit of development activities or projects however, 'sustainable development' represents primarily as a principle in international environmental law that should inform and guide development activities to a sustainable course in protection of the environment. The application of its elements in this case will depend on the kind of venture sought to be undertaken (mining, fishing, or manufacturing); by whom (whether foreign investment, government, or other); the nature and extent of use that must be made of natural resources (whether land, air, water and their components). And finally, the responsibilities of those embarking on such activities *vis-à-*

---

[53]For instance, a wider development agenda may need to incorporate almost all the principles of the Rio Declaration (or the NDD) including other principles known to international law, though particular emphasis will undoubtedly fall on International Economic law, Development Law, Human Rights Law and International Relations and Co-operation.

[54]Note the distinction between 'sustainable development' as a *principle* of International Law and 'International Law in the field of Sustainable development'. The latter body of law is identified through principle 27 of the Rio Declaration, and has been said to refer to processes, principles and objectives, as well as to large body of international agreements on environmental, economic, civil and political rights (see FIELD: Report of Consultation on Sustainable Development (1993) in *Reciel Vol.2 No. 4*, 1993 p. r2ff.

[55]Sands (supra n. 48) p. 39

vis the redress of those victimised (including species, flora and fauna) by the conduct of such activities. It is in the context of this latter articulation concerning regulation of economic activities, that the true value, purpose and objective of sustainable development find relevance and the element of 'integration' become paramount.[56] This is the meaning adopted in this book.

On this premise therefore, while not purporting to define the concept, it is submitted that 'sustainable development' has direct primary relevance for environmental protection in face of economic exploitation of natural resources to enhance country specific development goals. The imperative in the principle is to implore attention and consideration for the environment while exploiting natural resources. Lack of this attention and consideration, has, and continues to provoke adverse political, social, economic and environmental consequences. It is these consequences, wrought by unsustainable patterns of production and resource exploitation that aligns economic development issues to the 'principle of sustainable development', and thus usher in it a broader dimension - the Development Framework. True sustainability however starts and remains with the way resources are managed (or exploited), and accentuated by the legal mandates, policies or processes that direct it.

2:4 Legal Character of Sustainable Development

Like its definition, the legal character of sustainable development has also met equal scrutiny in scholastic literature. Fitzmaurice considers it an 'almost impossible task' to define the legal status of the concept.[57] This legal dilemma has been blamed on the rarity of legally formulated versions of the principle,[58] and on insufficient clarifications thereof from which to infer a legal content.[59] But Sands observes that sustainable development acquired

---

[56] The failure of the Draft MAI was in my opinion due to a faulty paradigm of articulation, based on this analysis – was it to influence development agendas or development activities? Giving that most investments would go to production processes that directly (or indirectly) connects environment and social issues, the 'Sustainable development activity' paradigm ought to have been the choice. This oversight may have caused the omission to include social and environmental objectives and inevitably, its collapse.(For analyses and criticisms on the MAI, see UNCTAD , *World Investment Report, 1999: Foreign Direct Investment and The challenge of Investment* UN, New York & Geneva, 1999; ILA, *Report of the Sixty-Ninth Conference*, London 2000, p. 700; Nieuwenhuys E., "Global Development through International Investment Law: Lessons Learned From the MAI" in *International Law and Sustainable Development*, Schrijver & Weiss (Eds.) 2004(supra n. 29) pp.295-338.

Also note the observation made by the UNFPA that 'human activity has affected every part of the planet, choices and interventions have transformed the natural world, posing extreme dangers for the quality and sustainability of our civilizations, and for the intricate balances of Nature' (see Report of the State of the World population 2001: Footprints and Milestones: UNPF- UNFPA, 2001 available at <www.unfpa.org>

[57] Fitzmaurice (supra n.23) p.59 In her opinion, it is this difficulty that has endeared authors to the concern with enumeration only of its characteristics and constitutive elements

[58] Layard (supra n.26) p. 46-52

[59] Malanczuk (supra n. 40)

both 'a legal function' and 'legal currency', pursuant to its mere invocation by international judicial bodies.[60] In my view, sustainable development applies to redefine the *legal parameters* of environmental and developmental objectives, emphasising their importance and discerning their role and proper place in addressing the needs of mankind and their interrelationship with nature. Thus 'legal function', 'legal content', 'legal currency' or 'legal use' of the term all indicate some form of legal relevance of the concept to the reorientation process.

However, the concept must have an appreciable legal context by which it can be understood, interpreted, transposed, implemented or achieved, whether at the international or national level. Drawing from the literature on the subject, legality of the concept could either be defined by the nature of the term, its status, or by its transposition and effect. In all three dimensions, 'sustainable development' is assessed not in the abstract of the phrase, but by reference, (implicit or explicit) to an identifiable set of core elements and principles. It is along this line that the legal character of the concept is presented.

2:4:1 Legal Nature: Legality and Obligation

The issue here is whether international law imposes an obligation on states to achieve or implement sustainable development. Scholars are not agreed that there is international legal obligation mandating that development activities must be sustainable.[61] This view is premised on the fact that substantial discretion is left with states in interpreting and giving effect to the 'alleged principle', and compounded by an absence of justiceable standards for review.[62] Some think of the concept as being set up in the mode of an aspiration,[63] while others blame its lack of substantive obligations on its 'declaratory codification approach'.[64] The principle has also been denied legality on grounds that it does not provide the basis from which 'specific obligations' can be deduced or 'individualised rights' tested.[65] Accordingly it is rather considered 'an area in which law-making and other law-related

---

[60]Sands (supra n. 48) pp.395 & 404

[61]Boyle and Freestone, *International Law and Sustainable Development*, Boyle & Freestone (Eds.) OUP, Oxford, 2001 pp. 16-18; Birnie and Boyle, (supra n. 19) p. 96

[62]Boyle and Freestone *Ibid.,* p.16

[63]Porras I, (supra n. 24) p. 246

[64]Malanczuk (supra n. 40) p. 26

[65]Handl G.,(supra n. 30) p. 36

activities take place'.[66]

But all is not lost on the legal character of the concept simply because in its nature, it is believed to confer no direct or specific legal obligation, or because application through its elements is discretionary. There is a sense in which its legal nature can infer an obligation. According to Boyle and Freestone, '...international law... does require development decisions to be the outcome of a process which promotes sustainable development,' and to establish appropriate processes for doing so.[67] In this context, the objectives and principles of the concept are set prescription on achieving sustainable development and are to be employed in policy formulations and decision-making, some of which may emerge as a legal rule rather than a norm. They could also assume high legal relevance when courts or international bodies have to interpret, apply or develop the law.[68]

2:4:2 Legal Status: Legality through Usage or Recognition

The second dimension of legality is tested by the extent to which the objectives of the concept are reflected in existing areas of international (and national) law, or how much influence they have on the development of general international law. The direction of the argument is that ample evidence of reference to the concept in international instruments, (binding and non-binding) policy documents of international bodies, or its application by judicial bodies, qualifies the legal status of the concept in international law. One should however distinguish between legality acquired through treaty obligations, or judicial pronouncements and legal status conferred by recognition, acceptance, adaptation or state practice. The former stands less challenged (because they are linked to sources of binding law), though the obligations they create may not be of universal application. This point is sealed with the official recognition that the concept does have clear treaty basis, from an international perspective.[69]

The issue of legality through recognition by state practice is not so clear cut and dry. In support of the normative significance of the concept, it has been argued that there is ample state practice of sustainable development, expressed in processes of decision-making on the applicability of

---

[66]Lang W., "How to Manage Sustainable Development" in *Sustainable Development and Good Governance* Ginther *et al* (Eds.) 1995 (supra n.33) p. 93

[67]Boyle and Freestone (supra n. 61) p. 17,18,

[68]Lowe (supra n. 40) p. 31 ff

[69]ILA: *Report of the Sixty-Eight Conference*, Taiwan (1998), London 1998. For an analysis of the treaty basis of sustainability principles in the WTO Agreements see Schoenbaum T.J., "International Trade and Protection of the Environment: The Continuing Search for Reconciliation" *AJIL*. Vol. 91 (1997) p.268;

sustainability elements.[70] According to Schrijver and Weiss, the concept has already successfully established its credentials as a legal concept in law through three dimensions of legality:- as 'possessing widely recognised legal core'; as a main policy objective of states and non-state actors, and as *'central to a bewildering variety of practice rooted in law'*.[71] Other scholars have observed that the 'process of legal socialisation' taking place within domestic practices and laws through the influence of sustainable development signifies a 'compliance pull'. It is argued that this 'compliance pull' is more relevant for determining the relevance of the concept as opposed to its precise legal nature (or of the legal text), the latter being less relevant otherwise than for dispute resolution purposes.[72] This school of thought is further embellished by reasoning in the *Gabcikovo case*, wherein the ICJ conceptualised the legal status of sustainable development in the 'consideration' and 'proper weight' that must be given to its objectives and standards in decisions initiating and continuing development projects.[73] It is further elevated to 'a principle with normative value' derived from its affiliation with 'principles of current international law' on the one hand, and from wide, general use and acceptance by the global community, on the other.[74]

With this status, Weeramantry affirms that 'the principle of sustainable development is thus a part of modern international law by reason not only of its inescapable logical necessity, but also by reason of its wide and general acceptance by the global community'.[75]

But presence of a number of environmental principles in conventions, directives, regulations, national codes, specialist analysis or case law, does not mean that they have achieved their full legal effect.[76] In Lowe's view, the concept of sustainable development is devoid of, and inherently incapable of having the status of a rule of law, (whether by the 'doctrine of necessity' or 'global acceptance'), that is binding upon States and purporting to constrain their conduct.[77] Frequent usage of the term is by no means the same as evidence of a general practice accepting the concept as law.[78] The crux of this submission is that sustainable development is incapable of acquiring

[70]Birnie and Boyle (supra n. 17) p.96

[71]Schrijver N. and Weiss F., in *International Law and Sustainable Development* (supra n.29) pp. xiii-iv (emphasis added)

[72]Campins-Eritja & Gupta (supra n.52) p.260

[73]*Gabcikovo Nagymaros Case* (supra n. 39), Paragraph 141 of the judgment

[74]Judge Weeramantry (supra n. 47) pp. 89 & 93

[75]*Ibid* p. 95

[76]De Sadeleer N., *Environmental Principles-From Political Slogans to Legal Rules*, OUP, Oxford 2002 p. 1

[77]Lowe (supra n. 40) p. 23

[78]*Ibid.*

normative status as a principle of international Law, through the traditional combination of 'state practice and *opinio juris*, for the reason that these methods create a primary obligatory rule that binds states.

Going by this reasoning, it would seem that any legal character that sustainable development may have acquired through states acceptance of it, or the necessity to use it as a tool in reconciling environment objectives and developmental goals, (whether in 'soft' or 'hard law' or other recognition thereof), will be legally defunct unless it entails a clear or specific obligation, that will constrain the behaviour of states or restrain other actors within the international legal system. This reasoning though legally plausible, does not however effect to limit the legal application of the concept or its elements. In my view, it only illustrates that there are degrees in legal capacity through which the concept can be applied. It might have failed the legal test of 'obligation', but not of 'responsibility' for environmental damage.

2:4:3 Legal Effects: Legality by Transposition or Application

The third legal investigation moves away from traditional legal analysis of the nature and status of sustainable development, to a legal character acquired through methods of transposition or application of the concept. Here, the legal effect borders around that of an informative, aiding or guidance principle that could be employed in judicial reasoning, administrative decision-making, treaty negotiations or policy formations. In this sense its legal effect is akin to a 'directing principle', providing guidance on choices and methods concerning measures to limit environmental risks and damage with the aim of guaranteeing citizens rights to enjoy a healthy environment.[79]

It must be stated that this third categorisation does seem to address an important concern about the subject, suggesting that indulgence in purely legalistic analyses of the character of sustainable development 'would not reveal whether it embodies a fair, useful and efficient method of achieving environmental goals in particular fields of protection in diversified society'. As emphasised by Higgins 'international law is a normative system, harnessed to the achievement of common values that speak to us all...' and which should be able to contribute to solving today's problems.[80] To a large measure, the international birth and breeding of sustainable development

---

[79]De Sadeleer, (supra n. 76) pp.5-6

[80]Higgins R., *Problems and Process: International Law and How We use It* Clarendon Press, Oxford 1994 p.2-3

Priscilla Schwartz

was intended to solve today's social and environmental problems engendered by economic biases that propagate uncontrolled and unconscionable exploitation of natural resources. Therefore, the legal character of the concept must be assessed from the point of view of its usefulness in society (regulating development activities), and analysed on a case-by-case basis.[81] International law as a process must encourage interpretation and choice that is more compatible with the values and objectives we seek to promote and achieve, and the possibility of including the actions of variety of authorised decision-makers within the fabric of international law.[82]

In this context, the goal-oriented value of sustainable development contributes to the strength and vitality of international law.[83] In other words, to limit the legality of the concept to 'treaty obligations', '*opinio juris*' or judicial pronouncements will not achieve this purpose. Thus, since the aim of this work is to capture the value and usefulness of sustainable development in international law, for environmental management and regulation, including imputation of responsibility for environmental damage consequent upon development activities, difference is given to this third dimension.

Lowe has made the case for this third line of investigation. He acknowledges that, sustainable development can properly claim a legal status as an element of the process of judicial reasoning in the application of the concept to resolve disputes in which environmental objectives and developmental goals conflict. Other vehicles by which legal identity is conveyed to the concept include usage by tribunals to modify the application of other norms; or by states when they negotiate on ways of reconciling conflicts inherent in sustainable development; and in making decisions that reflect its objectives.[84] Essentially, the regime of the principle allows for 'legal intervention [to] occur on a variety of levels'.[85]

Thus, through this third dimension of reasoning, one is able to grasp the true legal character of the concept. The plausibility and indeed merit of this reasoning in my opinion, is that it allows the principle to retain its peculiar character of adaptability whenever its elements are to be clarified,

[81]Fitzmaurice, (supra n. 23) pp. 61-63

[82]Higgins (supra n. 80) p.10

[83]Slinn P., "Approaches to the Relationship between International law and Development" in *International Law of Development: Comparative Perspective*, Synder & Slinn (Eds) Abingdon Professional Books, 1987 p.32 (see also p.36)

[84]Lowe (supra n. 40) p.31 Note also that this conflict-resolution character of sustainable development has bee identified as relevant for reconciling or resolving conflicts between economic, environmental and social treaties and regimes. (See Cordonier-Segger & Khalfan *Sustainable Development Law, Principles, Practice and Prospects*, OUP, Oxford New York, 2004, p. 53

[85]Layard A., (supra n. 26) p. 43)

interpreted, modified or distinguished in the context in which they may be employed.[86]

It is therefore submitted that while International Environmental Law is essentially a *'legislative process'*[87], the legal character of sustainable development as an aspect of that law goes beyond legislative and judicial processes (that may confer obligations relevant for pursuing sustainability) to include administrative, adjudicatory and deliberative processes. The latter defining measures which seek to regulate development activities for environmental protection, including responsibility for environmental harm.[88] It is this peculiar legal character of the concept that explains the richness of its content, justifies the broadness of its scope and enhances its transformationally oriented nature; and it is to this that the huge acceptance of its principles is credited.

2:5 Other Developments on the Concept since Rio

The increasing relevance and progressive application of 'sustainable development' in international (and domestic) fields have calmed its definitional uncertainties, dimensional variances and legal divergences. Efforts in other developments are more directed at extrapolating its useful values for the regulation of environmental and socially sustainable activities as the concept becomes further entrenched. Sustainable development is expressed to have evolved (from Rio–Johannesburg), from an environmental concept, into a shared global responsibility for the implementation of the Rio goals, especially in the protection of natural resources and the modification of patterns of production and consumption.[89] New wave of flexible pilot schemes of 'Voluntary Agreements' and 'Eco-Contracts' between industry and State organs in Europe, are reportedly, achieving the reconciliation of environmental protection in economic progress.[90]

Five years after UNCED, all members of the international community, as well as from major groups of civil society, reconfirmed the political

---

[86]Note also, the logic in this reasoning allows for legal development and enhancement of the concept, including the setting a framework for the reconciliation of conflicts between development activities and environmental protection.

[87]Boyle A., "Codification of International Environmental Law and the International Law Commission: Injurious Consequences Revisited" in *International Law and Sustainable Development*, (supra n. 61) p.63.

[88]Note that these may result in Agreements, voluntary initiatives, or other regulatory measures.

[89]Brandi M., " From Rio to Johannesburg: Toward Sustainable Development" in *Human Rights Law, Newsletter* (IBA/SLP) No.7 October 2004, p.13

[90]Rest A, "Implementation of Rio Targets-Preliminary Efforts in State Practice" in *EPL*, Vol. 25 No.6 (1995) p.139.

commitment to sustainable development at "the Earth Summit+5".[91] The CSD was established to continue the policy dialogue of the concept, including a more focused consideration of its elements for a possible legal instrument. Other initiatives on the development of the principle include a codification of its objectives in a draft covenant,[92] and the ILA NDD recognition and acceptance of general principles underlying the concept.[93] More recently, at the WSSD, in Johannesburg, South Africa, the principle was reaffirmed with renewed commitments.[94] Some of these developments are briefly examined hereunder.

2:5:1 The ICED (Draft)

The ICED aims to provide an integrated legal framework of sustainable development that will be a source for 'ecological and ethical guidance' to individuals, states and other entities.[95] The purpose of the covenant contemplates a legal framework 'to initiate further intergovernmental negotiation for a global treaty'.[96] However the comprehensive pull-together of sustainability objectives in one document provides an immediate reference for States and other entities on addressing sustainability issues, either in the spheres of policy direction, law-making, implementation, enforcement or compliance. The ICED has been assessed as having the potential of being of lasting importance in the global effort to introduce sustainability at the national level.[97]

It can primarily be credited with adopting a holistic approach that covers nearly all fields relevant for a balanced development with environmental protection. Generally, it reinforces some widely established and accepted principles of the concept. It further sets them out in general obligations, rights and duties of parties, states and individuals, which apply irrespective of environmental sectors or types of developmental activities. ICED also accommodates use of economic and legal instruments for the prevention of

---

[91] By the Earth-summit +5, many countries had enacted new environmental laws that are inspired also by the principles of the sustainable development. (See ILA *Report of the Sixty-Eight Conference*, (Taiwan) 1998, London 1998 p.702; Fitzmaurice, (supra n. 23) pp. 45-47

[92] IUCN & ICEL, *Draft International Covenant on Environment and Development* (EPL Paper No. 31 1995), IUCN, Gland, Switzerland, Cambridge, U.K (1995); see also Hassan P. "Toward an International Covenant on the Environment and Development" in *Proceedings of the American Society for International Law, Vol. 87, 1993*, and p.513f.(ICED was launched during the UN Congress on Public International Law, 13-17 March 1995, in New York and was officially presented to the UN in 1995 on the occasion of its fiftieth anniversary).

[93] ILA NDD (supra n.51); for an outline of the suggested principles see footnote 101 below)

[94] WSSD, UN GA Res. 55/199, 20: Dec. 2000

[95] ICED (supra n. 92) (preamble)

[96] Rest A*, (supra n. 90) p. 317

[97] Boer B, (supra n. 33) p.119

harm to the environment and several other legal innovations on sustainable development. Implementation and co-operation issues are addressed through procedures for controlling environmental impacts.[98]

It has received the most commendation for its well-balanced combination of 'State responsibility/liability concept with the civil liability regime, to achieve best compensatory effects'.[99] State responsibility for environmental harm is not limited to obligations under the covenant, but extends to include other rules of international law concerning the environment. This logical connection will no doubt enhance an integrated legal protection of the environment against harm, especially in pursuit of economic activities. Its very flexible, policy oriented compliance mechanism also enjoys this compliment.

The ICED does mark a significant step in the determination of sustainable development and formal legalisation of its principles since their consensual adoption at UNCED. It presents a context in which elements of an alleged 'vague' and 'meaningless' concept, find meaning and a logical legal purpose, through translation of broadly formulated policy targets into concrete and operable legal obligations and rights. It truly represents a formidable legal catalogue for sustainable development.

2:5:2 The ILA New Delhi Declaration

The NDD[100] identifies principles that will define sustainable development in international Law. It compresses the essential contents of sustainable development into seven principles in a manner that reflects the integrative and interrelated nature of the concept.[101] It expresses an objective of integrating economic, social and political process, aiming at sustainable use of natural resources, protection of the environment, fair standard of living and distribution of benefits, and participation, subject to due regards to the needs and interests of future generations.[102] The NDD has been described as building on three special areas of international law, provoking three legal

---

[98]*ICED* (supra n.92) parts 11-VIII & IX respectively.

[99]Rest A, (supra n 90) p.317; for analysis of ICED State Responsibility /Liability concept and compliance mechanism.

[100]ILA NDD (supra n.51)

[101]*Ibid* The relevant principles are:-The duty of states to ensure sustainable use of natural resources ; the principle of equity and the eradication of poverty ; the principle of common but differentiated responsibilities; the principle of precautionary approach to human health, natural resources and ecosystems; the principle of public participation and access to information and justice; the principle of good governance; and the principle of integration and the interrelationship in particular relating to human rights and social and economic and environmental objectives.

[102]*Ibid* para.13

connotations:- an emergence of international law *'for'* or *'relating'* to sustainable development; or a maturation of the concept into a distinct branch of international law *'of'* sustainable development.[103]

Closer scrutiny of the seven principles will reveal efforts primarily geared toward better regulation of development activities, (including accountability and responsibility) for a viable natural and human environment, from an international and national perspective. Thus while the reference *'relating to'* provides the basis for applicability of the principles to various fields of international law, its value and primary relevance for regulating domestic development activities for sustainability cannot be missed. The logical rationale underlying it hinges on sustainable utilisation of resources (in consideration of the environmental and social effects), and enjoyment of development proceeds within an over-all economic strategy for development. It is this fact that the NDD essentially seek to communicate when it considers that, 'the application ...[of these] *principles of international law relevant to the activities of all actors* involved, would be instrumental in pursuing the objective of sustainable development in every way'.[104]

2:5:3 The Johannesburg Summit Agenda for Sustainable Development

Since sown at UNCED, the concept of sustainable development has set deeper into international (and national) issues relating to environmental protection and development activities. The WSSD was convened in Johannesburg South Africa, primarily to reassert global commitment to the principle and to review the progress on implementation since Rio.[105] Two documents were adopted at the summit: The Johannesburg Declaration[106] and a Plan of Implementation (POI).[107] The former document represents a commitment from world leaders to advancing the goals of sustainable development at the national, regional and global levels.

The POI provides an action-plan on the way forward to achieving the objectives of sustainable development. Recognising that UNCED provided the fundamental principles for achieving sustainable development, the POI strongly reaffirms Agenda 21 processes.[108] Generally, it emphasises good

---

[103]Schrijver & Weiss, (supra n.71) p. xiii

[104]ILA NDD (supra n. 51) para 15 (emphasis added)

[105]*WSSD* (supra n.94) para.16

[106]Johannesburg Declaration: *Report of the WSSD*, Johannesburg, South Africa, (2002), UN Doc. A/CONF., 199/20 Res. 1, Annex at 1-5

[107]POI: *Report of the WSSD (Ibid), Res.* 2, Annex at 7-77)(Both Resolutions 1 & 2 available at http://www johannesburgsummit.org/

[108]*WSSD* (supra n. 94)

governance issues as essential both nationally and internationally for sustainable development.[109] It has been commended for extending the participation requirement from what it was under Rio (which limited it to environmental matters only), to applying to all decision-making with respect to sustainable development.[110]

An outstanding achievement of the WSSD especially for regulation of development activities for environmental and social sustainability is recognition by the international community of the need for private sector 'Corporate accountability', as an essential requirement for sustainable development at all levels. Corporate accountability has been noted as one of the most controversial issues in debates regarding implementation of sustainable development.[111] This is inextricably linked with the fact that most development activities are undertaken by corporate entities. Their peculiar legal personality not only blurs the legal scope of their environmental responsibility, but their often multinational or transnational character makes them more elusive and less subservient especially to developing third-world environmental regulations. Thus, the WSSD emphasis places regulation and control of corporate development activities at the 'center of concerns' for sustainable development, and ensures it through transparent regulations, international initiatives and public-private partnerships.[112]

But the POI in particular, has been criticised severally as being aspirational and 'short on specific actions to be taken';[113] as 'denoting more attention to municipal legal systems';[114] and as 'shifting the Rio accent from environmental protection to social and economic development'.[115] In my view, concerns in the POI with direction of national policies and laws, or economic and social issues do not affect or outweigh the environmental protection aspect of sustainable development. The core elements of the concept reflect the 'needs' (socio-economic) aspect, and they were to counterbalance with environmental objectives.

Also, WSSD was presented as a 'summit of implementation', not a 'norm setting exercise'.[116] It confirmed the Rio principles in 'globo' and attempts to

---

[109] See POI (supra n.107) para. 4.

[110] Pallmearts M. "International Law and Sustainable development: Any progress in Johannesburg?" *Receil Vol. 12. Issue 1, 2003* (cf. POI, *ibid* para. 164)

[111] Wilkins, H., (editorial), *Receil Vol.12 Issue 3, 2003*

[112] Johannesburg Declaration (supra n. 106) para.49; see also POI, (supra n.107) para. 18. For analysis on corporate accountability at WSSD, see: Cordonier Segger M., "Sustainability & Corporate Accountability Regimes: Implementing the Johannesburg Summit Agenda" , in *Receil Vol. 12 Issue 3, 2003)*

[113] Sands (supra n. 21) p.66

[114] Pallmearts (supra n. 110) p.4

[115] Rajamani L., "From Stockholm to Johannesburg: The Anatomy of Dissonance in the International Environmental Dialogue" *Receil Vol.12 Issue 1, 2003 P. 32.*

[116] Pallmearts (supra n. 110) p. 8

either strengthen or weaken their formulation were unsuccessful.[117] Thus, sustainable development, is firmly reinstated, reasserted, and entrenched as an international creature that is to guarantee environmental protection amidst the pursuit of development activities. Its constituent elements and principles are to champion this process by implementation at the national level through policies, laws, and other mechanisms clarified at the WSSD.

Part B

2:6 National Implementation of the Concept of Sustainable Development

2:6:1 Design for Adaptation and Implementation at the Domestic level

International law has achieved considerable success in developing, interpreting and applying sustainable development. But it is increasingly being accepted that domestic implementation is the most appropriate vehicle for conveying the valuable objectives of the concept, to truly enhance protection of development environments. The Principle's implications for *national* policy-making are deemed fundamental, especially in bringing countries to realisation of the limits within which they can exploit their natural resources;[118] and for eliminating the risk of 'blocking access to justice'.[119] This explains Lang's contention that sustainable development (as an international process), will never move ahead of the average performance within respective *domestic* processes.[120] These references present very plausible and rational arguments for the relevance of implementing sustainable development at 'home'.

Similarly, the importance of domestic implementation has also been emphasised in the major documents that provide guidance on the meaning and content of the term. The Brundtland report,[121] Rio Declaration,[122] Agenda 21,[123] and more recently the Johannesburg Declaration[124] and POI,[125] all hold important clues on the design for implementation and adaptation of sustainability objectives at national level. Scholars vary on specific emphasis,

---

[117] *Ibid*

[118] <http://www/gopher://gopher.Undp.org/00/ungophers/unep/publications/

[119] Cordonier Segger *et. al.* "Prospects for Principles of International Sustainable development Law after WSSD: Common But Differentiated Responsibilities, Precaution and Participation" in *Receil 12 (1)* 2003 p. 54

[120] Lang, (supra n.66) p. 102; see also Silveira (supra n. 19) p.9; Eliot J. A., *An Introduction to Sustainable Development* (2nd edn.) Routledge London 2001 p. 27

[121] WCED (supra n. 10) pp.308-336

[122] Rio Declaration, (supra n. 12) Principles 9, 10, 11, 13, 15, 16 and 17 respectively

[123] Agenda 21 Chapter 8 (supra n. 13)

[124] Johannesburg Declaration (supra n. 106)

[125] POI (supra n. 107), paras.4, 18, &163

but there is some unanimity of views on the methods of implementation. The general thematic content of these prescriptions including academic articulations on domestic implementation are explored in a general context, from three dimensions, respectively headed: Localisation, Legalisation, and Institutionalisation.

(i) Localisation: Nationalising the Concept

The rationale here is that sustainable development must transcend its 'conceptual cradle and made real and tangible, addressing real people, real developmental and environmental conflicts, and influencing real decisions in an altogether integrative local climate.[126] Valuable objectives and principles of the concept must be imported and localised as mandates primarily within state and government processes, policy planning and management.[127] Sustainability objectives must influence national decisions relating to economic policies, resources management, environmental protection, including the agencies and institutions responsible for these.[128] Policy instruments seeking to address the goals of sustainable development locally must be integrated to ensure minimum standards of compliance, as well as responsible voluntary actions.[129] As already observed, localisation process may raise questions of the limits of private property, particularly in terms of what governments can do to restrict or allow the use of resources through environmental law.[130]

The implementation process of localisation does not only rest with government, its agencies and institutions. Pursuing sustainable development must also be made an integral part of the mandates of international organisations (including UN Agencies), and of major private sector institutions (including businesses), that operate within nation states.[131] This strategy will ensure rapid and effective localisation of the principle.

Given the peculiar nature of sustainable development and the varying issues it seeks to address in an integrated manner (through its elements),

---

[126]WCED (supra n 10) p. 9

[127]Agenda 21 (supra n.13) Chapter 8 pp.87-88

[128]WCED (supra n.10) pp.310-319

[129]MMSD (supra n.33) p.24

[130]Boer B (supra n. 33) p. 115

[131]WCED (supra n.10) pp.310-319; All organisations and programmes of the UN system – FAO, WHO, WTO, World Bank, IMF, UNESCO, UNIDO, UNDP, UNCTAD –are required within their respective areas of expertise and mandate, to strengthen individually and jointly the support for national efforts at environmental protection through implementation of Agenda 21.(See Liobl G., "Environmental Protection & Sustainable Development", in United Nations Law and Practice (2000): Cede/ Sucharipa (Eds.) p 13)

implementation at the national level by localisation methods would require a more practical, direct and flexible framework. While policy statements or commitments are generally welcomed as efforts to adapt the concept nationally, a preferable primary initiative should be the development of national sustainable development programmes, strategies and action plans. The next step will be the adoption of legal measures within country specific conditions that consolidate it.

(ii) Legalisation: Legislation, Regulation, Enforcement and Compliance

National implementation of sustainable development would require certain legal representations that will enhance its gradual consolidation within national legal systems. This will primarily require the provision of an 'effective legal and regulatory framework'.[132] This seeming basic prescription does comprise varying legal methods through which the concept can be said to be effectively incorporated within national legal systems, and not as has been suggested, just 'a mere handmaiden to development'.[133] A legalisation process should therefore generally entail 'efficient rule-making mechanisms based on clearly articulated environmental ethic,[134] and reliable devices for supervising the application of rules.[135]

The first method of implementing sustainability within domestic legal systems is by introducing (or importing) laws, (international or regional), that promote sustainable development, and in a timely manner for enforcement.[136] According to the ILA, this mandate requires that legal texts and principles of international environmental law be made effective through municipal initiatives of ratification and/or implementation, using their legal, administrative and judicial authority and enforcements. It must also involve adjustments and modification on those texts that are necessary to give effect to the objective of enhancing the environment in the pursuit of development.[137] The development of these laws on the international scene must also be monitored, in order to provide continuous update on the local transplants.

The second implementing efforts concern actions in respect of existing and

---

[132] Agenda 21, (supra n. 13) p.91

[133] Boer (supra n. 33) p. 130

[134] *Ibid.*

[135] Lang (supra n. 66) p. 104

[136] Agenda 21 (supra n. 13) p.91

[137] ILA *Report of the 66th conference* (supra n. 32) p. 120

new laws. Existing legislation must be made effective, through a consolidation process. In other words, laws, rules, and regulations dealing with environmental protection or conveying sustainability objectives in other sectors must be identified, integrated, constantly reviewed, enforced and periodically assessed for compliance ratings. Similarly, the design of laws, regulations and agreements must reflect capacity to implement them.[138] A useful suggestion is to examine the socio-economic and environmental instruments in a holistic (as opposed to fragmented) manner.[139] In respect of new enactments (including laws, contractual or voluntary agreements), they must be based on sustainability principles, especially where they direct economic activities.[140] Also, this legislative process should be used to deal directly with prevention and punishment for environmental harm on the one hand, and to augment Common Law requirements through such statutes.[141] This process should in my view also cater for the speedy promulgation of rules to address environmental emergencies. As pointed out, sustaining the concept within legal precepts will bolster its capacity to provide for development alternatives within an enhanced environment.[142]

A very important and popularly acclaimed method of domestic implementation of sustainable development is through the use of effective economic instruments and other incentives.[143] The objective behind use of economic instruments and incentives is driven by the need to provide an effective legal and regulatory framework. The emphasis here is not so much on the legal system but on the results that such system can achieve in impressing environmental concerns within its development projects. It has found recognition in certain international environmental initiatives.[144]

The adoption of economic instruments for implementation of sustainable development have also been noted as instrumental in creating environmentally ethical investments, trusts, or development funds;[145] or for conduct of economic valuation and accounting of the environment to determine trade-offs.[146] Thus, regulation by economic instruments, incentives

---

[138]*MMSD* (supra n. 33) (Executive summary)

[139]Dowdeswell, E., "Sustainable Development: The Contribution of International Law" in *Sustainable Development and International Law* (supra n.19) p.7

[140]See Agenda 21 (supra n. 13) chapter 8.

[141]Wilkins H., (supra n.111)

[142]Eliot J.,(supra n.120) p.27

[143]Agenda 21, (supra n. 13) p.93

[144]See Principle 6(b) & (c), Bergen Conference: Ministerial Declaration on Sustainable Development in *EPL*, 20 (1990) p.104; Principle 13(c) Forest Principles (supra n. 18); World Bank: *WDR; Development and the Environment* (1992) OUP, Oxford, 1992, p 71.

[145]*MMSD* (supra n.33) p. 24

[146]Gillespie A., *International Environmental Law Policy and Ethics*, OUP, Oxford, p.124 This economic valuation technique is derived from what is termed 'Cost-benefit-analysis' (CBA) For a critical view on valuing the environment (in monetary terms) see Naess A., *Ecology, Community and Life Style*, CUP, Cambridge 1989, pp.106, 112-23.

and voluntary actions must be encouraged as compliment to traditional command and control regimes. This method possess great value for transmitting the concept, since it re-orientates economic policies by inclusion of environmental considerations, and combines different sets of regulatory techniques - economic, voluntary, and self-regulation - to promote sustainability.

It should be also mentioned that the WSSD also provide a special implementation prescription that is designed to improve the environmental performances of companies. Amongst these are voluntary systems, codes of conduct, certification, public reporting, and dialogue orientation between community, operators and stakeholders. Other global initiatives such as guide-lines and sustainability reporting are recommended.[147] Implementing and increasing corporate accountability at the local level has thus been summarised as requiring three approaches: voluntary actions (focusing on CSR); judicial punitive measures (based on corporate liability) and corporate citizenship Initiatives (based on international multi-stakeholder co-operation and treaty-making).[148] Similarly, standards of common usages such as 'Best Practice', 'Internationally Acceptable Practice' (IAP) or 'Best Standards', which often define corporate environmental obligations must be implemented in concrete set of sustainability objectives, obligations or goals to be achieved before, during and after the currency of development projects.[149]

Another fundamental implementing criterion is in law enforcement. An immediate emphasis in this measure is the facilitation of enforcement both in terms of appropriate remedies as well as of citizen's access to legal (and administrative) machinery.[150] It infers the use of court actions, tribunals and judicial inquiries to promote or implement sustainable development. The specific use of 'judicial ingenuity' to enforce environmental sustainability of economic activities has been eminently prayed.[151] Courts must be able to achieve sustainability principles in the 'environmental field, even with

---

[147]*POI* (supra n. 107) para 18; Note also other efforts in regulation of MNEs- OECD *Guidelines For Multinational Enterprises*, 21 June1976 (The Guidelines help ensure that MNEs act in harmony with the policies of countries in which they operate and with societal expectations); and OECD *Declaration and Decisions on International Investment and Multinational Enterprises*, (Paris 1992) both available at http://www.oecd.org/; Draft *UN Code of Conduct of Transnational Corporations* (1990) UN Doc.E/1990/94 of 12 June, 1990. (See generally Mulinchksy P.T., *Multinational Corporations and the Law*, Blackwell, Oxford 2003 for detailed analyses on MNEs regulation.

[148]See Wilkins H., (supra n.111)

[149]*MMSD* (supra n. 33) p. xxiii

[150]See Rio Declaration (supra n.12) Principles 10, 13, 20 &22

[151]Carnwath (Lord Justice) "Judicial Protection of the Environment at Home and Abroad" in J Env L Vol. 16, No.3, 2004.p.317-8

limited black-letter legal weapons'.[152] This process could give legal qualification to the concept and its elements, and consequential development of legal jurisprudence on the subject.[153]

A further need in fulfilment of the objective of law enforcement is that countries should put in place efficient and effective judicial and administrative system including the enabling procedures and logistics to facilitate enforcement. Where possible, special environmental courts, or tribunals must be established to deal with the peculiarities of interpreting the objectives of sustainable development locally. The elements and principles of the concept are designed to perform different functions and impose different restrictions, though they aspire to a common goal. In other words, they are not always capable of translation into precise binding laws and 'one size does not always fit all'.[154] This peculiarity is therefore likely to be best handled in judicial or (tribunal) forum, which will deal with their practical application on a case-by-case basis.

But an important aspect of implementation of the concept through enforcement is the need to encourage transnational enforcements against persons or entities that perpetrate environmental wrongs or violate established or recognized environmental principles. In other words it advocates the supranational application of law beyond national prescriptions and conditions. For instance, international courts and national courts of foreign jurisdictions, could aid this process by taking cognisance of both the domestic and international legal and policy framework in which business is conducted, having regard to the need for implementing sustainable development through both efforts. This issue is currently being addressed through various endeavours.[155]

---

[152]*Ibid*

[153]For examples on use of judicial *'ingenuity'* see: *Gabcikovo-Nagymaros Case*, (supra n. 39 & 47); *Minors Opasa et al. V. Sect. of the Environment & Natural Resources Fulgencio Factoras*, GR. No. 101083 30 July 1993. Reprinted in 33 ILM 173, (1994)

[154]Layard Antonia, '(supra n. 26) pp. 43-46

[155]See Draft "Hague Convention on Jurisdiction and Foreign Judgments in Civil and Commercial Matters" (negotiated under Hague Conference on Private International Law (HCCH)) available at http://www.cptech.org It codifies some principles of international jurisdiction which may be relevant in environmental disputes before the courts of most States; *ILC Report* of the 2001 HCCH on the Draft Convention on Jurisdiction and Foreign Judgments in Civil and Commercial Matters http://www.cptech.org; "ILC Draft Principles on Environmental Liability" in *JEL*, 2005 17, pp.155-157; Convention on Jurisdiction and the Enforcement of Judgments in Civil and Commercial Matters (done at Lugano on 16 September 1988 (88/592/EEC), (1988) OJ L 319/9; *OECD Guidelines on MNEs* (supra n. 147); Council Regulation (EC) No. 44/2001 on Jurisdiction and the Recognition and Enforcement of Judgments in Civil and Commercial Matters, (2001) OJ L12/1,(latest consolidated version in (1998) OJ C 27/1); The Alien Tort Claims Act ("ATCA") 28 U.S.C.S. § 1350 (2004)- It gives district courts original jurisdiction for any civil action by an alien for a tort only, committed in violation of the law of nations or a treaty of the United States. For analysis the application of these legislations, see ILA: "Transnational Enforcement of Environmental Law" (Second Report) (2004) (ILA/TEEL) Berlin Conference (2004) available at http://www.ila-hq.org/; and more generally, see *From Government to Governance- 2003 Hague Conference on Contemporary Issues of International Law* TMC Asser press, The Hague 2004.

A final and important requirement for implementation of sustainable development at the national level pursuant to the legalisation method, relates to promoting compliance with sustainability laws, rules, regulations and other policy requirements at all levels. A successful functioning of any legal system would require an orientation toward achieving complicity with its legal mandates. According to Wolfrum, while implementation would primarily require reflection of international obligations in existing laws, agreements and regulations of states (including other legislative and administrative measures necessary under national legal system), 'compliance' means that commitments entered into by states are fully effectuated in practice.[156] Compliance will therefore require action to be taken at the national and international level through enforcement in reaction to identified non-compliance. This will improve implementation failures.[157]

However, Charney has considered it unlikely that a specific formula can be discovered that could allow one to fashion norms to optimise compliance.[158] This view is not unconnected with the fact that compliance (as with sustainable development) is not static but a process, which must be susceptible to change over time to meet the social and environmental challenges that are engendered by development activities.[159]

A useful recommendation is to use compliance strategy that is tailored to the intent and capacity of individual states, and other actors to comply with particular instruments.[160] It is also deemed important to maintain the process and elaborate mechanism of accountability (for states and other relevant actors).[161] Lastly, 'civil society' must be recognised as having an essential role in furthering compliance, or in building the required consensus for negotiating or enacting binding legal instruments.[162]

(iii) Institutionalisation

The importance of this method of implementation cannot be over-emphasised. Broadly, it encompasses efforts at structural reorganisation,

---

[156]Wolfrum R. *Means of Ensuring Compliance with and enforcement of International Environmental Law, Academy of International Law*, Vol. 272 (1998), Martinus Nijhoff Publishers, 1999, The Hague/Boston/ London. Pp.27-29 & 30

[157]*Ibid.*

[158]Charney J.L., "Compliance with International Soft Law", in *Commitment and Compliance: The Role of Non-binding Norms in the International Legal System*, Shelton D. (Ed.), OUP, New York, 2000, p.117

[159]Wolfrum R. (supra n.156) p.30 (citing Brown Weiss)

[160]Brown Weiss E., "Understanding Compliance with Soft Law" in *Commitment and Compliance*: Shelton D. (Ed.), (supra n.158) p.553

[161]*Ibid*

[162]*Ibid*

capacitating institutions, introduction and application of efficient integrative systems, attitudinal reorientation, change in institutionalised practices, and provision of necessary financial mechanisms required to meet and sustain these demands. As was observed by the WCED, the interrelationship between development activities and ecological systems will not change; 'the policies and institutions concerned must change'.[163] This suggests both physical actions at institutional reorganisation, requiring integration of sectors and agencies responsible for environment and development related matters or enhancing cooperation and co-ordination between them. According to the report, 'separate policies and institutions can no longer cope effectively with these interlocked issues'.[164] In this same vein, Countries should integrate set of institutions that will be responsible for national environmental valuation and economic accounting of natural resources, so as to include them in conventional accounts. Old regimes which discounted social and environmental issues must undergo reorientation because 'the environment cannot be protected when growth leaves out of account the cost of environmental destruction...'[165]

The institutional rational entails a further requirement for attitudinal re-orientation of the perceptions of states, organisations, agencies, and people alike with regard to environment and development issues- that 'they are [both] linked in a complex system of cause and effect.'[166] Therefore institutionalisation demands more than just providing for individual elements of the concept, or institutions to promote specific principles (as is often done in the requirements for EIA). States systems must be made effective to apply broad array of elements and principles of sustainable development.[167] By implication, the methods of national implementation should equally be effectuated in practice. States should resist a 'pick-and-chose' adaptation technique and endeavour to source the valuable sustainability rationale embedded in the methods of 'localisation', 'legalisation' and 'institutionalisation' by applying them.

Finally, the reorganisation, and integration of institutions bring with it financial burdens which are likely to crumple the identified implementation processes. While it is paramount that states maintain the responsibility to budget necessary finances for institutional and legal capacity to pursue

---

[163]WCED (supra n. 10) p.310

[164]Ibid p.37

[165]Agenda 21 (supra n. 13) Chapter 8:D

[166]WCED (supra n. 10) p. 37

[167]Okidi, C. "Incorporation of General Principles of Environmental Law in National Law with Examples From Malawi" in EPL 27/4 (1997) p.331

sustainable development at national and local levels, they would also require assistance with financing and technology.[168] One such effort is evidence in the UNEP GEF in terms of financing of environmental projects.

Conclusion

The aim of this chapter was to bring out the value oriented nature and relevance of the concept of sustainable development in international law, for resource management and environmental protection in conduct of development activities. It also sought to present the methods by which the concept can be implemented at the domestic level. This effort has revealed that despite definitional questions and legal divergences, sustainable development does have primary purpose and direct relevance for the regulation of development activities for environmental protection, including an appreciable legal context in which it could be applied to fulfil its primary purpose.

It has identified a legal character in the concept beyond legislative and judicial processes (that may confer obligations relevant for pursuing sustainability), to include adjudicatory, administrative and deliberative processes; with a flexibility that allows for the interpretation of its principles within legal rules to enhance environmental protection at the global or domestic level. Through, an illustrative paradigm of implementation methods, the value of the concept for regulating domestic activities is further emphasised. It has also been established that national implementation represents an important and necessary means of applying sustainable development in order to achieve its purpose of protecting domestic development environments.

Having identified the primary purpose, legal parameters and its national application, the next chapter will analyse relevant elements and principles for directing or achieving sustainable development. These principles convey the practical value of the concept by defining the social and environmental parameters within which natural resources can be exploited for economic purposes, for the ultimate objective of sustainability.

---

[168]See Malanczuk.P (supra n. 41)

3 ELABORATION OF ASPECTS OF SUSTAINABLE DEVELOP-MENT MOST RELEVANT TO THE ENVIRONMENT

3:1 Introduction

The previous chapter established the place of sustainable development in international law. Its primary purpose was revealed as rooted in the protection of the environment amid economic exploitation of natural resources. The chapter also established an appreciable legal context and implementation methods by which domestic development environments can be protected as a goal of sustainable development. Discerning the purpose, legal nature and domestic implementation methods of the concept represent as conditions for initiating sustainability. Underlying this theme is the rationale that sustainable development in international law provides social, environmental and resource management parameters that must define the way resources are exploited in development activities pursuant to the initiating conditions. These parameters are represented by some pertinent element and principles that embody the concept.[1] These principles convey the practical value of sustainable development, fulfil its purpose by instilling social and environmental considerations into development activities, and impute responsibility on developers for the ultimate objective of sustainability. This chapter entails an elaboration on identified principles which represent aspects of sustainable development most relevant to protection of the environment (as opposed to socio-economic development), and which this book considers to hold environmentally valuable objectives.

---

[1]Note that the references to the term 'elements' and/or 'principles' in this thesis only reflect the distinction between principles that are commonly recognised as inherent in the concept and are described as its elements; and principles derived from general International Law, and deemed relevant for achieving the objectives of the concept. (See Fitzmaurice M.A., *International Protection of the Environment*; Hague Academy of International Law, Martinus Nijhoff Publishers, Hague/ Boston/ London (2002) p. 51); but note also, that the demarcating line between 'elements' and 'principles' has been considerably eroded as they continue to be adopted in treaties, declarations and legislations. Their effect in fostering the goals of sustainable development is however not affected by this distinction and therefore they are used in this work interchangeably.

The relevant principles are-: Environmental Protection, Integration, Inter and Intra-generational Equity, Sustainable Utilisation, Polluter-Pays and Precautionary Principle, EIA and Public Participation. These will be analysed, bringing out their value-oriented nature especially the capacity to afford environmental protection in resource exploitation. They are presented as deriving severally from the legal characterisation of sustainable development adopted in chapter 2. Therefore, an in-depth individual assessment of the legal nature of the various principles will not be addressed here. Also, the principles will be analysed as independent components though they may overlap or complement each other in their functions. The chapter ultimately seeks to bring out the values in the individual objectives of these principles (as components of sustainable development) that are necessary for regulating development activities to ensure environmental protection.[2]

3:2 Principles Relevant for Sustainable Development Activities

The least disputed aspect of sustainable development is an acceptance that it constitutes distinct set of elements by which development activities can be made environmentally sustainable. This fact is recognised in scholastic interactive on the subject.[3] There may be slight variances in the general appreciation of the principles, usually placed in context of attempts to distinguish between their nature, function, application, or the means of achieving their individual objectives. In the absence of clear substantive obligation, the principles have severally been deemed to serve variegated functions in aid of directing sustainability. For instance some elements are said to impose political obligations on governments when they set the framework for the exploitation or use of components of the environment.[4]

Other principles are considered a 'reiteration and precisation of existing customary law';[5] while some guide specific substantive policy choices or relate to procedural and institutional behaviour, directed by a process by

---

[2]Note that the environmental protection dimension of sustainable development employed here goes beyond the natural environment to include the social environment as well; (see Introductory Overview supra p.22, A(ii)); social concerns are therefore to be generally implied in references to 'environmental protection' , 'domestic' or 'development' environments.

[3]Handl G., "Sustainable Development: General Rules Versus Specific Obligations" in *Sustainable Development and International Law*; Lang, W. (Ed.), Graham &Trotman/ Martinus Nijhoff, London/Dordrecht/ Boston (1995) p. 40

[4]Wolfrum R., "International Environmental Law: Purposes, Principles and Means of ensuring Compliance" in *International, Regional and National Environmental Law*, Morrison & Wolf rum (Eds.) (2000) Kluwer Law International, The Hague/London/Boston, 2000, p.23

[5]Rest A, "Implementation of Rio Targets-Preliminary Efforts in State Practice" in *EPL, Vol. 25 No.6* (1995) p.313. Note that principles reiterating and making customary law precise are those embodied in numerous international treaties.

which future environmental impacts can be considered and addressed.[6] These relevant principles can also provide for the application and further elaboration of the concept by states, international organisations, courts and tribunals.[7]

Two fundamental inferences can be drawn from the respective distinctions and categorisations. First, they suggest a basic common agreement in the least, on certain elements and principles of the concept through their functions or the manner in which they may be employed is likely to vary depending on the context in which they may be used. Second, the various formulations give ample legal capacity to the principles, as they prescribe the important contexts in which their values can be interpreted and harnessed. To my mind these references mark the corner stone for applying and achieving environmental protection in conduct of development activities.

3:2:1 Environmental Protection

Environmental protection has been a constant challenge on the international arena, especially when it is often erroneously understood as coming up against development activities.[8] Yet environmental protection is recognised as a fundamental principle in international law, expressed primarily through the sovereignty principle.[9] But it is also recognised in treaties directed either at protecting the environment generally, or in respect of particular environmental components, mostly in effort to protect renewable natural resources that are shared between States.[10]

A distinction must be made between environmental protection generally as a

---

[6]Gaines S.E., "International Trade, Environmental Protection and Development as a Sustainable Development Triangle" *Receil Vol. 11 Issue 3*, (2002) pp.259-273, at 264; Birnie & Boyle, *International Law and the Environment*, second edition, OUP,(2002) p.90; Boyle and Freestone, *International Law and Sustainable Development*, Boyle & Freestone (Eds.) OUP, Oxford, 2001 pp.8-9).

[7]Sands P., "International Law in the Field of Sustainable Development – Emerging legal principles" in *Sustainable Development & International law*, (supra n. 3), p.66; Cordonier Segger et. al. "Prospects for Principles of International Sustainable development Law after WSSD: Common But Differentiated Responsibilities, Precaution and Participation" in Receil 12 (1) 2003 p.54

[8]The 1962, UN GA Resolution 1831(XVII) on 'Economic Development and Conservation of Nature' expresses concern over the environmental wealth of developing countries which was being jeopardised by economic development, and endorsed a call by UNESCO to enact effective domestic legislation covering *inter alia*, the preservation and rational use of natural resources. (See UNYB (1962) pp 68-9); For a comprehensive insight, see Schrijver N. *Sovereignty over Natural resources*, Cambridge University Press, Cambridge, 1997 pp 120-40.

[9]Note that primarily applied in transboundary context, this principle now finds direct application to protection of domestic environments.(see Experts Group on Environmental Law of the WCED, *Environmental Protection and Sustainable Development* (Experts Group) Monroe & Lammers (Eds),Graham &Trotman, Martinus Nijhoff 1996 , London/ Dordrecht/Boston p.ix;

[10]Some protection efforts are in:- Convention on Nature Protection and Wildlife Preservation in the Western Hemisphere, 1940 (nature and wildlife); The African Convention on the Conservation of Nature and Natural resources, 1968 (soil, water, flora and fauna); CITES 1973 (endangered species); UNCLOS 1982 (marine environment); Convention on the Protection and Use of Transboundary Watercourses and International Lakes, 1992 (water resources) and Biodiversity Convention 1992 (biological diversity).

principle of international environmental law,[11] and environmental protection as an element of sustainable development. The latter is more narrowly defined in connection with natural resource management within the framework of sustainable development. This dimension of protection will find specific application 'to all instances of the use of a natural resource, or of an environmental interference in any part of the world'.[12] The requisite protection will therefore interpret in context of particular development activities, as undertaken in particular environments, and in relation to the environmental resources that would be employed or affected. It is in this sense of resource exploitation that emphasis is placed on the protection of the environment for sustainable development. In other words, environmental protection forms the basis upon which resource exploitative activities can be said to be sustainable. Thus, environmental protection as an indication of sustainable development, has acquired several connotations.

It has been taken to mean 'a commitment to reducing pollution and environmental degradation and to the more efficient use of resources' so as to maintain environmental capacities.[13] It has also been understood to have an economic and social component, by which protection should not be seen as limitations for utilization, but rather as the right to utilize the 'resource environment' in a certain manner.[14] In the extreme case, environmental protection implies imposing a limitation or qualifying the exercise of the right of States in exploitation of their natural resources. Whatever the connotations, the operation of this element for sustainable development has been clearly stated in the Rio Declaration. 'In order to achieve sustainable development, environmental protection shall constitute an integral part of the development process, and cannot be considered in isolation from it'.[15] So that, the effects of any form of development activities on the environment must be contemplated in order to avoid, reduce or minimise the impact on the natural, human and cultural environment.

Furthermore, in so far as 'human beings are the center of concerns for

---

[11]This envisages a wider scope of regulation under international environmental law, and will include issues like, protecting the environment from Wars, hazardous substances, technologies and wastes, Transboundary pollution, protection of global atmospheric components, trade and the environment, and control mechanisms (liability regimes) for environmental protection at the international level.

[12]Experts Group, (Supra n. 9) p. ix; For example, the revised 1975 constitutive treaty (Lagos Treaty) of ECOWAS members (revised in 1993) endorses one of its objectives as '... to protect, preserve and enhance the natural environment of the region'. See *Revised Treaty of the Economic Community of West African States* (ECOWAS), 1993, article 29, reprinted at (1996) 8 *Afr.J.I.C.L* 189

[13]See Jacobs, M. "Sustainable Development as a Contested Concept" in *Fairness and Futurity*, Dobson A.(Ed.) OUP Inc, New York, 1999 p.85; Shiva V., "Resources"; in *The Development Dictionary*: Sachs W. (Ed.), Zed Books, London, (1992) p. 217

[14]Liobl G., "Environmental Protection & Sustainable Development", in *United Nations Law and Practice* (2000): Cede/ Sucharipa (Eds.)

[15]Rio Declaration on Environment and Development, June 13, 1992, adopted by the UNCED at Rio de Janeiro. UN Doc A/CONF. 151/26 (Vol.1) (1992);*ILM* 874, 1992 (Rio) Principle 4

sustainable development', they are entitled to pursue developmental activities so as to 'equitably meet their developmental and environmental needs...'[16] The latter 'needs' becomes very important in the protection mandate, because it enables humans to fulfil both their 'right to development' and their entitlement 'to a healthy and productive life in harmony with nature'.[17] It is in respect of this fundamental implication of environmental protection for sustainable development that states assume the following responsibilities under the Rio Declaration:- to conserve, protect, and restore the health and integrity of the earth's ecosystem;[18] to take cost effective measures to prevent environmental degradation;[19] to enact effective environmental legislations, employ environmental standards and management objectives and priorities; and are required to develop national laws regarding liability and compensation for the victims of pollution and other environmental damage.[20] Environmental protection efforts have also been championed through institutions both at national and international levels.[21]

More importantly, the Principle has been viewed as conferring environmental rights, generally referenced in context of human rights.[22] Environmental rights have been sought from other internationally protected rights, advocated as deriving from democratic values (procedural rights) and even given constitutional status or judicial pronouncements in national legal systems.[23] According to Judge Weeramantry, 'the protection of the environment is also a vital part of contemporary human rights doctrine... such as the right to health and the right to life itself'. Damage to the environment can impair and undermine this right. The Principle is thus surmised to mean that: 'while therefore, all peoples have the right to initiate development projects and enjoy their benefits, there is likewise a duty to ensure that those projects do not significantly damage the environment'.[24]

[16]*Ibid* Principle 3

[17]*Ibid* Principle 1

[18]*Ibid* Principle 7

[19]*Ibid* Principle 15

[20]*Ibid* Principle 13; (other pertinent protection measures states could adopt are evidenced in Principles 8,9,10,17, 18 &19 respectively).

[21]UNEP and the CSD urge environmental protection through implementation of Agenda 21; Also Environmental protection institutions have been established through a number of framework environmental treaties (Secretariats of CBD, FCCC, and Montreal & Kyoto Protocols) including financial mechanisms (GEF).

[22]For analysis on environmental rights, see Experts Group,(supra n.9) p. 38-42; Redgewell, C., "Life, the Universe and Everything: A Critic of Anthropocentric Rights" in *Human Rights Approaches to Environmental Protection,* Boyle & Anderson (Eds.) Claredon Press, Oxford, 1998; Handl G., "Human rights and Protection of the Environment" in *Economic, Social and Cultural Rights* Eide/Krause/Rosas (eds) 2001; *'The Right of a child to a Clean Environment',* Fijalkowski/Fitzmaurice, (Eds.) (2000). See also the application of this principle in the *Lopez-Ostra Case in HRLJ, Vol.15, and No. 11- 12.*

[23]See the ILA Report of the *70th Conference,* (New Delhi) London 2002 pp. 832 f.

[24]Separate opinion of Weeramantry in the *Gabcikovo-Nagymaros Case* (1997), *ICJ Reports* 15 September 1997, GL No. 92 p.92

But some have questioned this 'right' to a clean environment because of its inherent anthropocentricity, understood as ignoring the rights of animals and nature.[25] For others there is envisaged 'complications' in using the notion of rights in environmental protection giving that it has' imprecise definition and limited justifiability'.[26] Yet further concerns suggest that the rights perspective is not helpful because of the danger of having a situation where 'preference confronts preference'. This might make the accommodation process advocated by the integration principle more difficult, as it will be harder for the right-holders to accept a compromised situation.[27]

Notwithstanding the forgoing, there is no denying that the element of environmental protection is vital and a value-added requirement for sustainable development that must be recognised in the conduct of development operations. As Redgewell puts it, 'a clean, healthy or decent human environment is also a clean healthy or decent environment for non-humans'. This effect she contends is inevitable even without recognition of such a human right, since it is not possible to separate human interests from the protection of the environment.[28] Central to the element is an overwhelming concern and need to protect and preserve components of the environment for the benefit of mankind between generations, but 'it does not rule out the protection of nature for its own intrinsic value'.[29] What sustainable development implies is a development pursued in an environmentally sound and friendly manner. Such an activity should *inter alia*, have integrated within it, general environmental concerns.

3:2:2 Integration of Environment and Development

The meaning and concept of the integration principle can be discerned from a combination of principles 3 and 4 of the Rio Declaration. While Principle 3 justifies and sanctions the conduct of development activities, Principle 4 seeks to condition such conducts by recommending the integration of environmental concerns and initiatives into such activities. By this element the declaration indicates that environmental preservation and promotion of development are interrelated and therefore require an integrated approach.

[25]Churchill in Redgewell C, (supra n.22), p.71

[26]ILA *Report of the 69th Conference*, (London) London 2000 p. 693

[27]Ximena F.,(citing Merrills) "International Law-making in the Field of Sustainable development: The Unequal Competition Between Development and Environment" in *International Law and Sustainable Development: Principles and Practice*, Schrijver & Weiss (Eds.) Martinus Nijhoff Publishers, Leiden/Boston 2004p p.34

[28]Redgewell, C., (supra n. 22) P. 87

[29]Wolfrum, R., (supra n. 4) p.22

The implications of the integration element for sustainable development are far reaching, as it seeks to reconcile environmental and developmental differences, recognise and absorb social issues, influence economic policies and political decisions including the way laws are made and implemented. Rio is said to also integrate the needs of both present and future generations.[30] Policy makers and developers should therefore, always consider the social effects of their development policies and activities.

The practicalities of integrating environment and development in decision-making and the prescriptions for implementing it are dealt with in chapter 8 of Agenda 21. In that context, integration requires ensuring that economic activities and environmental protection are integrated at the policy, planning and management levels. The principle has accordingly been interpreted as injecting 'sustainability' concepts into both macro and microeconomic policies.[31] At the 'macro' level, traditional national accounting systems must be changed to rather measure the quality of life in the face of development ventures by reflecting environmental damages caused by pollution, or otherwise to exclude efforts aimed at controlling such damages. Microeconomics shifts calls for imposing the costs of environmental damage on the developer causing the damage, while product pricing should be made to reflect environmental and social costs as the true cost of production costs.[32] This integration approach has been described as 'most legalistic', its formal application requiring the collection of appropriate environmental information and its dissemination. It may also serve as the basis for allowing or requiring 'green conditionality' in development loan institutions.[33]

This holistic approach and diversified application engendered by the integration element, truly makes it priceless in the pursuit of sustainable activities. It is therefore not surprising that the principle is described as the very 'backbone' of the concept of sustainable development.[34] Thus, the key to sustainable development in resource use, exploitation and the achievement of environmental protection and conservation is through the integration of environmental safeguards and economic decision-making. 'Integration remains the most likely means to secure a balanced view of environmental needs within competing priorities'.[35] People in the business of resource

---

[30]Such needs also includes environmental ones; see ILA (supra n. 23) pp 390, 391

[31]At <http://www.gopher.undp.org/oo/ungopher/unep/publications/monographs/law> p.2

[32]*Ibid*

[33]Sands, P., (supra n. 7) p.61

[34]ILA (supra n. 23) pp. 390, 391

[35]Birnie and Boyle., (supra n. 6) p.87

exploitation for economic reasons are able to empathise with the demands of this element, because it translates environmental concerns into a language they understand. Above all, the other elements find easy application through it, because it explains *inter alia* why 'posterity' matters in the environmental protection imperative of sustainable development.

3:2:3 Intergenerational Equity

This element of sustainable development is primarily defined by the concept of needs. As recognised by the ILA, the integration element also calls for the integration within development plans, of the 'needs' of future generations in relation to developmental and environmental materials and components.[36] The WCED definition also suggests that 'development' does not imply only the pursuit of economic activities to meet our needs, but one that is also sustained to meet future needs.[37] This principle should form a new global ethic that is needed to find an answer to the environmental *problematique*.[38] In other words, while the formulation does not question the principle of 'development' as a method for satisfying the 'needs' of current generations, it at the same time explicitly recognises that future generations also have interests deserving protection.[39]

Principle 3 of the Rio Declaration also gives formal recognition to the concept of 'intergenerational equity', indicating that there is a balance that must be maintained for sustainable development.[40] The search for this balance continues to generate various interpretations of the element. First, intergenerational equity is said to infer that present generation should not use resources or degrade the environment, and thereby to leave future generations in worse position than the present generation.[41] It also indicates that generations must have equal chances for development while they

---

[36]ILA (supra n. 30 above)

[37]WCED: *Our Common Future*, OUP, Oxford, 1987; (WCED) p.43

[38]*Ibid*

[39]See Pallmearts M., "International Environmental Law from Stockholm to Rio: Back to the Future?" *Reciel Vol. 1, No.3* (1992), p.261

[40]Some example of international recognition of the principle include: article 30 "The 1974 UN Charter on the Economic Right & Duties of States" UNGA Res.3281 (XXIX) 1974; Principles 1 & 3 "Historical Responsibility of states for the Preservation of Nature for Present and Future Generations" UN Doc. A. /RES/35/8 (1980) 30 Oct); The 1980 Brandt Commission, North-South: "A Programme For Survival", (Pan, London 1980, p. 115;The Nairobi Declaration, 18 May 1982, UNEP Report. 37 UN GAOR.

For a number of national Constitutions that reflect the principle, see Weiss E.B., *In Fairness to Future Generations: International Law, Common Patrimony & Intergenerational Equity*, Falk R. (Ed.) UN University, Japan, Dobbs Ferry, New York, 1988. App. B.

[41]Boer B., "Implementation of International Sustainability Imperatives at the National Level" in *Sustainable Development and Good Governance*, Ginther et al (Eds.) Martinus Nijhoff Publishers Dordrecht/Boston/London, 1995 (citing Edith Brown-Weiss) p. 115

inhabit the environment at any given time.[42] In this sense, the element operates to limit economic developments if such developments would result in significant or lasting deterioration on the environment and thus impose the cost of present developments upon future generations.

Others view the element as placing policy discussions in a 'fresh context', by adding a temporal component to the evaluation of whether a particular policy assists in the development process and protection of the environment for the future.[43] This interpretation becomes particularly important in cases where the concept has received a strict interpretation, requiring that natural capital should be preserved intact for future generations - 'strong' sustainability, - as against substitution between different forms of natural and manmade capital -'weak' sustainability.[44] In my view, the balance required to be maintained in the operation of the concept evidences in the 'weak' version of sustainable development but to the extent that it includes the preservation and bequeathing of some form of environmental assets, renewable and non-renewable alike. This understanding is echoed elsewhere, suggesting that the nature of intergenerational interests relates to human needs on the one hand, and other environmental interest that are based on the intrinsic value of nature, flora and fauna.[45] Thus, the ideology of intergeneration equity allows for environmental issues of distribution and access to goods (both environmental and manmade) among people of present and future generations.

Similarly the element has been understood as entailing two issues that define the meaning of equity in sustainable development especially in context of the environment; these are 'allocation of natural resources' and 'responsibility and liability for pollution'.[46] In other words the concern of the concept is not limited to our consideration of the interest of future generations and what or how much we should bequeath to them. It includes the actions taken and measures we implement to safe guard that interest, even as we exploit nature for development. The scope of the 'interest' is discerned as extending to considerations of 'fairness and justice' in the formulation, application and interpretation of laws aimed at regulating development activities; and to the

---

[42]Wolfrum R.,(supra n. 4) p.22

[43]Gaines S., "International Trade, Environmental Protection and Development as a Sustainable Development Triangle" *Receil Vol. 11. Issue 3, (2002)* p. 264

[44]Both 'strong' and 'Weak' forms of Sustainable development are common adjectives used to describe the extent or limits on the claims in respect of present and future generations, regarding 'rights and interests' in Environmental resources, and how these can be guaranteed in the decision-making process.

[45]ILA (supra n. 23) p.392

[46]Brown Weiss E., "Environmental Equity – The Imperative for the 21st Century", in *Sustainable Development and International Law* (supra n.3) p.17

environmentally adverse consequences that result from resources utilisation or exploitation.[47]

At another level Brown-Weiss interprets the principle as symbolising an obligation owed to future generation, which is expressed in notions of 'duty of care' and 'a right' in relation to our dealings with environmental resources.[48]

She maintains that, members of the present generation hold the earth in trust for future generation, and also as beneficiaries, with entitlement to use it.[49] The scope of the formers' interests or claims on the environment have been identified as 'quality', 'options' and 'access,' implying that they should be giving the opportunity to enjoy no less environmental quality, should have no less option for development and no less access to a viable environment than the present.[50] This 'rights-based' analysis effectively suggests that future generations have 'rights' in certain environmental components which present generation is obliged to protect.

The ICJ has recognised the interests of future generations to an undamaged environment. It identified existence of a reasonably defined set of 'interests' of the future generation in environmental protection expressed in the ability to secure food from it, the luxury of enjoying its ecosystems and yields of nature, and their well-being, but did not define them in terms of 'Rights'.[51] Essentially, these are vital interests that ought to be contemplated by this generation in the conduct of development activities; but whether future generation can claim them from a 'Rights' perspective is not clear-cut. At the national level, the Philippines Supreme Court has recognised protection of intergenerational interests in the *Minors Opasa Case*.[52] In securing their interest, the court acknowledged 'the right of future generations to be represented by the present generation' to protect the quality of the environment (substantive standard) and to target grave abuses of administrative discretion which are exercised in the detriment of the environment (remedial standard).[53] This case is said to have established the

---

[47]See ILA (supra n. 23) p.392.

[48]Brown-Weiss E., (supra n. 40) pp.47-93 & 95-117

[49]*Ibid*; see also Brown-Weiss "The Planetary Trust: Consequences and Intergenerational Equity", *Ecology Law Quarterly*, 11 (1984) 511.

[50]See Report of the Expert Group meeting on identification of Principles of International Law for Sustainable Development, Geneva Switzerland, 26-28 Sept 95, and Background paper 3 for the CSD Fourth Session, 1996, at p. 12.

[51]Advisory Opinion to the UNGA on The Legality of the Threat or use of Nuclear Weapons, *ICJ Reports* 1996, p.339 Para. 29 – 35.

[52]*Minors Opasa Case* (supra chapter 2, p.67, n.153); (see concurring opinion of Feliciano) In that case, the court, applied the principle in the management of natural resources and the environment, and granted standing to forty-two children as representatives of themselves and future generations to protect their right to a healthy environment, against timber development decisions that would affect the environment. They accorded them standing to sue on behalf of succeeding generations based on the concept of 'intergenerational responsibility in so far as the right to a balanced and healthy ecology is concerned'.

[53]Antonio G.M. La Vina "The Right to a Sound Environment in the Philippines: The Significance of the Minors Opasa Case", *Receil* Vol. 3 No. 4 1994 pp. 246-249.

principle as a legal concept with practical and potentially far-reaching implications for the right of both present and future generation.[54]

However, there are scepticisms elsewhere on this whole debate on the 'rights' of future generation or the scope of obligation it imposes on present generation. This generational obligation has severally been considered as an ethical one,[55] as a moral one based simply on humanitarian objective[56] and as a matter of justice.[57] Similarly, Birnie and Boyle suggest that references of 'intergenerational equity' in Declarations and Treaties only indicate the importance of the principle in international policy for environmental protection. They do not demonstrate an endorsement of generational right, or endowment with justiceable rights in international law.[58] Equally, the reception or expression of the principle in national courts do not represent generalised generational rights in national laws, as this will turn on procedural rules in context of each legal system.[59]

In rejoinder to the immediate arguments let me add that intergenerational equity by its nature, is reflective of what it entails - equity. The symbolism of fairness in equity is what drives the Principle, not legal rights. The present generation must use the components of nature in exercise of their own option for development, but in an environmentally responsible manner so as to protect the interest of future generations. Even though 'rights' could be accorded in equity when prayed, it is a right that only present generation can claim and identify a common interest of future generation in it.

It is however important to clarify and caution that the 'rights' issue debate on the principle, is particularly engendered towards the goal of general environmental rights and has little effect on the ideology that defines the element for sustainable development - that in dealing with nature, consideration should be given to 'posterity'. For only in line with this rationale would all parties with varied interests in the environment adopt a responsible concern in interaction with it - whether in the exercise of 'right to development', 'right to protection', administrative discretion or judicial functions. And all the other elements of sustainable development would derive from it.

---

[54]Boer B., (supra n.41) pp.135 - 136)

[55]Gower B., "What Do We Owe Future Generation"; in *The Environment in Question - Ethics & Global Issues,* Cooper D & Palmer J. (Eds) Routledge, London, 1992

[56]Beckerman, W., "Sustainable Development and our Obligations to Future Generations" in *Fairness and Futurity* (supra n. 13) p. 91

[57]De Shalit A., *Why Posterity Matters- Environmental Policies and Future Generations,* Routledge, 1995 p.11

[58]Supanich in Birnie and Boyle (supra n. 6) p. 90

[59]*Ibid*

3:2:4 Intragenerational Equity

Sustainable development is not just about protecting the environment in the interests of future generations, but also advocates for the needs and interests of the present.[60] They are the 'center of concern' for sustainable development, and are 'entitled to a healthy and productive life in harmony with nature'.[61] Intragenerational equity therefore implies that people within the present generation have the right to benefit from the exploitation of resources (to fulfill their right to development) and are equally entitled to a clean and healthy environment in the process of such exploitation. The principle encapsulates varied set of implications especially for environmental protection in conduct of development activities for ultimate sustainability.

Primarily, it allows for the employment and utilisation of environmental resources by policy planners and developers, as a means of meeting the economic and developmental needs of present generation. But they must also always consider the extent to which adverse impacts generated thereby, (social and environmental costs) would take away from the aspired development benefits to the public.[62] This delicate balance must be maintained, as it facilitates the controlling objective of sustainable development- ensuring that ecological and economic concerns go hand in hand. Similarly, the element also implies maintaining social sustainability through *inter alia*: fair and equitable distribution of income; access to, and allocation of resources; sustainable social infrastructures and institutions; provision of redress for victims of pollution, apportioning responsibility for environmental degradation and improved decision-making on alternative uses of environmental materials. But socially sustainability issues in natural resource development ventures have equally been increasingly allied with impacts on 'human right, especially were projects entail forced resettlement of populations and pollution of shared water resources.[63] Thus, equity in the principle seeks to guide development planners to recognise, that human well being is constituted by more than just income growth, to include more significantly the 'quality of life.[64]

Finally, the operation of the element demands that meeting the needs of present populations and protecting their interests within an interdependent

---

[60]Note that the analysis centers on equity within states, in the sense of peoples right to benefit from development activities not on aspect of intra-generational equity between states (including issues of differentiated responsibilities).

[61]Rio Declaration (supra n. 15) principle 1

[62]On this point see Auty R.M and Mikesell R.F., *Sustainable Development in Mineral Economies* OUP, Oxford 1998 p. 67.

[63]Handl (supra n. 22) p. 40

[64]For an analysis of 'quality of life' as an indication of social sustainability, see Jacobs, M., (supra n. 13)

environment is to be achieved 'in harmony with nature'. It means that humans and nature have a common existence and interdependence on the environment that must be considered in the pursuit of development activities. In other words, for the principle to have its full compliment environmental capacities must be maintained, its resources efficiently managed and its components must be sufficiently guarded through effective environmental controls like conservation on the one hand, and standards that ensure sustainable utilization or employment of natural resources, on the other.

3:2:5 Sustainable Utilisation or Employment of Natural Resources

Generally, the principle sustainable utilisation (or employment) of natural resources represents a mandate for states to 'maintain ecosystems and ecological processes essential for proper functioning of the biosphere, to preserve biological diversity, and to observe the principle of optimum sustainable yield in the use of living natural resources and ecosystems'.[65] From this formulation, one observes that the principle is deeply rooted in preservation and protection of environmental components as a priority over economic activities; save that, living natural resources of the environment are to be regulated for optimality of use. In all other situations, however, all development activities must be conducted within the capacity of the environment.

Internationally, sustainable utilisation as an element of sustainable development requires states and peoples to pay due care to the environment and to make prudent use of the natural wealth and resources within their jurisdictions,[66] including the elimination of 'unsustainable patterns of production and consumption'.[67] In this context, utilisation seems to warrant regulation in terms of the total natural capital wealth of a nation. The principle has been severally reflected in international (and national) instruments and practice, to warrant the suggestion that it might be sufficient to crystallise conservation and sustainable use of natural resources into an independent normative standard of international law.[68] It has especially found relevance in the areas of nature conservation, and natural

---

[65] Article 3 of "General Principles, Rights and Obligations Concerning Natural Resources and Environmental Interferences", Experts Group (supra n.9) p. 9

[66] Principle 1:1:2 ILA NDD (supra chapter 2, p. 49 n.51); (also ILA (supra n. 23) p.391)

[67] Rio Declaration (supra n. 15) Principle 8; (see also Principle 2 of Stockholm Declaration)

[68] Birnie and Boyle, (supra n.6) p. 89

resource exploitation, including those shared by two or more States.[69] In one view, the principle is said to condition the traditional international duty on states (to avoid or prevent extraterritorial damage) by imputing concern for domestic environmental damage.[70] In this sense, states assume several duties on their sovereign right over national resources such as: protection of biological diversity, elimination or reduction of the effects of over-exploitation of soil, deforestation, over-fishing and pollution. This necessitates that during economic activities, environmental resources are used rationally (non-renewable resources), sustainably (for renewable resources), or equitably (renewable and non-renewable resources). Their environmental impacts must be considered and integrated into the decisions effecting such interactions, and certain legal standards must be developed to ensure this.

It must be pointed out that, this principle is traditionally rooted in regulation of renewable natural resources, especially in context of fisheries,[71] but has extended to regulation of forests[72] and water resources.[73] For instance, ITLOS ruled that measures had to be taken to preserve the rights of parties (in the exploitation of exhaustible resource as southern blue-fin tuna) while at the same time averting further deterioration of the Stock. The issuance of 'provisional measures' held a balance between resource protection and fisheries development, thereby implementing the principle of 'sustainable utilisation'.[74] Similarly, the Forest Principles recognises the rights of states to utilise, manage and develop their forests pursuant to their national policies, but 'consistent with sustainable development and legislation, including the conservation of such areas for other uses within the overall socio-economic development plan and based on rational land-use policies'.[75] This dimension of sustainable development allows for competing uses of forests to be balanced through rational land use policies that allow for other uses of

[69]For examples see: - Principle 3 of Rio Declaration (supra n.15); Para. 4 of the World Charter for Nature 1983) (Non-binding) GA Res. 37/7(Annex), UN Doc A/37/51, 22 ILM. 455 (1983); Art. 5 ICED (supra chapter 2, p.60 n.92); Art. 30 Charter of Economic Rights and Duties of States (1974), GA Res. 3281 (XXIX) 12 Dec.1974; UNEP: "Principles on conservation and Harmonious Utilisation of Natural Resources Shared by Two or More States" (1978) (UNEP Principles) UN Doc. UNEP /IG12/2 (1978), 17 I.L.M 1097 (1978); UNCLOS (1982), 21 ILM (1982) 1261; Convention on Biodiversity (CBD)(1992) 31 ILM 818;

[70]Schrijver N J., (supra n. 8)

[71]See Southern Bluefin Tuna Cases, (Australia v. Japan; New Zealand v. Japan)(SBT Cases) Provisional measures Order of 27th August 1999 at <http://www.itlos.org/case documents/1999/document en 123.doc ; The Shrimp-Turtle Case, (supra chapter 2, p.49, n.48); the Appellate Body in that case held the US imposed restriction on shrimp and shrimp products was provisionally justified under Article XX (g) of the GATT Rules to further conservation of exhaustible natural resource.

[72]See Forest Principles (supra chapter 2, p. 44 n.18)

[73]UN Convention on Non-Navigational Uses of International Watercourses, 1997, 32 ILM 700 (the Watercourse Convention) (see also Gabcikovo Nagymaros Case (supra chapter 2, p.47 n.38)

[74]SBT Cases (supra n. 71)

[75]Principle 2 (a) Forest Principles, (supra n.72)

forests than for development projects. And where such development projects become necessary, cognisance must be taken of other interests that may benefit from the forest.

International law has equally extended the principle to regulation of use of water resources for development purposes especially where the resources are shared by two or more states as competing users.[76]   However, as observed by Suebedi, the objective of sustainable development anticipated by the regulation of water resources of states also has implications outside sustainable use of shared international watercourses. He reasons that since, the convention requires the 'co-riparian' to use and share the waters concerned on an equitable, sustainable and rational manner, whether the convention is applicable or not, the ideology behind it is what defines the application of the principle.[77]   It can therefore be applied to regulate domestic watercourses and channels, streams and rivers employed in development activities.

It is important to point out that the principle of sustainable utilisation does find equal relevance and application to the regulation of exploitation of non-renewable resources. The rationale is not only limited to concerns over their potentially depleting tendency, but that employment or utilisation of other environmental assets needed for their exploitation and operational consumption are often adversely affected. Thus, sustainable utilisation as evidence of sustainable development calls for the need to regulate the rate of depletion of these resources on the one hand, and to effect proper environmental management and controls over the manner in which environmental resources are employed, including the utilisation of its renewable components- like, waters, streams, lakes, rivers and forests.

An important aspect of sustainable utilisation of natural resources which has remained elusive in scholastic literature, but which is vital for ensuring sustainable development activities relates to human resources. Labour and human ingenuity are fundamental natural resources, often required and exploited in economic processes. The importance of including human resources in the categorisation of natural resources that must be employed and used sustainably in conduct of development activities is advocated because it is deemed 'exhaustible', needs to be maintained and must always be exploited within its regenerative capacity if it must continue to contribute to the bank of man-made capital that could benefit present and future

---

[76] Watercourse Convention (supra n 73)

[77] Suebedi S. P., (supra chapter 2, p.43 n. 7) p. 270 ; (Cf. Art. 6, of the Watercourse Convention) *Ibid*

populations.[78] Whilst recognising the role played by improved technology in modern economic activities, human resources and endeavours are always a major component. This explains the connection of the concept with international emphasis on recognition of aspects of human rights and labour standards in conduct of development activities.[79]

In a domestic context therefore, sustainable utilisation would imply that development projects effect sustainable utilisation or 'employment' of natural resources (both renewable, non-renewable and the human component) in the environment within which they operate, so as to equitably meet the 'developmental and environmental needs' of present and future generations.[80] In this case, the employment of natural resources in development activities has both a social and environmental content as the basis upon which natural resource utilisation may be said to be sustainable.

Whatever the context of appreciation, the value of this element for sustainable development activities cannot be overstated. It suggests that environment, as a resource base for development, must be conserved, managed, maintained and sustained. The principle is said to facilitate the realisation of the generational principles, in so far as efficient management and utilisation of environmental and human resources by states allows for both present needs to be met while at the same time securing the interests of future environmental needs.[81] Thus, states are required to take measures both through laws, regulations and standards to ensure that resources employed, utilised or affected in development process are preserved, managed and protected.

To this end nature conservation becomes important for enhanced and sustained utilisation. Yet still, other important efforts required to give effect to the principle will include environmental management and monitoring capacity, setting of acceptable user and pollution standards, use of economic instruments, (taxes, charges and permits) and above all, liability and responsibility for environmental damage. The latter is what defines the polluter-pays principle.

---

[78]Man-made capital could either be manufactured, financial, social structures, institutions and more specifically, a bank of information from human knowledge and skills.

[79]See ILO Declaration on the *Fundamental Principles and Rights at Work* of 18 June 1998 which urges states to recognise several ILO Conventions including those relating to Equal Remuneration (No.100, 1951), Forced Labour (No. 29, 1930) and Minimum Age (No.138, 1973) (available at http <www.ilo.org>); WSSD Pol (supra chapter 2, p.63, n.107) para. 47(d) recognise the need to support the ILO (also paras 10(b), 12, & 13); also see generally the UDHR 10 Dec.1948, GA Res. 217A, UN GAOR, 3rd Sess., UN Doc. A/810 (1948); its two implementing treaties- ICESR, (1966), 993 UNTS 3 and ICCPR, (1966), 993 UNTS 171

[80]Rio Declaration (supra n. 15) Principles 3 &4

[81]See Okidi C.O, " Incorporation of General Principles of Environmental Law in National Law with Examples from Malawi"; *EPL* 27/4 (1997) p.330

3:2:6 Polluter-pays Principle

In its most general formulation the 'Polluter Pays Principle' is a reflection of what it entails - that persons who pollute or cause damage to the environment (and individuals) in the conduct of economic activities, must bear the cost of cleaning-up, reparation, or remediation of such pollution or damage. The principle is recognised in a number of international instruments,[82] including its more prominent adoption by the OECD[83] and EC.[84] Conventional forms of the principle have been interpreted as requiring regulated entities to pay the costs of meeting national environmental standards.[85] However, under certain treaties polluters may incur primary liability or direct accountability for environmental harm at the national level.[86] In addition to the conventional references, the principle is also incorporated in Principle 16 of the Rio Declaration.[87] In that context, the polluter-pays principle is made a national endeavour to be directly promoted or implemented by national authorities, based on economic rationale. Authorities should ensure that both environmental and social costs[88] resulting from development activities are met by the polluter either through the internalisation of such costs, (through investment or trade programmes), or by use of economic instruments like environmental taxes, charges and permits. However, while these efforts are being made at home, the authorities should also ensure that international economic transactions are not distorted.[89]

Though the practical application of the principle will depend on the particular economic activity to be pursued, yet its values and objectives hold far-reaching implications, not only for environmental management,

---

[82] See The 1992 Helsinki Convention on the Transboundary effects of Industrial accidents (preamble); The 1992 Helsinki Convention on the Protection and Use of Transboundary Watercourses and International Lakes, 31 *ILM* 1312 (Article 2.5(b)); the 1993 Lugano Convention on Civil Liability for Damage Resulting From Activities Dangerous To the Environment (preamble); These instruments generally describe the Principle as a general principle of international Law.

[83] The 1972 OECD "Council Recommendation on Guiding Principles Concerning the International Economic Aspects of Environmental Policies", *OECD Council Recommendation C(72) 128 (1972)*; http://www.oecd.org/

[84] The EC First Programme of Action on the Environment (1973),(O.J.(112) 1 (1973)

[85] Gaines S.E., (supra n.6) p. 265

[86] See Annex III, Article 22 of the 1997 Convention on Civil Liability for Oil Pollution Damage Resulting from Exploration for the Exploitation of Seabed Mineral Resources (London)(nif); the 1998 Wellington Convention on the Regulation of Antarctic Mineral Resource Activities (nif) Article 8) It must be stated however that the application of the principle under national law must be seen as an alternative to state responsibility under International Law, and the liability rules which apply may differ. For analysis on the deferring rules that apply, see Lefevere R., *Transboundary Environmental Interference and The origin Of State Liability*, Kluwer Law International The Hague/London/Boston, 1996, p.299-310.

[87] Rio Declaration (supra n.15); note its implicit recognition in Agenda 21(supra chapter 2, p.43 n.13) paras. 30:3 & 2:14 - requiring that the price of goods and services reflect environmental costs.

[88] This is implied by reference to 'due regard to the public interest'.

[89] This latter condition seeks to guard against usage of the principle in a manner that upsets 'National Treatment' or 'Most Favoured Nation' (MFN) trade principles; it will therefore be erroneous to read the principle as being subject to general international trade and investment rules.

regulation, and liability, but also for the general ideology of environmental protection. For instance, while the principle aims to 'eliminate the deleterious effect of over-exploitation' (by cleaning up or restoration), it also demands that where such actions are technically impossible, 'the destruction must instead be compensated, by providing or improving the protection accorded to as yet undamaged assets.[90] A stronger version of the principle includes *'its users-pay cousin'*, suggesting that polluters and *resource users* should internalise all the environmental externalities of their activities.[91] The plausibility of these determinations in my opinion rests on the fact that they present the principle not only in its 'polluting and paying' context, but that it's environmental value (user value) and saving content (conservation) must also be explored and promoted.

Similarly, the principle impresses the close relationship between development and environmental protection through emphasis on achieving environmental and social objectives using economic rationale. Its 'internalising', 'redistributive' 'preventive' and 'curative' functions,[92] combine the different objectives of sustainable development - economic, social and environmental - thereby making it an invaluable tool for directing economic activities towards sustainability. Within this framework, therefore, the principle can be used to promote environmental awareness, to attract responsibility for environmental damage (regardless of the legitimacy of the economic activity) and for enhancing environmental capacity. It is not surprising therefore that the principle has been regarded as the essential conceptual basis for a range of legal instruments at the core of environmental legislation.[93]

A further value of the principle for environmental regulation is the centrality of concerns with responsibility and liability. Its relationship to the development of rules of civil and state liability for environmental damage from pollution as a social adverse is said to have received broad support.[94] The way it combines compensatory and preventive functions, has been commended as surpassing conventional civil liability regimes.[95] Yet another valuable aspect of this regime of responsibility is the evolution by it, of notions of compensation funds, environmental trust funds, development funds and even insurance schemes. The question of liability is totally absent

---

[90]De Sadeleer N., *Environmental Principles-From Political slogans to Legal Rules*; OUP, Oxford 2002 p.15

[91]Gaines S., (supra n.6) p. 265

[92]De Sadeleer (supra n. 90) pp. 34-37

[93]*Ibid* p. 22

[94]Sands (supra n. 7)

[95]De Sadeleer (supra n. 90) p. 21

from the ideology of these measures, as they usually derive from show of support, solidarity or some sort of general concern. More importantly, such funds can be accessed even where the polluter is unavailable or unknown.[96] It must be mentioned however that to achieve the objectives of the polluter-pays principle necessitates the institution of methods that could value the environment correctly in an economic setting.[97] The goal of environmental valuation is intended to assist the decision maker not to make decisions that are wrong from both economic and environmental points of view.[98] This 'environmental valuation' aspect of the principle and concerns with financial reparations has its scepticisms. Valuing the environment in monetary terms has been considered 'an environmentally dangerous and intellectually deceptive exercise'.[99] It has also been criticised for having the attraction of setting few constraints on production activities, and that concerns with compensation effects a misrepresentation of social and ethical values. But in my view, these concerns must be noted mainly for reflective guidance by national authorities in the promotion and implementation of the objectives of the principle,[100] rather than as an adoption thereof in condemnation of it. For to uphold the latter view would suggest a limited perception of the objectives which the principle seeks to achieve, which cuts across economic and financial connotations, to a practical appreciation of environmental issues.

That said the value of the principle for effecting sustainable activities remains unfettered. It is most likely to find easy and practical application in domestic environmental management and regulation, especially because it impresses a flexible public regulatory function. This allows for the use of different economic mechanisms to address varied types of environmentally adverse consequences, with further potential of developing voluntary initiatives. To this end, its consequential value for the promotion of precautionary approach in economic activities cannot be over emphasised.

---

[96] Ibid

[97] A new form of economic equation has been developed that seeks to establish the 'total economic value' (TEV) of the environment. 'TEV' represents total economic aggregate of three separate economic factors, namely-*Consumptive or direct use values* (the calculation will reflect market prices); *Indirect use values*, (Corresponds to ecologists concept of ecological functions); and *option values* - relates to the amount an individual will be willing to pay to conserve nature see Gillespie, A (supra chapter 2, p.65 n. 146) p.69

[98] Ibid p.38; For instance, national authorities must be able to determine that taxation does correspond with the estimated economic value of the environmental damage; or that regulatory standards do in fact prohibit or limit damage associated with the economic activity.

[99] Jacobs M, (supra chapter 2, p.47 n. 36) p.202; similar concerns have been expressed elsewhere:- See Point 6(c), "Ministerial Declaration on Sustainable Development" (Bergen Conference) *EPL20 (1990), 104*); Naess A., (supra chapter 2, p. 69 n. 146) pp. 106, 112-23; For contrary views, see the World Bank: *World Development Report 1992: Development and the Environment*, OUP Oxford 1992, p.71 Pearce, D., "An Economic Approach to saving the Tropical Forests", in *Economic Policy Towards the Environment*; Helm D. (ed), (Blackwell, Oxford 1992) 239

[100] For instance it may form a guiding reference for further development of liability and taxation regimes to enhance the environment.

3:2:7 Precautionary Principle

The Principle requires the exercise of due care, caution and prudence in carrying out socio-economic activities, in order to prevent any possible damaging environmental consequences. 'Precaution' means that if a risk is not certain, this will not be used as an excuse to prevent measures that could mitigate harm. It differs from 'prevention' which applies when risk is known and preventive measures are needed.[101] It does not 'posit a perfect understanding of any given risk: it is sufficient that a risk be suspected, conjectured or feared', to warrant its application.[102] The principle is deemed central in international law relating to sustainable development because it expresses a 'duty on states' to take preventive measures to protect human health, natural resources and the environment.[103] Precautionary principle does occupy a central place in any realistic strategy for achieving sustainable development, and particularly sustainable use of the planet's natural resources.[104] It is therefore not surprising that the 'approach' has marked presence in most international environmental treaties, natural resource management regimes, application by courts and tribunals, and is increasingly being adopted by national legal systems.[105]

These endorsements of the principle have been read as suggesting a pattern of state practice and a breadth of application, that supports 'a good argument that it has emerged as a principle of customary international law'.[106] The principle is also explicitly incorporated in Principle 15 of the Rio Declaration, as an approach that will secure protection of the environment and efficient use of natural resources in the conduct of development activities.[107] It was reiterated at the WSSD, with a prominence directed at social issues such as human health, and the importance of science based decision-making for

---

[101]Cordonier-Segger *et al* (supra chapter 2 p. 62 n.119) pp. 55-61

[102]De Sadeleer (supra n. 90) p.191

[103]ILA NDD (supra chapter 2, p.49, n.51) Principle 4:4:1; (see also ILA (supra n. 23) p. 682

[104]Freestone D., "International Fisheries Law since Rio: The Continued Rise of the Precautionary Principle", in *International Law and Sustainable Development*, Boyle & Freestone (Eds.) OUP, Oxford, 2001 p. 135.

[105]Some examples of instruments endorsing the precautionary principle or approach include: Helsinki Convention on the Protection of the Baltic Sea Area (1992) 3 *YBIEL* (Article 3(2); Convention on Transboundary Watercourses (supra n.82)(Article 2(5); The OSPAR Convention, 1992, 32 *ILM*, 1069 (1993) (Article 2(2)(a) (also in *International Environmental Law-Multilateral Treaties* (W.Burhenne, ed.) 1992:71); Maastricht Treaty on European Union, (1992) 31 ILM 247; ITLOS *SBT Cases* (supra n.71); ICJ *Gabcikovo Case* (supra n. 73) and the WTO (*Hormones case*; European Communities- Measures Concerning Meat and Meat Products, Complaint by the United States (WT/DS26) and Canada (WT/DS48), *Report Of the Appellate Body; WTO DSR 1998, Vol.1*, Cambridge pp.135ff)- have all applied the principle. For regional and national endorsement of the principle see Hey, E., "The Precautionary concept in Environmental Policy and Law: Institutionalising Caution" in *Georgetown Environmental Law Review* IV, (1992) pp.303-318. Note also that the principle is reflected as a general principle for environmental policy for most Organizations.

[106]Freestone (supra n. 104) p. 13 (citing Cameron and Abouchar)

[107]Rio Declaration (supra n.15) See also CBD (supra n.69) (ninth recital); UNFCCC (1992) 31 *ILM* 848 (Article 3(3))

sustainable development[108].

The Rio formulation however brings out the distinguishing features of the principle, by indicating the time, manner and the circumstances in which it could be applied. First, the approach is triggered only for environmental protection (and not as reasons for holding a balance between development and environmental goals). The relevant environment must be under threats 'of serious or irreversible damage'. In any such case, irrespective of whether or not there is scientific proof of, or the likelihood of damage occurring, measures should be employed in order to prevent or contain the damage. Thus, as has been observed, Principle 15 resolved the controversy on scientific uncertainty in favour of not requiring complete knowledge in case of serious threats,[109] and provides 'a new lens with which to view existing obligations'.[110] The next feature in the application of the precautionary principle relates to the manner and the extent of the measure to be taken. These are to be employed in accordance with states 'capabilities' and are to be 'cost effective'.[111] The obligations created hereunder are of a relative nature since they depend upon economic and financial capabilities.[112]

The ILA NDD also identifies some precautionary measures as including: accountability for harm caused (including state responsibility where appropriate), planning based on clear criteria and well-defined goals and EIA.[113]

The principle is deemed capable of implementation through different types of measures.[114] As a peculiarity in its nature, the precautionary principle could be applied in the regulation of diverse economic activities, which have deferring ways of affecting the environment. The value in its application criteria therefore allows the principle to reflect some flexibility within which decision makers can determine every potential impact which turns out on the facts of the particular development activity, and assess the method of prevention or contention that is cost effective to be adopted.[115] The capability will determine the cost effectiveness of the measure to be applied,

---

[108]WSSD POI (supra chapter 2, p.60, n.107) para.23

[109]Sands (supra chapter 2, p.44, n. 15) p. 17.

[110]Freestone (supra n.104) p.141

[111]Rio Principle 15 (supra n. 15)

[112]Wolf rum (supra n. 4) p. 11

[113]ILA NDD (supra n. 103) Principle 4:2 (a)-(c)

[114]Nollkaemper, "What You Risk Reveals What You Value and Other Dilemmas Encountered in the Legal Assault on Risk" in *The Precau-tionary Principle and International Law: The Challenge of Implementation Freestone and Hey (Eds.), Kluwer Law International, The Hague/ London, 1996) p. 80

[115]Note that EIA, ERA, Environmental Auditing and Monitoring all have direct connections with the implementation of the principle, as mechanisms to determine the propensities of risks.

but in all cases, it must have an effect of prevention of harm or protection of the environment.

The *Southern Bluefin Tuna Cases*[116] represent a useful illustration of the application of the precautionary principle, bringing out its value-added incentive for sustainable development. In that case, ITLOS considered that the conservation of the living resources of the sea was an element in the protection and preservation of the marine environment, and therefore the parties were required to act with *'prudence and caution'* to ensure that measures were taken to effect such conservation and prevent serious harm to the stock.[117] In Judge Treves' view, the application of the precautionary 'approach' was warranted by the purpose which it would serve (of avoiding any environmental harm or damage to the fish stock), as opposed to concerns with the legal status of the concept.[118] In his opinion, 'precautionary approach,' 'caution' and 'prudence', are one and the same thing, signifying the 'stopping of a trend towards' environmental deterioration or collapse.[119] The tribunal seemed to be suggesting that measures which had the objective of preserving resources and protecting the environment, were reason enough to impress on persons undertaking development activities to exercise 'prudence and caution', so as to avoid damage to the environment notwithstanding that scientific evidence has not confirmed such danger of damage. ITLOS also seemed to have appreciated the flexibility in the legal character of sustainable development, by not limiting the application of the principle to treaty application or customary law (legality by obligation). Instead, it realistically pursued the concept of legality based on its effects.[120] Adoption of this 'approach' it has been suggested, underlined the appreciable awareness of ITLOS' members, of the existence and significance of environmental rights and duties of states, in modern international law.[121]

It must be pointed out that, similar 'approach' was contemplated in the

---

[116]*SBT Cases*, (supra n.71) The tribunal was required to stipulate provisional measures that would impose restraints on Japan so as to allow for the recovery of the stock which the complainants alleged was at its lowest. In such a case, the tribunal could by authority of Article 290 of UNCLOS and Article 25 of ITLOS, prescribe such measures if it considered among other things that '...the urgency of the situation so requires' for preserving the rights of the parties or preventing serious harm to the marine environment. Despite the inconclusive nature of the parties' scientific evidence, ITLOS ruled 'that measures should be taken as a matter of urgency to preserve the rights of the parties and to avert further deterioration of the southern bluefin stock'.

[117]*Ibid* Order Para. 77(emphasis added)

[118]*Ibid* Separate Opinion, para. 9; (see also clause 90 (1) (a) & (b) of the Order).

[119]*Ibid* para 8

[120]Note that this dimension of 'legality' is hinged on what this book submits as 'deliberative processes' - which is geared towards 'defining measures which seek to regulate development activities for environmental protection, including responsibility for environmental harm' (see supra chapter 2 p.57, n.87)

[121]Kwiatkowska, B., "The Southern Bluefin Tuna (New Zealand v Japan; Australia v Japan) Cases", *The International Journal of Marine and Coastal Law* Vol.15, No.1, Kluwer Law International, 2000 p.35

Gabcikovo-Nagymaros case,[122] when Judge Weeramantry observed that '... the growing awareness of the risk to mankind have led to the development of the new norms and standards', which have to be continuously applied.[123] In his opinion, the 'larger general principle of caution' is undoubtedly one such standard, (applied through EIA), and it requires 'continuing watchfulness and anticipation'.[124] The inference here is that, the precautionary principle should often be implied within environmental agreements and given proper effect to- through adoption of corrective, preventive, or abstention measures- when likely environmental damage presents itself. The yardstick is not one of certainty (or not) of damage, but potentiality.

A further clarification on the purpose and application of the principle was made in the *MOX plant case*.[125] According to Judge Wolf rum, the Principle reflects the necessity of making environment- related decisions in the face of scientific uncertainty, about potential future harm of a particular activity.[126] Therefore, in implementation of the principle, the burden of proof must shift on the party interested in pursuing the potentially harmful activity rather than the one making the allegation.[127] The NDD acknowledged this shift, but qualifies its application to 'activities which may cause serious long-term or irreversible harm'.[128] Regardless of the instance of the burden, the measure is likely to allow for proper consideration to be given to environmental concerns, in discharging this evidential burden, and consequently enhance environmental awareness.

Further in *Mox-plant*, the principle was said to connote several procedural initiatives that must be inferred from uses of the terms 'caution' and 'prudence'. They represent requirements to consult, cooperate, exchange information, monitor risks and even devise appropriate measures for preventing harm to the environment.[129] In other words, compliance with procedural requirements epitomises 'due diligence' which in turn is an indication of fulfilment of the obligations under the precautionary principle.

---

[122]Separate Opinion in the *Gabcikovo Nagymaros Case* (supra n. 24) para 112. p. 64

[123]*Ibid* p.110 (citing para 140 of the Court's Judgment.)

[124]*Ibid*. It seems the precautionary approach was used to interpret the relevant Agreements in that case.

[125]*The MOX Plant Case (Ireland v. United Kingdom), Request for Provisional Measures Order of 3rd Dec. 2001, (2002) 41 ILM* 405 also at http://www.itlos.org. Note in this case, ITLOS rejected Ireland's request for Provisional measure because it did not consider that the urgency of the situation required prescription of such measures, in the short period before the constitution of the Annex VII tribunal. It however undertook on its own to do so, upon reasoning that 'prudence and 'caution' required that both countries needed to cooperate in exchanging information concerning risk. (para18).

[126]*Ibid*, Judge Wolfrum (Separate Opinion)

[127]*Ibid*

[128]ILA NDD (supra n. 103 (Principle 4.3 (d))

[129]Judge Julio Treves (Separate Opinion); (Cf ITLOS Order of 3rd Dec 2001, para 84)

A further beneficial value of the Principle is its application through an 'approach' (as opposed to a principle). Judge Laing observes that adopting the 'approach' rather than the 'principle' imports a certain degree of flexibility in its application.[130] In this sense, the principle is not only to be identified and defined by name, but could be generally implied in development agreements, or inferred from certain obligations or duty of care owed to the natural and social environment by developers in the conduct of economic activities. But it is interesting to note that the subsequently constituted tribunal, decided that it was not appropriate to provide provisional measures in order 'to prevent serious harm to the marine environment'. In their view, Ireland had not established that any harm that might be caused to the marine environment by the Mox-plant would be 'serious'.[131] This is a departure from the plausible argument set by Wolfrum regarding the instance of 'burden of proof' and the underlying purpose of caution or precaution. This consequence suggests that the precautionary 'approach' was not taken, because as has been pointed out, had it been applied, the tribunal would have reached a different conclusion.[132]

Apart from the lack of general consensus as to its legal implication, the principle has drawn scant criticisms in respect of its operation. Concerns have been raised over the principle's inherent reliance on some form of scientific and/or economic assessment for its operation, necessitating the need to conduct a Cost-benefit-analysis (CBA), which itself is deemed to be ruled by uncertainties.[133] This uncertainty increases the possibility for ecological interests to be systematically compromised and for non-targeted risks to arise.[134] While noting these concerns, it must be stated that the operation of the principle is always going to require a balancing process in decision-making. But since the emphasis on 'precaution' is primarily in favour of environmental protection, it is hard to see how ecological concerns could be compromised.

Thus, the merits of the principle bear testimony to their value for environmental protection and natural resource management in the conduct

---

[130]*Ibid* Sep. Op. of Judge Laing; Note also that the WTO's Dispute Settlement Bodies have analysed the principle some cases concerning health measures, including the *Hormones Case* (supra n. 105); see Pauwelyn J., "The WTO Agreement as Applied in the First Three SPS Disputes", (1999) *Journal of International Economic Law*, 641.

[131]The *Mox-plant Case* (Ireland v United Kingdom) Order No. 3 "Suspension of Proceedings on Jurisdiction and Merits and Request for further Provisional Measures" at http://www.itlos.org.

[132]Churchill R. & Scott J*, "The Mox Plant Litigation: The First-Half" in ICLQ vol. 53, July 2004 p.651 (see article for detailed analysis of Jurisdictional issues in this case).

[133]K.von Molkte in De Sadeleer, (supra n. 90) p. 169-170

[134]*Ibid* p. 171

of economic activities. Its objective bias in favour of environmental protection in sustainable development is evidently grafted at the threshold of decision-making, anticipating environmental harm before they occur. Precaution evidences in several characters and measures, by which its goal is achieved, and with flexibility that allows developers, decision-makers, policy planners and judges to be able to interpret, infer from obligations, or implement policies that promote environmental objectives. The principle can foster useful and legitimate environmental law and policy, but fundamental amongst its strategies, is the assessment of environmental impact of development activities.

3:2:8 Environmental Impact Assessment

EIA is a very prominent policy tool in the pursuit of sustainable development in international environmental law and regulation, though it is initially of domestic orientation.[135] As a strategy for sustainable development, it seeks to mitigate the destructive potential of development activities (or ameliorate their impact), by basing action on greater and widespread knowledge, and thereby enhancing 'ecological rationality' of policy decisions.[136] Its goal is to integrate environmental issues into development planning, in order to maximise the potential for sustainable and environmentally sound decisions and plans.[137] Over 70% of the World's nations (including Sierra Leone), have reportedly adopted either informal or mandatory EIA requirements.[138] Also the principle is deemed a mandatory 'legal' fundament of international environmental law.[139]

Representing a global endorsement of EIA, the Rio Declaration requires that 'as a national instrument, EIA shall be undertaken for proposed activities that are likely to have significant adverse impact on the environment, and are subject to a decision of a competent national authority'. This mandate does reflect the relevance of the EIA mechanism for the regulation of domestic developmental activities and effectively warranting suggestion that the presence of EIA in the global arena is a reflection of each state's

---

[135]US/NEPA (1969) is the first to institute EIA; (see *40 C.F.R1500.1 -1517.7* and also *42 U.S.C ss. 4321-4370, 2000*).

[136]Bartlett R., "Ecological Reasoning Administration: EIA and Administrative Theory" in *Managing Leviathan – Environmental Politics and the Administrative State* (Paehllee & Torgerson Eds.) London, Belhaven 1990. p.83

[137]Pring & Noé "The Emerging International Law of Public participation Affecting Global Mining, Energy and Resource Development", in *Human Rights in Natural Resources Development* Zilman, Lucas & Pring (Eds.) OUP(2002) p.38

[138]"Rio Declaration on Environment and Development: Application and Implementation"- *Report of the Secretary General, UN Commission on Sustainable Development*, 5th Session, UN DOC. E/CN.17/1997/8 (1997)

[139]Experts Group (supra n.9) article 5

environmental law.[140] A distinction must be made between EIA as a requirement under international law and EIA as a domestic mandate. Despite the Rio endorsement international law does not generally purport to require EIA for projects with solely domestic effects.

For international law to apply, the environmental consequences of any proposed project must have a transboundary effect, pursuant to the sovereignty principle of state responsibility for transboundary environmental damage.[141] But presently, apart from the Antarctica regime,[142] there is no global MEA that certifies its legal status, or that requires EIA of development activities, with transboundary effect, though such efforts are being made.[143] The closest to that is a declaration by the UN General Assembly, ranking it as an equivalent with the Polluter-Pays Principle, the Precautionary Principle and the Common but Differentiated Responsibilities principle.[144]

But EIA has been catapulted on the international arena through regional EIA regimes[145] and efforts of other multilateral lending institutions.[146] There are also other instances of EIA requirements as obligations in some major treaties,[147] laws,[148] declarations or as policy initiatives for sustainable development.[149] Its importance as a principle for sustainability of development activities has also not been an oversight in judicial pronouncements.[150]

The Espoo regime can be credited for putting an EIA mechanism in place that will address transboundary environmental harm, albeit through

[140]Gray* K.R, "International Environmental Impact Assessment: Potential for a Multilateral Environmental Agreement" in *Colorado Journal of International Environmental Law & Policy*, Vol.11, No.1, 2000 p. 83

[141]Knox, J.H (citing N.A Robinson) in "The Myth and Reality of Transboundary EIA" *AJIL* Vol. 96:291 2002 p. 297

[142]See Wellington Convention (arts. 4(2) & 5(2); Antarctic Environmental Protocol (1991) 30 *ILM* 1461 (art. 25 (1)); the 1991 Protocol on Environment Protection to the Antarctica Treaty (Madrid Protocol) 30 *I.L.M* 1461 (1991). Generally, the regime (including its protocols) requires an assessment or 'comprehensive environmental evaluation' on all proposed mineral resources activities in the Antarctica or other designated areas.

[143]See "ILC Draft Articles on Prevention of Transboundary Environmental Harm from Hazardous Activities" in *Report of the ILC*, 53rd Sess., UN GAOR, 56th Sess., Supp. No. 10, at 370- 436, UN Doc.56/10 (2001).

[144]See Programme for the Further Implementation of Agenda 21, UN GAOR, 19th Spec. Sess., Annex, Agenda item 8 UN DOC. A/S - 1929 (1997)

[145]See UNECE Convention on Environmental Impact Assessment in the Trans-boundary Context 1991(Espoo); 30 *ILM* (1991) 802; also at <www.unece.org/env/eia>; The NAAEC, (1993),(Can.-Mex-US), 32 *ILM* 1480 (1993) also at <http://www.cec.org/ pubs-info-resources/law-treat-agree/> (for NAFTA parties)

[146]World Bank Operational Manual (OP) 4.01 (1991), at http://www.worldbank.org- (reissued as Operational Policy 4.01 in Dec. 1998); See also World Bank Environment Department: *The Impact of Environmental Assessment: A Review of World Bank Experience*, World Bank, Washington DC. (1997)

[147]See Art. 14(1)(a) CBD (1992) 31 *ILM* 818 (1992); Art.206 UNCLOS (supra n.69); Art. 3(1)(h) Convention on Transboundary Watercourses & Lakes (supra n.82)

[148]EEC: EC Directive on EIA, Directive 85/337 (1985) *O.J. L175/40*, amended by Directive 97/11/ EC (1997) *O.J.73/5*. (also at http://europa.eu.int/eur-/ex/en/index.html>)

[149]See UNEP Principles (supra n.69); UNEP Guidelines on Goals and Principles for Environmental Impact Assessment, (1987) (UNEP Guidelines) UN DOC. UNEP/Z/SER. A/9 (1987); WCN (1982) (supra n.69); Agenda 21 (supra n. 87); See further "Africa and EIA" in *EPL* 25/6 (1995) 322

[150]*Gabcikovo-Nagymaros Case* (supra n. 73)

domestic EIA requirements. Generally, parties are required to take into account the extra-territorial effects of limited range of projects that are subject to domestic EIA or government approval.[151] While focusing primarily on the project level of proposed activities (including post project analysis), Espoo also urges parties to apply EIA principles to policies plans and Programmes'. Procedurally, parties are to 'notify' 'assess,' and 'consult' with potentially 'affected states' about likely transboundary impacts. They must also apply these requirements to the public in 'affected areas' on an equal access and non-discriminatory basis.[152] It is probably in light of these arrangements that Espoo is said to extend rather than rewrite domestic EIA law.[153] However, nothing in Espoo obliges the 'state of origin' to prohibit a proposed activity or even minimize its adverse extra-territorial effect. It is sufficient that an 'affected' party is notified of the final decision on the proposed activity, including the considerations on which it was based.[154] Evidently, the parties use EIA as an informational tool rather than a substantive prohibition of environmentally harmful projects.[155]

Thus far, it can be safe to suggest that the state of the principle of EIA as it stands in regulation of environmental harm derives validity through domestic law which basically requires the decision maker to weigh environmental, economic and social concerns in deciding whether to allow a project to go on. As a mechanism it necessitates an assessment of certain development activities primarily for their environmental impact and impresses the need for consultation and public participation in the decision-making process. It does not necessarily prohibit, prevent or halt activities with significant environmental impacts from being implemented. As has been observed, the legal requirement emphasises the objective of EIA in environmental protection, but the procedure relies on political and not legal means to reach an end.[156] One should however caution on some possible consequences engendered by the inherent domestic character of the principle. It allows for variances, discretions and flexibilities that not only effect to undermine any legal obligation created thereby, but also presents the likelihood of political or other factors outweighing environmental concerns. Also, Pring observes that 'EIA are both inadequate predictors of,

---

[151] Art. 2(1) Espoo (supra n. 145); It includes Major mining, and other Extraction and processing activities (Appendix 1(14))

[152] *Ibid* Art. 3 -5

[153] Knox (supra n.141) p.305

[154] Espoo (supra n. 145) Art. 2

[155] Knox, (supra n 141) p. 307

[156] *Ibid* p.289; this implication underscores the submitted legal character of sustainable development as deriving from several processes, including administrative action. (Supra chapter 2, p.57)

and inadequate controls for sustainable development standing alone'.[157]

Despite these concerns, EIA is still a formidable and well-recognised tool in the regulation of development activities. Its greatest and primary merit lies in its capacity to assess environmental and social effects of proposed (and ongoing) development projects, thereby improving environmental decision-making and enhancing environmental awareness. Others accredit its flexible environmental management strategy that allows firms and industries to incorporate environmental concerns into their rationale.[158] EIA is also perceived as amounting to greater environmental protection than would otherwise occur[159] and has potential for greater usefulness if it is sufficiently linked formally or informally, to the ways problems are defined, structured and addressed.[160] This re-echoes Judge Weeramantry's call for a 'continuing environmental impact assessment'.[161]

The broad implication of this analysis is far-reaching for directing sustainable activities. It recognises that environmental concerns are alive and continuing, irrespective of when the project under which they arise may have been inaugurated. It also means that the relevant environmental standards that will be applicable will be those prevailing at the time. EIA mechanism is thus destined to become very valuable as a continuing assessment process, but only within a legal mandate that guarantees participatory rights and holds authorities accountable for taking its results into consideration.

3:2:9 Public Participation

The principle of Public Participation has a peculiar identity that must be understood for a better appreciation of its place in the sustainable development discourse. It derives from three parallel paths: First, it is an integral and essential component of EIA procedure.[162] Second, it obtains from other spheres of general environmental decision-making, such as in environmental planning, conservation of shared natural resources and resource allocation and distribution issues.[163] Third, it represents as a distinct

---

[157]Pring G .W (Rock)., "International Law and Mineral Resources" in *Mining Environment and Development*, UNCTAD, p. 34

[158]Gray (supra n. 140) p. 89

[159]Sadler B. *Environmental Assessment in a Changing World: Evaluating Practice to Improve Performance* (1996) p. 52-53.

[160]Bartlett R., (supra n.136) p. 90

[161]Sep. Op of Judge Weeramantry, (supra n. 24) p. 112

[162]Common facets of participatory requirements portrayed herein could also condition EIA participatory obligations.

[163]This dimension represents in general international environmental law and policy, and the broader developmental perspective of sustainable development, which now interprets in the concept of 'Good Governance' or an evolving 'environmental Human Rights'. (See ILA (supra n.23) pp.834-5

element of sustainable development in regulation of economic activities.[164] It is with emphasis on this latter perspective that the relevance and contents of public participation are analysed.[165]

Public participation has been deemed especially relevant and valuable in the sustainable development triangle. It has marked recognition in the global, regional and national arena. The general direction of the principle under different international postulates is to create participatory rights for their public to have either access to environmental information, participate in environmental decision-making, or gain access to a form of redress for environmental wrongs, commonly described as 'access to justice'. This latter component usually infers three adjudication possibilities, which are either: to challenge the refusal of access to information, to seek prevention of and/or damages for environmentally harmful activities and to enforce environmental laws directly.[166]

These three participatory elements have been employed diversely in international resources management, and environmental protection efforts, through varied instruments, including policy prescriptions of institutions and organizations. But while some of the international instruments would clearly require all three elements, (information, participation and justice),[167] others represent only one.[168] A third set of instruments (usually requiring public participation in EIA procedures) generally adopts two forms of the elements.[169] However Rio Principle 10 provides guidance on the general application of the principle with evident practical dimensions. Firstly participation 'of all concerned citizens' is made a precondition for any effective determination of environmental issues. Second, its proper breeding

---

[164]Addresses participation in a narrow and specific context of regulating development activities for social and environmentally sustainable development and appreciates in an immediate local context (See Rio Principle 10).

[165]Note that the participatory ideology in all three dimensions may be similar and have interrelated goals, yet participation for directing sustainable activities is distinguished in the sense that it goes beyond concerns with public influencing of environmental decisions, (or creating environmental awareness or simply exercising a participatory right) to their implementation, and enforcements; and is not limited to citizens, or government processes, but includes other actors (corporations, organizations or institutions), whose interests may lay one way or another, in the pursuit of economic activities

[166]Pring &Noe supra n. 137) p.44

[167]Some examples include: - WCN (supra n. 69) arts.16 &23; Rio Declaration (supra n.15) Principles 10,13,20,21 and 22 respectively; Johannesburg Declaration (supra chapter 2, p.60 n. 106) para 26; WSSD Pol (supra n.108) paras. 25, 40, 42, 44, 45 & 46(b) respectively; UN/ECE: Convention on Access to Information, Public Participation in Decision-Making and Access to Justice in Environmental Matters (Aarhus) UN Doc. ECE/ CEP/ 43 (1998) at http://www.unece.org/env/pp/treatytext.htm; ILA NDD (supra n. 103) Principles 5:2 & 5:3

[168]See: - UNFCCC (supra n. 107) art. 6(a)(ii); Convention on Transboundary Watercourses and Lakes, (supra n. 82) art.16(1) & (2); OSPAR Convention (supra n.105) art.9(1) (Information); Watercourse Convention (supra n. 73) art. 32 (access to justice)

[169]UNEP Principles (supra n. 69), Principle 4; UNEP Guidelines (supra n.149) Principles 7-9; Madrid Protocol (supra n.142) annex 1 art. 3(3); Espoo (supra n.145); NAAEC (supra n.145) art.5 (2) & 6(3); EEC Directive on Access to Environmental Information, Council Directive 90/313/1990, O.J. c158/56; ASEAN Agreement on the Conservation of Nature and Natural Resources (1985) (art. 16(2)) at http://sedac.ciesin.org/entri/texts/asean.natural.resources.1985.html

ground is at the national level, where the relevant public authorities must make available to the public two categories of environmental Information: - those that generally concern the state of the national environment and those concerning environmentally-adverse development activities conducted in particular local communities.[170] In respect of this latter category, a further responsibility is imposed on States to '*facilitate*' such participation. Primarily, this means *inter alia* that responsible authorities have to identify and give individuals the opportunity to participate in the decision-making process of the development related activities.[171] Agenda 21 further extends this participatory right to 'groups' and 'organizations'.[172]

Beyond identifying participants and providing 'wide availability' or 'accessibility' to environmental information, facilitating participation will also include responsibility to educate the public of the likely environmental impacts of development activities, and require continuous notification of the public about environmental issues even when concerns are not raised.[173] Further, facilitative efforts must cater for measures that enhance citizens' right of access to institutions (administrative or judicial proceedings) for redress or remediation of environmental wrong, damage or threat of harm. By effect of this requirement, citizens should be able to compel the release of information, seek restoration, reclamation or obtain an injunction against damaging or wrongful activity, or compensation. It is in this regard that states are obliged to 'develop national law regarding liability and compensation for victims of pollution and other environmental damage'.[174]

The Aarhus Convention[175] is the first legally binding 'participation-specific' international instrument, said to contain the broadest and most detailed requirements to date, for public participation in decision-making.[176] In one eminent view, Aarhus is by far the most impressive elaboration of principle 10 of Rio, with global effect, despite its regional application.[177] The convention defines participatory rights in terms of its three elements, (information, participation and justice), as a means through which the public

[170]The latter distinction is relevant for directing sustainable activities. (see supra ns 162-164).

[171]See Rio Declaration, (supra n. 15) Participants must include Women, Youth, other local communities and Indigenous people (Principles 20, 21 &22) respectively

[172]Agenda 21, (supra n. 87) chapter 23:2

[173]Pring & Noé (supra n. 137) p.30; Perceived as a 'proactive' and 'reactive' duty imposed on governments.

[174]Rio Declaration (supra n. 15) Principle 13

[175]Aarhus (supra n. 167)

[176]Pring & Noe supra n.137) p.43

[177]Kofi Annan (UN Secretary Genera); UNECE, Environment and Human Settlements Division: "Introducing the Aarhus Convention" at < http:// www.unece.org/env/pp >

can exercise their right to life and well-being in a healthy environment and also perform their duty to protect it for future generations. It furthers this objective by extending the category of persons with obligation to provide these elements beyond governments, to include persons (natural or legal), performing public administrative functions under national law, have public responsibility and specified institutions of any regional economic integration organization.[178] Even the content of requisite environmental information is broadened to include information on the state of environmental materials and resources,[179] on factors and development activities,[180] or administrative measures that 'affect' or are 'likely to affect' prescribed environmental resources.[181] In effect, access to information cuts across different facets of factors - physical and institutional - that affect the state of environmental elements. And the public must be informed early in environmental decision-making process, in an 'adequate, timely and effective manner'.[182]

Aarhus also extends the category of participants referenced as the 'public' beyond 'citizens' to include human beings, corporations, companies, organizations, associations or groups formed by these and which are recognised under national law and practice.[183] Participatory right is triggered where any of the above mentioned 'public' is 'affected', 'likely to be affected', or have 'an interest' in the environmental decision-making.[184] This provision effectively widens the scope of participants, as 'interests' could be inferred based on either the right to a 'healthy environment' or a duty to protect it for posterity. In a truly innovative way Aarhus does help to shed light on what participation under the Rio declaration must entail, in order to achieve the objectives of sustainable development.

Another important responsibility in effecting the participation principle was identified at the WSSD. The Johannesburg Principles on the Role of Law and Sustainable Development (Johannesburg Principles)[185] reiterate the crucial role of the judiciary for promoting compliance with the implementation and enforcement of international and national environmental law. More particularly, their role must be effective in improving the level of public participation in environmental decision-making, access to justice for the

---

[178] Aarhus Convention Article 2(a), (b), (c) and (d)

[179] Ibid art. 3(a)

[180] Ibid Annex 1

[181] Ibid art. 3 (b)

[182] Ibid art. 6(2)

[183] Ibid art. 2 (4)

[184] Ibid art. 5

[185] Adopted at the Global Judges Symposium, Johannesburg, South Africa, 18-20 august 2002, available at www.unep.org/dpdl/symposium p.1

settlement of environmental disputes and the defence and enforcement of environmental rights and public access to relevant information.[186] Building on this requirement, it has been suggested that the specific role of the judiciary in a particular case may either be supervisory, determined by the regulatory competence of individual countries;[187] or in cases where administrative systems are relatively underdeveloped, by using ingenious articulations to 'fill in the gap'.[188] But in either case, cost of court proceedings has to be removed as an obstacle, if the courts' role is to be widened. A preferable solution could be sought in enhancing the state machinery for local inquiry or in the development of new environmental tribunals.[189]

Similarly, the participatory principles have also been variedly interpreted or affirmed by scholars. For instance it has been understood as requiring education of the public about the relationship between environment and development;[190] as not limiting 'access' to citizens and victims of development activities but also available to other entities and private corporations;[191] as posing the strongest argument for Human Rights to the environment,[192] or as catering for 'legal standing of intermediary groups on the basis of right to development'.[193] Yet others have deemed it 'actually necessary in order for any development-related decisions to be sustainable'.[194]

The specific importance of the various legal and policy formulations in Aarhus, Rio, other international instruments (including the Johannesburg principles) and scholastic interpretations, is not so much in there substantive objectives, but in the fact that they contribute in diverse ways to clarifying or adding value to the content of public participation as relevant implement for environmentally sustainable activities. They all attest to the value of the principle in enhancing sustainable development. As an element that must inform environmental policies, environmental laws and development decision-making at the national level, 'public participation' cannot be

---

[186] *Ibid*, para.4 (b)

[187] Carnwath (Lord Justice) "Judicial Protection of the Environment at Home and Abroad" in *J Env L* Vol. 16, No.3, 2004 p.318; For example, where countries have well-developed codes of environmental law and systems for policing it, the judicial role is likely to be more supervisory such as in promoting access to justice, including public access to environmental information and the publics role in the enforcement of environmental laws designed for their protection.

[188] *Ibid* Here courts may have recourse to 'imaginative interpretations of constitutional guarantees'

[189] *Ibid* p.327

[190] Malanczuk P., (supra chapter 2, p.48 n.40) p.12

[191] *Ibid* p.16

[192] See ILA (supra n. 23) p.390; Picolotti R. "Agenda 21 and Human Rights" in *Linking Human Rights and Environment*, Picolotti and Taillant (Eds.) Tucson, Arizona, University of Arizona Press, 2003. p.56

[193] ILA (supra chapter 2, p.47, n.32) p 133

[194] Pring & Noé (supra n. 137) p. 23

assumed under one encompassing definition, but must be structured within the forgoing ideals to deal with the situations that present themselves.

However, its main precept must always be that of creating awareness in the public of any general or specific environmental threats posed by development activities; and such efforts must include mechanisms for its appreciation at 'grassroots' level. A public that is aware, is one that is educated enough to understand the implications of the issues upon which they are expected to comment, challenge or defend. It is upon this basis that effective participation is achieved, fair and equal access to justice is maintained, environmentally friendly laws, regulations and decisions are encouraged and development activities are helped toward sustainability.

Conclusion

The chapter sought to bring out the value-oriented nature of sustainable development through selected relevant principles, especially their capacity to regulate development activities and promote environmental protection in resource exploitation. This effort has portrayed the relevant principles in the several dimensions they assume under international law, each serving useful purposes and important functions essential for steering resource exploitative activities through an environmentally-friendly sustainable path. It argued that the ultimate value of the principles is ensuring that development activities are conducted to improve human well being between generations, but with consideration, due care and attention to the consequences wrought on other environmental components. The elaboration proves their capacity to ensure environmental protection through varied facets of measures, ranging from ethics to legal dictates, standards and processes, all applying within a flexible system of regulatory endeavours, and with a co-ordination that allows each   principle to work individually or concertedly, with little or no conflict between them. Their relevance and value for directing sustainable development has been proved.

The next chapter will seek to apply the concept of sustainable development in the specific context of mineral resource developments. This will be effected through a practical illustration of how the identified sustainability principles namely: Environmental Protection, Integration, Inter and Intra-generational Equity, Sustainable Utilisation, Polluter-Pays and Precautionary Principle, EIA and Public Participation - operate to ensure protection of domestic mining environments.

4 SUSTAINABLE DEVELOPMENT AND MINING

4:1 Introduction

The previous chapter has demonstrated the relevance and value of the concept of sustainable development in international law, primarily for directing or achieving socially and environmentally sound development. Principles of Environmental Protection, Integration, Inter and Intra-generational Equity, Sustainable Utilisation, Polluter-Pays and Precautionary Principles, EIA and Public Participation were identified as relevant components of the concept, that define the social and environmental parameters within which development activities should generally be conducted, so as to regulate resource management and enhance environmental protection for ultimate sustainability. This chapter seeks to apply these principles in the specific context of the regulation of mining activities for sustainability.

The chapter is divided into two parts. The first attempts to displace arguments suggesting that mining is not sustainability oriented by demonstrating the applicability of the concept of sustainable development to mining. It will present a practical illustration of ways in which these principles can achieve the objective of sustainable mining activities within a protected environment. Part B makes up a general summary of the components of sustainable development identified generally in international law and specifically in relation to mining. The purpose of this general summation is to form an instant reference for discerning or integrating sustainability objectives within policies and legal frameworks for the protection of domestic mining environments.

Part A

4:2 Applicability of the Concept of Sustainable Development to Mining

Perspectives vary on the application of the concept of sustainable development to mining minerals. One popular contention is that mining is not sustainability-oriented.[1] This perspective denies applicability of the concept to mining by arguments relating either to the nature of such operations, or on scepticisms over fundamental objectives of the concept. The first argument is premised on the perception that mining generally results in ultimate degradation of the environment, appalling social conditions and depletion of natural resources. This view advances the adverse resultant effects of mining operations as defeating of the goals of sustainable development. But such arguments effectively underscore the relevance and value of the concept in the sense that it is designed to ameliorate such adverse effects.

As regards the nature of sustainable development, sceptics have suggested that the concept finds 'difficult application' to development of non-renewable resources like minerals, in the sense that mining permanently removes resources from a country and forecloses the right to 'access' or 'option' of future generations' benefit of it.[2] In other words, since the intergenerational principle is one of the fundamental ideologies of the concept, it is deemed by this reasoning to be difficult to tie in with mining. Though this view suggests an effect of mining on future generations, it tends to interpret the generational concept narrowly. The interests aimed to be protected by the principle and the methods of such protection are varied.

A third perspective moves away from concerns with the nature of mining activities and the concept, to blaming inapplicability on those with responsibility for its application. For instance, it has been maintained that non-sustainability in mining is as a result of the reluctance of governments and companies to use array of regulations to chart such developments towards a sustainability path, because of 'the lack of thinking going on in the process of such developments'.[3] By this reasoning, the adverse consequences of mining are not an end in themselves that cannot be corrected. It requires willingness of the responsible parties to desire sustainability and put the necessary conditions in place to achieve it.

---

[1] Almost all writers on the subject will allude to this point, usually termed an 'oxymoron'.

[2] Westin, R., "Intergenerational Equity and Third World Mining" in *University of Pennsylvania Journal of International Business Law* Vol.13 No.1, 1992, p. 181

[3] Bhattacharya, J., "Sustainable Development of Natural Resources: Implications for Mining and Minerals", in *Mineral Resource Engineering*, Vol.9, No.4 (2000) p. 462.

But several reasons and interpretations have also been proffered in support of the applicability of the concept of sustainable development to mineral resource development. According to one author, it is not impossible to combine the concept with the 'seeming contradicting development of non-renewable resources'.[4] Achieving 'sustainability' is also said to be possible if the term is acknowledged as 'an ethic' rather than as a public relations 'buzzword' that is without content.[5] Natural resources (especially non-renewable resources), have been deemed particularly relevant to sustainable development in the sense that its environmental dimension must respond to the 'taking' of a 'resource' of 'nature' for humanity's often transient and wasteful uses.[6] Therefore, sustainability applies as an overall description of environmental 'good practice', entailing a number of government and corporate policy prescriptions, direction and regulation, including ESIA, stakeholder consultation procedures and internalisation of costs.[7] The concept has been predicted to play an increasingly significant role in negotiations surrounding mining developments in resource-based economies, especially in the absence of specific and uniform international standards applicable to the industry worldwide.[8]

Further, the concept is believed to hold a peculiar application to mining, which is distinct from its generally considered development criteria in the sense that it goes beyond satisfying basic human needs.[9] In this context, sustainable development encourages the preservation of all aspects of a country's environmental, cultural and socio-economic heritage, including the rational use of non-renewable resources.[10] Similarly, sustainable development is also deemed applicable to mining through adoption and transposition of 'internationally acceptable [mining industry] practice' into local mining environments and consolidating them by iterative processes that generally cater for measuring sustainability, methods for trade-offs and balancing of conflicting interests.[11]

Put together, these views severally tend to emphasise the need for a

---

[4]Porter J.A., Santana L.S., & Culbertson KD; "Reconciliation of Mining with the Concept of Sustainable Development, Miners Gerais, Brazil", in *Mining Latin America: Challenges in the Mining Industry* (The Institution of Mining and Metallurgy eds) p.381

[5]*Ibid* p.382

[6]Wälde T.W. (supra chapter 2, p.46, n. 29) p. 120

[7]*Ibid* pp 133-135

[8]Pring (Rock), (supra chapter 3, p.98 n.157) p.6

[9]*Ibid* p.8

[10]See Novoa V.L., "Sustainable Development and Its Relationship with Mining and Law" Special Institute On Mineral Development in Latin America 7-1 Rocky Mountain Mineral Law Foundation ed. 1997, p.20

[11]MMSD (supra chapter 2, p. 47 n.33) p. xxiii & 28

reorientation of perception of the concept to allow for its application, suggests *how* and *why* sustainable development is relevant to mining, establish an applicability criteria and reaffirm the goals to be achieved by adaptation of the concept to mining. It is therefore safe to infer from these various positions that the concept does truly have a place, purpose and meaning for mining. Its place implied in the ultimate interaction with the environment; its purpose, in the objective of steering the interaction to a social and environmentally sustainable path; and its meaning explained in ensuring that mining contributes to the well-being of the current generation with little or no disadvantage to future generations. This conclusion is affirmed elsewhere, suggesting that '...a mining project that is developed, operated and closed in an environmentally and socially acceptable manner can be seen as contributing to sustainable development'.[12] It is however paramount that the concept is always adapted to the needs and demands of local mining environments. Sustainability principles must be identified for each individual and isolated component of mining life cycle and implemented within integrated mechanisms and manageable decision-making structure.[13] Essentially, '...sustainable development is a concept that has to be unpacked along the way. There is no single point of arrival'.[14]

4:3 Principles of Sustainable Development in Mining

4:3:1 Protection of the Mining Environment

Mining has acknowledged crosscutting impacts on the natural and human environment in which such activities take place.[15] This fact underscores the logical necessity for protection of mining environments and the WSSD support for efforts to address environmental, economic, health and social impacts of mining minerals and metals, and for fostering sustainable mining

---

[12]Berlin II Guidelines For Mining and Sustainable Development (Berlin Guidelines) UN, 2002 available at ttp://www.mineralresourcesforum.org/Berlin/index.htm (also in 10 *Journal of Natural Resources and Energy Law* 355-357 (1992))

[13]See MMSD (supra n. 11)

[14]Minnitt R.C.A, "Ensuring the Mining Sectors Contribution to Sustainable Economic Development:" *The Challenge of Sustainable Development for the Minerals and Metals Industry*, July 2001, Witwatersrand, South Africa, p. 90; see also pp 36-43

[15]For examples of mining impacts particularly in Sierra Leone, see supra chapter 1, pp. 30-35; for more general analyses see: Cohen M. "A New Menu for the Hard-Rock Cafe: International Mining Ventures and Environmental Cooperation in Developing Countries", 15 *Sanford Environmental Law Journal* 130 (1996); Wälde T., "Environmental Policies Towards Mining in Developing Countries", 10 *Journal of Energy and Natural Resources Law* 327 (1992);UNESCAP & UNEP: *Mineral Resources Development and the Environment* (1992); World Bank: Environmental Health and Safety Guidelines for Mining and Milling open Pit, 1995; World Bank: Environmental Assessment of Mining Projects (EAMP)- *Draft: Environmental Assessment Sourcebook Update* (Feb. 1997), also at http://www/worldbank.org/html/fpd/technet/decade/assess.htm; Auty R.M and Mikesell R.F., *Sustainable Development in Mineral Economies*, OUP, Oxford,1998, pp 67ff; Pring (supra n. 8) p. 7ff.

practices.[16] The application of environmental protection to mining is considered as deriving mainly from ethics, demanding *inter alia*, determination of equitable cost and benefits, contemplation of reciprocal relationships and the impact of such operations on the scale of communities.[17] The principle's main thrust suggests a protection of the mining environment for the benefit of present and future generations, though it generally represents in protecting, preserving, managing and maintaining natural capital and other components that such operations interact with. This emphasis connotes varied implications and responsibilities.

For example, it means that exploitation of mineral resources to satisfy a human population must not be done at the expense of animal species. All possible efforts should therefore be made to secure them in their immediate habitat or provide suitable alternative.[18] It also implies that in conduct of mining operations, steps must be taken to maintain and enhance environmental capacity. Ensuring such capacity would necessitate that once resource development in a given area has reached its environmental capacity, or in the threshold, that area should not be used for mining till some environmental capacity has been generated.[19] Equally so, the principle will require that any activity in a protected area should be compatible with the overall objective of the protected area in question and demarcated 'protected areas' must be respected and maintained.[20]

In sum, these rationales suggest that people who undertake mining activities (including those who regulate them) should respect and protect the environment from degradation, pollution, ecosystem instability and ensure biological diversity in the interest of posterity. They also infer a duty to take necessary and appropriate measures to rehabilitate exhausted mining areas and adoption of conservation measures. Environmental protection in mining will thus require considerable efforts and commitments from miners and public authorities alike. While mineral planning must be tailored to deal with all round development around the mining area, mineral laws and agreements, environmental laws, regulations, guidelines and policies, must also reflect these protection objectives.[21] A more useful recommendation is to

---

[16]WSSD POI (supra chapter 2, p.60, n.107); see chapter 3 on CSR and "Changing Unsustainable Patterns of Production and Consumption".

[17]Bhattacharya, J., (supra n. 3) p. 451; Porter *et al* (supra n. 4) p.382

[18]Minnitt (supra n.14)

[19] Bhattacharya J., (supra n. 3)

[20] See IUCN/WCPA "Position Statement on Mining and Associated Activities in relation to Protected Areas" in *EPL Vol.29 No.6, 1999 p 286*; "IUCN Guidelines for Protected Area Management Categories- Part 11" in *EPL Vol. 29*, No. 6 1999 p. 285; Bellini M., "IUCN Mining Policy", in *EPL, 26/6 (1999)*. 270

[21]See Auty and Mikesell, (supra n.15)

have special environmental legislation and regulations for extractive industries that will reflect the peculiar environmental conditions in mining.[22]

4:3:2 Securing the interests of Present and Future Generations in Mining

The generational elements of sustainable development stand at crossroads of mineral resource development initiatives. At one end, it favours mining in order to provide for the 'material welfare' (basic needs) of present population 'within an environment that is adequate for their well-being' and in 'harmony with nature'. At the other end, it requires the adoption of certain measures and controls that will also secure the interests of future generations. Both elements generally necessitate that human welfare is improved thereby, and environmental as well as the social impacts of the industry's activity (including mine life and closure), are addressed and mitigated.

For intra-generational equity in mining, the most common expectation is that local communities must be better advantaged (economically), both during and after the life of the mine, as a consequence of mineral investment.[23] It also interprets to mean that mineral depletion should produce value for society through the most efficient and functioning system of mineral licensing, environmental taxes, (including a charge for depletion), and a system of governance which ensures that economic benefits from mining flow to those affected by mining.[24] More specifically, the principle can be applied by reinvesting capital gained from mining activities, in profitable enterprises directed at environmental restoration, remediation and reclamation.[25] This idea has been described as 'the most potential [and] truly sustainable strategy for non-renewable resources development if applied to a region or individual mine, and could be of more value to communities impacted by mining development if applied locally.[26]

A further guidance on the adaptation of the principle to mining is given by Auty and Mikesell. In their view, social welfare in mining is maximised by

---

[22]*Ibid*

[23]Minnitt, R.C.A (supra n. 14) p. 72

[24]Wälde (supra n. 6) p.140

[25]See Westin (supra n.2) p.190

[26]Porter *et al* (supra n. 4) p. 382; for the application of this model of GNP accounting, in context of renewable resources, see (Cf El Serafy, S. and Lutz, E., "Environmental and Resource Accounting: An Overview": in *Environmental Accounting for Sustainable Development*, (1989), Ahmad, El Serafy and Lutz (Eds.), The World Bank, Washington, DC, 1989, 8, 1–7; Also, El Serafy, S. (1989) "The Proper Calculation of Income from Depletable Natural Resources" in Ahmad et al (Eds.) *ibid*, pp. 10–18.

equating 'marginal social costs' to 'marginal social benefits'. The social costs range from air, water and soil pollution, to disturbing the economic and cultural lives of indigenous people.[27] Evaluating social cost would also include the determination of alternative uses of land for social benefits such as production of minerals, or by providing amenities to those enjoying undisturbed natural areas.[28] So that where issues of social costs and benefits (including resource allocation) are not given equal considerations, it makes for inequitable effects which could affect both the quality of life of the present generation and the quality of their environment, thus making mining operations unsustainable. Overcoming this consequence requires informed environmental controls by government, its agencies and mining entities, in setting and enforcing environmental standards through use of economic incentives or requirements for the use of specific technologies, or adoption of voluntary actions.

On the other hand, securing the interests of future generation must equally be made a necessary goal in all mining operations. The relevance of inter-generational equity to mining has been explained by categories of ways in which the conduct of present population could be said to violate the interests of future generations: Present mining generation can cause uncorrected environmental degradation; they can consume the higher quality resources which leads to real prices in the future; they can consume resources not yet identified as valuable to the present generation, or they can consume resources prior to their best use; finally, they can exhaust resources, resulting in a narrower range of available natural resources for future employment.[29] These wrongs explain the concern in sustainable development with imputing responsibility on the present mining generation to conserve and enhance 'access' (to an undamaged environment), conserve its 'quality' (including its materials and components) and allow future generations the opportunity to exercise their 'options' in the extractive industry.

The principle also has implications for regulating depletion of non-renewable minerals in order to preserve future generation 'options'; while for renewable resources (such as forests, fish, rivers and lakes), it effects to enhance the 'option' by controlling or minimising the stresses placed on them. Several suggestions have been made regarding some practical initiatives that could fulfil the objective of the principle in regulating resource depletion. One view considers that the best way is to 'appeal to reason and basic concepts

---

[27] Auty & Mikesell (supra n. 15) p. 80

[28] Ibid p.80

[29] Westin (supra n.2) p. 197

of economic equity'[30]. Wälde explains that concerns with global depletion of non-renewable resources for future generation should be addressed if the systems for maintaining ingenuity, change and responsiveness to market signals are maintained.[31] By another view, intergenerational interests affected by depletion of natural capital can be addressed if the flow of mineral income from the liquidation of natural assets is reinvested in other forms of natural capital (and man-made capital) that can provide an equivalent or similar benefit to future populations.[32] This strategy of investing 'resource rents', (including the current value of minerals removed from the ground) in 'durable reproducible capital goods' (such as buildings, machines, extra- research and development *etc.*), connote 'reciprocity across generations'.[33]

This approach is at the heart of 'weak sustainability,' implying that net receipts from the sale of non-renewable minerals, contain an element of capital that has to be set aside and reinvested to compensate for depletion of the asset. From this point the policies and mechanisms that determine the compensatory methods become the true instruments of sustainability. Their direction must not be concentrated only on man-made capital, though they make an important part.[34] It can also be allocated to projects with environmental content. More importantly, this model does not justify complete depletion, but rather advocates rationality. The goal here is that our offspring should be able to enjoy the benefits of mineral development in the same way that the current generation has, including the ability to make the choice to develop minerals. Conservation is thus an important part of the rationality.

Another relevant strategy to cover for physical depletion of minerals, explains in recycling. Where possible, minerals and metals should be recycled, recovered and re-used so as to add to the physical stock of mineral resources that is passed on to future generations.[35] This strategy, works to

---

[30]*Ibid* p.184

[31]Wälde (supra n.6) p.128; this reasoning suggests that the real problem in mining is not in depletion of minerals (especially those necessary for the global economy) because the main factors predicting that this occurrence is not in sight, are a combination of social, economic and technological change and the response of economies to price signals in a functioning market. He argues that, based on the interplay of these factors, scarcity of individual minerals (or energy) may inevitably lead to higher prices, search for substitutes and more efficient production and consumption methods. Therefore the real issue is not the question of 'depletion' but the sudden 'obsolescence' of demand for particular minerals, which provoke grave social and economic disruption for the communities, countries and regions dependent on individual minerals. In sum, minerals may not vanish; but the demand for them may vanish (p.129).

[32]Minnitt (supra n.14) p. 62

[33]Hatwick J. M & Olewiler, N.D., *The Economics of Natural Resource Use* (second edition); Addison-Wesley Educational Publishers Inc., Reading Massachusetts, p. 165; see also Auty and Mikesell "Policies for sustainable Development of Mineral Economies" in *Sustainable Development in Mineral Economies*, Oxford/New York , Clarendon, chapter 13 at p.130.

[34]See supra chapter 3, p.86

[35]Minnitt (supra n. 14) p. 14

also reduce the rate of depletion of other natural assets, since the regulation of unsustainable levels of consumption will consequently affect the patterns of production. Similarly, the 'green conditioning of loans' and imposition of environmental guidelines and standards on application of funds for development of mining projects given by MDBs, DAAs, and other public and private finance and insurance institutions identifies among the strategies for off-setting the 'bill' of present mining on future generation.[36]

Thus far, these expressions of intergenerational equity in mining suggest specific measures and strategies that are infused with economic and environmental implications, and emphasising their interrelationship for sustainable development in mining. But equally significant are measures designed to regulate the stress of mining on other environmental resources, which may affect the interest of future generations either as regards the quality of the environment that will be inherited or maintaining its capacity. It has therefore been suggested that environmental damage created by the extractive industries should be 'internalised' on a current basis, as a means of either avoiding the environmental degradation, or of compensating future generations for the loss of environmental capital.[37] This strategy is a recurring strategy in the application of sustainable development to mining and is further emphasised by the 'integration', 'polluter-pays' and 'precautionary, principles.

4:3:3 Recognising 'Integration', 'Polluter- Pays' and 'Precautionary' Principles

The controlling objective of sustainable development is ensuring or facilitating ecological and economic concerns to go hand in hand. Development activities are no longer to be conducted in isolation, or in disregard of the consequences they wrought on the natural and human environment. In mining, 'integration' is applied primarily through emphasis on transforming concerns with maximising material gains, or reliance on technology to afford mass production for benefit of the present populations, to concerns with improving the non material quality of life of mining communities; and to protect the environment for future generation use and

---

[36]Westin (supra n.2) p.189; see also Auty & Mikesell (supra n. 15); Wälde T., (supra n. 13) p. 55; Cohen M., (supra n. 15) p.155; World Bank: *Mainstreaming the Environment: The World Bank Group and the Environment Since the Rio Earth Summit*, Fiscal 1995, The World Bank, Washington DC (1995); World Bank: EAMP (supra n. 15); Pring (supra n. 8).

[37]Auty and Mikesell (supra n. 15) p. 65

enjoyment.[38] The latter concern drives the application of the principle and necessitates several economic and accounting adjustments and techniques within mine planning and operations, including a re-evaluation of environmental law and policy to reflect the true environmental and social costs of such developments.

For example, the principle will require appropriate accounting for all natural resources that are engaged in mineral operations, in the traditional national economic accounts. It is argued that the rate of depletion of mineral resources, including exploitation of other natural resources in mining have been exacerbated primarily because the structure of payments for mineral rights do not reflect the depletion of minerals in national accounts;[39] and because such accounts have treated the value added environmental assets (like water air, rivers, forests, and lakes) used in mineral resource operations as free gifts of nature.[40] Thus for sustainable development in mining, calculations of mineral rights purchase values and the national accounting techniques must integrate both mineral depletion costs and natural resources- user costs.

Other expressions of the integration principle to direct sustainable mining would require the industry to inculcate a culture of including cost of reclamation and remediation in the product price, which hitherto has been determined only by constant change and use of technology.[41] The principle also extends to include an ethical compulsion, which suggests that mining firms must avoid the 'soft spots' of developing countries, where easy accessibility of the reserve, poor regulating framework and non-accrual of actual remedial costs generate low price results.[42] It further implies that sustainable technological innovation choices should also be encouraged for non-renewable resources.[43] Thus, to realise the optimal value of 'integration' in mining, it is recommended that government power be used to impose a price on all external effects, so that agents are forced to include them in their calculations of planning, production and consumption.[44] This measure is commonly known as 'internalisation'.

---

[38]Smith, S. L., 'Ecologically Sustainable Development: Integrating Economics, Ecology, and Law', 31 *Willamette Law Review*, 1995 p. 263

[39]Minnitt (supra n. 14) p.3

[40]Hatwick and Olewiler (supra n. 32) p.382; On this rationale, see also WCED (supra chapter 3, p.68 n.37) p. 220; Pearce, D., "An Economic Approach to Saving the Tropical Forests" in *Economic Policy Towards the Environment*, Helm D. (ed) Blackwell, Oxford 1992 p. 239.

[41]Bhattacharya, (supra n.3)

[42]*Ibid* Note that Principle 6 of the Rio Declaration, (supra chapter 2, p.43, n.12), emphasised the environmental vulnerability particularly of LDCs

[43]Rio Declaration *Ibid*, Principle 9

[44]Hatwick and Olewiler (supra n. 32) p. 382

The principle of 'internalisation' also marks the regime of the polluter-pays principle in mining activities, generally requiring the developer to bear the cost of pollution control and remediation. 'Pollution' in mining is said to effect where mining causes or is likely to cause disturbance that is 'permanent' or quasi 'permanent', with discernible impacts on the 'natural capital' and on the welfare of the associated living beings. In other words, polluter-pays principle, would apply as a responsibility to not only correct air, water and soil pollution, but any disturbance with discernible impact on the natural and human environment, including efforts to maintain the welfare of living beings,[45] and provide growth to the natural capital by rehabilitation or alternative conservation options. These 'environmental cost of mineral production' should be borne by the mineral firms creating the damage rather than being absorbed by government or borne by members of society who are victims of pollution and other natural asset degradation.[46] Effecting 'internalisation' in mining will generally necessitate actions and commitments by government and mine developers.

Government and its agencies must put in place environmental controls including uniform extraction standards and mechanisms for enforcing same, while the industry must develop environmental culture, ethics and co-operation.[47] It is along this line, that Rio recommends the application of the principle by way of national laws on liability and compensation, and through economic regulatory instruments.[48] Economic and environmental policies, legislations and mining agreements must be tailored to reflect this need through allocation of civil liability, imposition of emission charges, taxes, fees, trade permits and other incentives, voluntary mechanisms, 'best practice' and up-to-date technology.[49] Social benefit and cost accounting could also be internalised by the producer, through compensatory mechanisms, insurance schemes development funds and projects.[50] It must also include the development and implementation of EMS, (ESIA, planning, pollution control and mitigating measures) and channelling mining investments within clear environmental standards and criteria.[51] All these must however be determined upon proper valuation of external effects and

---

[45]Bhattacharya, (supra n. 2) p. 462

[46]See Auty and Mikesell, (supra n. 15) p. 68

[47]Bhattacharya, (supra n.3)pp 462ff

[48]Rio Declaration (supra n 42) Principles 16, 13 and generally principle 11

[49]See Wälde (supra n. 6) pp 133ff; Porter et.al. (Supra n. 4) p. 80; Auty and Mikesell (supra n. 15) pp 64-65; Hatwick & Oriella (supra n. 32)

[50]Auty and Mikesell, *ibid* p 64

[51]Berlin II Guidelines (supra n. 12)

allocating such effects to a particular actor.[52]

A further dimension of the 'internalisation' strategy for sustainable mining is the adoption of precautionary approach in the whole development process. Mining firms must absorb the cost of avoiding environmental damage to the natural and human environment especially where there are threats of serious or irreversible damage, and regardless of lack of scientific proof of the effects.[53] Put succinctly, mineral developments cannot insist on access to mine, or unconditioned mining rights or permits simply because critics have not proved the validity of their concerns over serious or irreversible impacts.[54] Mining companies and industries must therefore take 'cost effective measures' whenever the possibility of harm unfolds.

Internalising 'precautionary costs' could take varied forms: Primarily it will involve investments on sophisticated damage-reduction technology and equipments, undertaking environmental research of proposed mining environments and meeting costs of monitoring including emergency response measures. It also assumes all costs of relocating or resettling humans, habitating animal species and alternative conservation efforts. More importantly, it extends to 'costs of forbearance', suggesting that if damage potential is so great as would severely and lastingly affect environmental capacity, then that activity should be avoided in that area. Above all, it must include the cost of carrying out EIA.

4:3:4 EIA: A Prerequisite for Mineral Developments

EIA as an element of sustainable development finds very easy application in the regulation of mining activities. In fact, it is so far the main and direct regulatory technique required by most international and national instruments, for testing the environmental sustainability of mining plans, projects, programs and ventures.[55] Nearly unanimous reliance is said to be placed on this mechanism,[56] as policies and guidelines of public and private international institutions and organisations adopt it as necessary for

---

[52]Wälde (supra n. 6) pp 133ff

[53]Rio Declaration (supra n. 42) Principle 15

[54]Pring (supra n. 8) p.31; See further Pring, Otto & Naito, "Trends in International Environmental Law Affecting the Minerals Industry" in *Journal of Energy and Natural Resources Law*, (1999). 39-35 and 151-177

[55]See Wellington Convention; Antarctic Environmental Protocol and the Madrid Protocol respectively (supra chapter 3, p. 106, n 142)

[56]Cohen M. (n. 15) p. 158

sustainable mining operations.[57] In addition, most international mining companies working in developing countries have adopted detailed internal environmental management guidelines and systems that recognise the relevance of EIA mechanism;[58] and so too have most national laws and modern agreements between mining companies and governments.[59]

While the popularity of the EIA mechanism for regulating the mining business stands unquestionably well in laws, guidelines and agreements (explicitly or implicitly), its true value in enhancing sustainability rests with its practical application to particular mining environments. EIA has been observed as valuable to mining because of its capacity to predict and evaluate potential impacts, identify alternatives and mitigating measures, and using its conclusions as a tool in planning and decision-making.[60] It is also suggested that unless a comprehensive environmental assessment study has been undertaken, the agreement may lack specific commitments.[61] In this observation is embedded the true objective of EIA, which requires detailed procedures for assessing, the likely environmental and social impacts of proposed mining programmes or projects, before embarking on them. Such procedures should be effected early enough (preferably, during the negotiation stages) before commitments are made or mining rights are bought. A useful recommendation is that EIA is initiated and applied in the decision-making of regional land-use planning, rather than as a reaction to project proposals.[62] Comprehensive impact assessments done prior to formulating plans for exploration and development will often reveal strategies to protect the environment without extensive increases in costs; and will further cater for risk-reduction and likely environmental emergencies.[63]

---

[57]UNEP Guidelines (supra chapter 3, p. 96 n.149);(see also UNEP's Guidelines on Offshore Mining and Drilling (1982); UNRFNRE 'Revitalization Plan': *Achieving Sustainable Development of Mineral Resources in Harmony with the Environment* (brochure 1995);The World Bank EAMP (supra n.13); OPIC is required by the United States Foreign Assistance Act (22 U.S.C. § 231(n)) (since 1985) to perform EIA on any Programme or project significantly affecting the environment of any foreign country that they finance, see http://www.opic.gov; Berlin Guidelines (supra n.12) paras, 2-10 and 14.

[58]Armstrong, Kit, "The Green Challenge - Managing Environmental Issues in Natural Resources Projects in Developing Countries" 42 *Rocky Mountain Mineral Law Institute* , p3-30 (1996).

[59]MMSD (supra n. 11) p.28

[60]MBastida E.; "Integrating Sustainability into Mining Law: The Experience of Some Latin American Countries" in Schrijver and Weiss (Eds.) 2004 (supra n.6) p.591

[61]Auty & Mikesell (supra n. 15) p.67

[62]Minnitt (supra n. 14) p.20

[63]See Auty & Mikesell (supra n. 20). The experience with the *Ok Tedi copper-Gold Mine Case* in Papua New Guinea (PNG) best illustrates the value of applying the principle of EIA to mining; a 1976 concession agreement between the PNG government and an international consortium had provided inter alia for submission by the consortium to the government of a development proposal, and an undertaking to prepare an EIA with a maximum budget of only $200,000. But the consortium later argued that it could not undertake exhaustive EIA before the mining license was granted. When actual mine construction began in February 1981, many of the environmental problems were not foreseen and therefore not addressed in the development plan. Serious environmental problems arose which gave rise to disputes between the consortium and the government. (See <http://dte.gn.apc.org/cstd1.htm> for case illustration)

The EIA procedures may vary from country to country, but its substantive objectives need not vary in their application to mining proposals, since it is accepted that all mining activities would have some impact on the environment. Therefore, it is pertinent for sustainable mining, that there be undertaken a comprehensive assessment study that will capture the least environmental impact, and a continuing role through monitoring of mining operations and their environments. More importantly, EIA must include full participatory dialogues before a decision is made.

4:3:5 Defining the Role of the Public in Mining

The strategic location of the public as targeted beneficiaries of mine proceeds on the one hand, and as victims of mine developments on the other, determines the importance and relevance of their role in such activities. Their role has been defined as a 'new law of public rights to control private development' and is deemed the most significant new trend or change facing mineral, energy and resource developments in the 21st century.[64] The contexts in which the public can be said to exercise their 'right to control' public and private mineral developments to enhance sustainable mining practices are varied. One perspective suggest that it must be a requirement at national, and industrial level that the decision-making process fully integrates a consideration of socio-economic and environmental issues with input from a broad range of public perception at an early stage before the commencement of operations.[65] This perception has both a factual and practical implication. It implies that a factual determination must be made of the environmental and socio economic effects of proposed mining activities; and the public's perception of those issues must be considered in the decision-making process. This distinction is crucial because firstly, it corrects situations were people would often not generally be disposed to appraising social and environmental impacts beyond themselves. Second, compilation of environmental and socio-economic facts will often serve as reference for testing the substance upon which decisions were reached, giving that 'the decision on how to use the environment [for mining] is usually a political one'.[66]

From another dimension, public participation relates to the issue of

---

[64]Pring & Noe` in "International Law of Public Participation" in *Human Rights in Natural Resource Development*, Zillman/Lucas/Pring (Eds.) OUP oxford, 2002 p.14 (citing Pring, Otto & Naito)

[65]Minnitt (supra n.14) p 20

[66]Hanemann P., *Economics and the Preservation of Biodiversity*, Wilson, E.O (ed.) 1988, National Academy Press, Washington pp.193-194

apportioning of mineral wealth including the determination and actual receipt of compensations. More specifically, mining communities must have a fair and equitable share in the distribution of mining proceeds that is commensurate with their share of the social and environmental impacts;[67] and such benefits must be made sustainable beyond the life span of mining projects. Ideally, these must be determined through a democratic process, and incorporated into initial agreements between governments and mining companies.[68] Such a process will address concerns over compensations and other mining benefits not reaching locals either because of lack of knowledge or cultural inadequacies. Thus public participation must be secured in the decision-making process and the decisions must also reflect effective and transparent strategies for distribution of the benefits.[69] To this end, the principle interprets to mean forming an alliance between government, NGOs and local communities in order to address social and cultural impacts in traditional value systems, especially since mining often takes place within traditionally communal remote settings.[70] Because of this peculiarity, participation in mining should not be daunted by assessments on aggregate of individual economic wants, but must be based on consensus that must obtain from an open process, where the consequences are made clear.

A final aspect of participation in mining is the need to provide for an accessible forum – administrative or judicial, where people can challenge and call to question decisions, laws, regulations and mining agreements on the one hand or seek their enforcements. The latter objective defines participatory right of 'access to justice', usually extending the determination of issues from the executive or administrative realm, to judicial authority. As has been observed, the absence of clear-cut international standards of liability and effective international dispute-resolution forums, has increased the potential for national courts stepping in and 'filling the void', to regulate mining activities.[71] The judiciary has capacity to confer liability on mining companies for environmental harm, and to enhance legal development of some environmentally related principles of national and international relevance. Participation will therefore necessitate that victims of mining activities or persons interested in enforcing legal precepts in protection of mining environments be provided with a right to institute actions in courts

[67]Westin (supra n. 2)

[68]MMSD (supra n. 11) (executive summary)

[69]Benefits must not necessarily interpret only in monetary terms, but includes development projects that will improve the general social and environmental capacities of mining environments.

[70]Bhattacharya, J (supra n. 2) p. 461

[71]Pring, (supra n. 8)

pursuant to law and clear procedures, without undue delays and respecting due process. Legal access should be equal, non-discriminatory and made effective both at home and abroad. This is said to warrant the creation of judicial standards for the mining industry in three venues; - by courts in developing countries where mining is occurring;[72] by courts in developed countries where companies are incorporated or headquartered;[73] and by courts of some developed countries applying their own national laws extraterritorially.[74]

The forgoing analysis no doubt, clarifies the role of the public in effecting sustainable decision-making, sustainable laws, policies and mining agreements, sustainable environmental litigations and sustainable mining practices. Their role has generally assumed importance and popularity in EIA procedures, but it is clear that several other concerns are regulated through such participatory right. It is however important to encourage co-operation and dialogue among all interested parties in furtherance of environmental objectives especially the sustainable utilization of resources.

4:3:6 'Sustainable Use' of resources in Minerals Production Processes

The principle of sustainable utilisation has received only lukewarm reception in its appreciation for non-renewable resources such as minerals. The immediate emphasis in this element for mining is directed not at the products but at the regulation of renewable resources and other environmental materials employed in mining. Such operations are highly water intensive (usually making use of rivers, lakes and streams), they affect landforms, vegetations, trees, animals and in some cases forests, including other interests in these resources.[75] Therefore the goals of the principle are two-fold: to ensure rational use of resources in mining operations and to implore consideration in their engagement in a manner that will cause little

---

[72]Access in local jurisdiction is explicitly portrayed in the following cases:- First, a local court in Turkey is reported to have cancelled gold mining license of Eurogold, a multinational French-Australian-Canadian mining company, in a 1997 lawsuit brought by local villagers fearful the company's cyanide process would pollute their region; Another example is the *Chañaral case* in Chile, in which citizens are known to have successfully sued a division of the State-owned Codelco copper company in the late 1980s for remediation of the environmental damage done by years of dumping of its mineral-processing tailings in the Salado River and Bay of Chañaral (available at ESCAP Virtual Conference, <http://www.unescap.org/> ; Finally, in the *Huasco Case*, olive tree farmers and fishermen successfully sued Compañía Minera del Pacífico for air and water pollution remediation at its pellet plant in Huasco (available at<http://www.natural-esources.org/minerals/CD/docs/unctad/pring.doc>)

[73]For example residents of Ecuador and Peru chose United States federal courts to sue Texaco for over US$1 billion for air, water and soil pollution arising out of its historical oil and gas operations in Ecuador. See Prince & Nelson, "*Developing an Environmental Model*: Piecing Together the Growing Diversity of International Environmental Standards and Agendas Affecting Mining Companies", *7 Colorado Journal of International Environmental Law & Policy*, 243

[74]Pring (supra n. 8) p. 27

[75]See supra chapter 1, pp 33-37; Pring (supra n. 8) p. 9

disturbance to other interests or avoid harm to the environment.

Thus, by operation of the principle human resources (exemplified in labour and skills) being both natural and exhaustible must be employed in mining in the manner that reflect the value and sustainability of labour through adoption of standards that cater for better working conditions (including health and safety), the development and transfer of skills and elimination of child labour.[76] In other respects, water resources employed in such activities must be used in a rational manner, free from pollution, and diversions that could affect their channels, and in consideration of other users. Other environmental materials and resources are to be employed or utilised with due care, within their regenerative capacities, and must be sustained during and after mining operations. This will require reclamation measures designed to restore to acceptable standards the physical, chemical and biological quality of environmental resources disturbed by mineral exploration or development.[77] Similarly, land management, responsible stewardship and aftercare become critical factors in ensuring responsible engagement of resources in mining. Such effort will necessitate use of sound technology, rehabilitation measures, remediation works, environmentally safe tailings and waste management, dam treatments and over-all monitoring of land and water quality including the effects of operations on fish stock.

Accordingly, 'sustainable utilisation' in mining does effect both to regulate the manner and rate at which human and environmental resources are utilised in mining operations on the one hand, and to encourage responsible management of land, soil, and water capacity on the other. Achieving the value of the principle on the above characterisation will require government regulation and standards to determine appropriate utilisation. One suggestion is that there is put in place specific legislation governing mine closure and reclamation, and tailored to apply to current and future mines.[78] Above all, the land-ethic must be made a close companion of mining policies, laws and agreements.

---

[76]This goal could be enhanced by the observance of internationally established principles relating to employment and labour standards; see supra chapter 3, p.86, n.79; and generally http://ilo.org

[77]Minnitt (supra n.14) p. 39; these must start even before a mine is actually opened.

[78]Ibid p. 40

Part B

4:4 Summary of the Components of Sustainable Development Identified Generally in International Law and Specifically in Relation to Mining

So far, this work has illustrated the importance of sustainable development in international law for the regulation of development activities generally, and mining in particular. Relevant principles of the concept have been identified both in international law and specifically in regulating mining activities for environmental and social sustainability. This section presents a summary of the objectives embedded in the said principles as reference criteria for any investigative analysis of the sustainability of legal regimes aiming for the protection of mining environments. Their value or significance for environmental legislation, regulation, and management of natural resources in mining is a recurring emphasis in this summation.

Foremost emphasis is the principle of 'environmental protection', a rationale or 'ethic' that must constitute an integral part of all mineral resource development processes. The legal regime for environmental protection must guarantee protection in connection with adverse environmental interference, ensure efficient use and management of natural resources, commitment to reducing pollution, minimising mining impacts, avoiding environmental degradation and maintaining environmental capacities. Such protection regime must have viable environmental institutions, effective environmental legislations, adequate environmental standards, management controls and the capacity to protect rights of individuals from pollution, damage and general environmental concerns.

To fulfil the principle of 'integration', mineral development plans and activities should be designed and conducted with due consideration to the environmental and social issues engendered by such activities. Environmental issues must also be made to infiltrate into, or influence national planning and economic policies, and the way laws are made and implemented. The cost of environmental and social damage of mineral production activities must be given priority consideration and such costs reflected in the laws, regulating purchase of mining rights, product pricing and taxation schemes.

In meeting the element of inter-generational equity, the legal regime regulating current mining ventures must give consideration to addressing the rate of depletion or reduction in mineral wealth, must seek to preserve environmental materials and components by arresting environmental degradation, promoting conservation and eliminating unsustainable patterns of production. The objective should be in maintaining a safe and healthy environment among generations. This should be assured through regulation of mining activities generally for environmental sustainability; through formulation, application or interpretation of laws that impose responsibility for environmental damage and through the rational allocation of resources.

In seeking intragenerational equity, legal rules must guarantee and protect the interests of present populations especially those in mining communities and their environments, in the midst of mineral development activities. Legislation and agreements must be tailored to yield them fair and equitable distribution of economic benefits obtained from exploitation of resources, protection of shared environmental resources, impose liability for pollution or damage, afford redress to environmental victims and avoid adverse interference with their livelihood. The quality of life in mining environments must be maintained and the human rights impacts of mining activities must be addressed and made enforceable by legal prescripts.

To ensure sustainable utilisation, legal dictates must emphasis on the one hand, that living natural resources of the environment used or affected by the conduct of mining operations be regulated for optimality of use; and that in all other cases, such activities must be conducted within the capacity of the environment. Laws should stress the prudent, rational and equitable use of natural wealth and resources so as not to severely diminish or exhaust their levels. Such laws and policies must impress among other things, proper forests management, planned and rational land-use policies, conservation and protection of species, preservation of watercourses, steams, rivers and lakes, enhanced management standards and monitoring controls.

The polluter-pays principle is effected by imputing on national authorities the responsibility to ensure that all costs generated from mining activities - environmental, social, and economic - are met by persons (including legal persons) undertaking such activities, through measures like cost internalisation, environmental taxes, fees, charges, permits and so on. The effect desired by the principle goes beyond polluting and cleaning up, remediation or reparation, to include environmental responsibility and/or liability regardless of damage or the legitimacy of the economic activity. A legal regime implementing the principle must equally emphasise issues of redress, compensation, development of trust funds and insurance schemes as environmental and social security in resource development operations. As a complement to traditional systems, more innovative strategies such as use of economic instruments and voluntary schemes must be encouraged through corporate social responsibility. Agreements must be designed or adapted to improve environmental performance and accountability of mining companies. This objective must be enhanced through adoption of guidelines and standards (national and global), codes of conduct, certification schemes and reporting on environmental and social issues.[79]

The precautionary principle must be expressed by imposition of a general and legal duty on states, corporate entities and individuals engaged in mining, to exercise caution, prudence and due care with the objective of preserving resources, and protecting the natural, human and cultural environment against potential harm, deterioration or damage. Legal rules must mandate the use of preventive measures that could mitigate environmental harm, protect natural resources,[80] human health and the social environment.[81] The principle must be transposed to effect continuously, always maintaining a standard by which existing and new environmental obligations are assessed, and irrespective of whether harm is perceived, conjectured or proved. Laws and agreements should require developers and decision-makers to consult, cooperate, exchange information, monitor risk, use and demand modern safe practice and technology with a flexibility that will appreciate the particular activity in the given environment.

A legal regime promoting EIA in mining for sustainability must emphasise environmental protection and seek to regulate environmental harm. It must charge decision-makers and developers with the responsibility to weigh environmental concerns together with economic and social ones in deciding whether to allow mining projects to go on. Specifically, it must require an assessment of mining programmes or activities, seek consultation and public participation in the decision–making process. Laws requiring EIA should not necessarily prohibit, prevent or halt activities with significant environmental impacts from being implemented, but this could be mandated in extreme cases. It must be designed as a flexible environmental management strategy that allows mining firms and operators to incorporate environmental concerns into their rationale, improve decision-making on environmental effects, their mitigation, and enhance environmental awareness. The mechanism must recognise environmental concerns, as alive and continuing, and represent the principle as mandatory irrespective of when a mining project may have been inaugurated; and should further ensure that the applicable environmental standards must be those prevailing at the time.

To effect sustainable mining through the principle of public participation, environmental and mining policies, laws and decision-making must create participatory rights for the public, mining communities and individuals, and

---

[79]See supra chapter 2, p.69-70, and ns. 143-149 on categories of regulations through economic instruments, Voluntary actions and CSR generally

[80]ILA: *Report of The Seventieth Conference, New Delhi, April 2002*, London 2002

[81]See WSSD POI, (Supra chapter 2, p.63, n.107)

provide for effective access to institutions (administrative, tribunal or judicial) on environmental and social issues. Groups and individuals must be granted rights, jointly or severally, to have access to environmental information, participate in environmental decision-making processes, and 'access to justice' through provisions that cater for redress. This latter component must find legal reflection in three adjudication possibilities: It must accord the capacity to challenge the refusal of access to information, to seek prevention and/or damages and compensation for environmentally harmful activities and to enforce environmental and mining laws directly. Importantly, participatory mandates must *facilitate exercise* of these rights through provisions for environmental education, research, reporting and financial assistance to promote these, including public interest litigations.

Finally, an appreciation of the foregoing sustainability objectives in mining would require an enabling environment for their implementation through the paradigm of localisation, institutionalisation and legalisation.[82] The emphasis must not be solely on the 'nature' of mining operations, but also on the policies, decisions, laws, regulations and agreements that chart them. These are the true torchbearers for effecting, enhancing and entrenching sustainable development in mining.[83] Generally however, implementation will require an integration of environmental and mineral development concerns as a national strategy at policy, planning and management levels; the ratification and/or implementation of applicable conventions and principles of international environmental laws; ensuring that the design of mining laws, agreements and regulations are properly articulated with capacity to implement, interpret, review, supervise, monitor, and update them continuously; and facilitating the use of legal, administrative and judicial authority for their enforcements.

Conclusion

This chapter set out to apply relevant principles of sustainable development in the specific context of mining, through practical illustration of ways in which these principles can achieve the objective of sustainable mining activities. It also sought to present a summation of the relevant sustainability principles identified generally in international law and specifically in

---

[82]See supra chapter 2, pp. 62-70

[83]MMSD (supra n.11); A useful recommendation is for governments to have a sustainable development policy for the minerals sector which would provide a useful tool to integrate, coordinate, and harmonise the missions of different departments, in pursuit of different the objectives. The departments that should be involved in adopting and implementing sustainable development policy should at a minimum include those dealing with minerals exploration and development, the Environment, trade and industry, labour and economic development.

relation to mining, as an instant reference for discerning or integrating sustainability objectives within policy and legal frameworks for the protection of mining environments. The chapter has established a direct relationship between sustainability and mining, translating its value for mineral resource developments through analysis of its relevant principles. And a summary has been set out representing specific contents of separate and distinct (but complementary) set of sustainability objectives in international law and in mining that mark the corner stone for applying, directing and achieving sustainable mining. It is upon this framework that the legal aspects of environmental regulation of mining in Sierra Leone are examined in subsequent chapters of this work, to test their sustainability content, adequacy or effectiveness in protecting the country's mining environment.

5 SUSTAINABILITY AND MINING LAWS OF SIERRA LEONE

5:1 Introduction

A major incidence of mineral resource development in Sierra Leone is the attendant damages mining activities cause to its environment. The spiralling effects go beyond physical damage to the natural environment to include severe impact on the social and cultural well-being of mining communities.[1] The previous chapter has identified and proved the relationship between mining and sustainable development by revealing how the valuable objectives of the concept (expressed through some relevant principles) can be adapted or applied to regulate domestic mining environments for sustainability. It set out a summary representing specific contents of separate and distinct (but complementary) set of sustainability objectives in international law and in mining that must mark the corner stone of legal regimes, in applying, directing and achieving sustainable mining.[2] The objectives identified generally recognised environmental protection as a mandate in mining; integrating environmental concerns into economic aspects of such activities; infusing the concept of posterity, fairness and equity in mining across generations; addressing social needs and environmental concerns of present generation; utilisation of natural resources in a sustainable manner; imputing or assuming responsibility for environmental harm, disturbance or damage caused by mining; exercising due care and taking precaution so as to avoid or prevent environmental harm; conducting EIA of mining programmes and activities; including the public in mining decision-making and enforcement and an enabling environment for implementing the defined objectives.[3]

---

[1] For examples of such impacts see supra chapter 1, pp. 33-37

[2] Note that references to sustainable development connotes sustainable development in international law, represented by the relevant principles and objectives identified in international law generally and related to mining specifically.

[3] The implementation aspects of all identified sustainability principles within legal dictates will be examined in chapter 7.

This chapter will examine the legal regime of environmental regulation in mineral resource development in Sierra Leone as a case study, dwelling only on mining specific laws and regulations, including selected mining agreements.[4] The structure of these mining laws will be examined, in three parts to determine the extent to which the principles of sustainable development in international law are represented in them. Also, the aim is to ascertain whether by expressed term or implication, they seek to apply, direct or achieve the objectives of the concept in protection of the country's mining environment, judging from the investigative criteria of sustainability objectives set out in the foregoing chapter. Part A will examine the Mines and Minerals legislation which is the parent act that validates categories of mineral rights and agreements. Part B will elaborate on two major agreements in respect of Rutile and Diamond mining, as representative samples. The third part will analyse the law regulating Petroleum development, including a model agreement in respect thereof.[5]

Part A

5:2 The Minerals Act, Environmental Provisions and Sustainability

The Mines and Minerals Act of 1994 (the Minerals Act), generally regulates mining activities in Sierra Leone, and is the parent legislation from which regulation, rules and agreements relating to mining claim their validity.[6] The Minerals Act holds a separate part for environmental protection, with general provisions that contemplate damage caused by mining to the natural and social environment, including the welfare of communities. It also creates defined environmental obligations within specific mineral rights and for general administration of the industry.[7] The act requires that, in the determination of whether or not to grant a mineral right to any applicant, the

---

[4]The laws of Sierra Leone that are examined in this and subsequent chapters, derive their authority pursuant to s. 170(a)-(e) and s.170 (4) and (5) of *The Constitution of Sierra Leone 1991*, Act No. 6 of 1991, (the constitution). These generally include the constitution; Parliamentary enactments, orders, rules regulations, and statutory instruments made pursuant to the constitution or any other law; the Existing Law, the Common Law or Modifications and adaptations made to any of these that conforms or gives effect to the constitution.

[5]This work recognises that the legal regime of mining in Sierra Leone is inextricably linked with land-use and land tenure issues. But this study excludes debates on the viability of Sierra Leone's legal dualism on tenure or title to land in its provinces. References to legal rules regulating land use for mining are discussed in the context of their relevance or capacity to enhance or inhibit the environmental goals that they are meant to safeguard in diverse ways.

For perspectives on the viability of Sierra Leone's legal dualism whether for economic purposes, legal efficiency, social justice and equity, see:- Johnson O.E., *Economic Analysis and the structure of Land Rights in Sierra Leone* Dissertation (PhD), University of California., L.A 1970; Renner- Thomas (supra chapter 1, p.28, n.48); Codjoe, V.S., *Land as a factor of Inequality in Kenema District*; B.A Dissertation (unpublished)1986, FBC, USL, respectively.

[6]The *Mines and Minerals Act* (1994), Act No. 5 of 1994(Minerals Act); Note that the 1994 Minerals Act does not cover the development of Mineral oil, which is regulated by the 2001 Petroleum Act.

[7]*Ibid* 'Mineral Right' is defined in the act to mean a prospecting licence, an exploration licence, a mining lease, or an artisanal mining licence; (Part 1 on Interpretation).

Minister 'shall take into account' the 'need to conserve natural resources which are in or on neighbouring land' during the conduct of mining activities.[8] The dedication of a whole part (Part XII) of a predominantly minerals development act to the objectives of environmental protection, fulfils the integration principle for sustainable development. The provisions represent the environment as an integral part of mineral development, by emphasising consideration for environmental concerns at the decision-making stage of granting mineral rights.

The act also provides for the inclusion into mineral rights of conditions for the protection of the environment or the rehabilitation of areas damaged or deleteriously affected by mining or exploration operations.[9] The indicated protective conditions include prevention, limitation or treatment of pollution and more generally, minimisation of the effects of mining on the natural and human environment.[10] Rehabilitation condition is one of the paramount environmental obligations in respect of artisanal and SCM rights holders, who must carry out 'effective' rehabilitation and reclamation of mined out areas.[11] Alternatively, they must deposit some form of security with the DoM, for the performance of such conditions.[12] These requirements are in line with the objectives of environmental protection in sustainable development to the extent that they reflect commitments to avoiding environmental degradation and maintaining environmental capacities. There is concern however regarding the efficiency of accepting fees without reference to the nature and extent of the reclamation or rehabilitative exercise that would be required before and after mining.

Under the act, the grant of a mineral right does not automatically enable the holder to dredge any river, stream, watercourse, pond, lake or waters of the continental shelf.[13] A license is required to be obtained upon payment of

---

[8]*Ibid* Part XII 'Protection of the Environment' s. 92 (1)

[9]*Ibid* s. 94(1); the act distinguishes between conditions for rehabilitation on the one hand, and environmental protection or damage prevention on the other. The latter conditions would not require 'security for performance'.

[10]*Ibid* s. 93 (1) (a) & (b); the scope of the protection to be afforded in this case will include those environmental assets or inhabitants on 'adjoining or neighbouring areas' covered by the mineral right. Compare with s. 92(1), which includes natural resources 'in or on the land over which the mining right is sought', in consideration of the need to conserve natural resources.

[11]*Ibid* s. 78(3)(d) and s. 79(1)(h); see also Clauses 7(a)(b)&(c) *Details of New Policy Measures Relating to Small Scale and Artisanal Mining and marketing of Precious Minerals* 2002 (Mining Policy), MMR, Freetown 2002. Note however, that there is nothing inhibiting the inclusion of further conditions in artisanal or SCM rights for environmental protection, pollution prevention and damage minimisation pursuant to the environmental provisions under Part XII of the Act.

[12]*Ibid* s. 94(1-2); artisanal right-holders are required to pay prescribed fees into a rehabilitation fund before the grant of artisanal license, while SCM right-holders have the option to rehabilitate or pay the requisite fees to defray the cost;(see Mining Policy (supra n. 11) clause 7(a) &(b)). The applicable rehabilitation fees in respect of diamond mining is set at Le.100,000 (per acre per year) for Artisanal mining; Le 200,000 for SCM; for Gold mining, at Le.50, 000 (per acre per year) for Artisanal mining; Le 100,000 for SCM (see Schedule 1)

[13]Minerals Act, (supra n. 6) s. 89; fees for dredging licences is set at $250.00 (per acre per year) (Mining Policy *ibid, schedule* 1)

prescribed fees. Such licenses could contain environmental conditions, breach of which becomes an offence on the one hand, and warrants liability for any damage arising in consequence of such contravention.[14] Similarly, reliance is placed on the use of fees for regulating land and river use,[15] and taxing scheme is employed on some products on export (diamonds) for mining communities. These provisions, suggest regulatory trend toward rational allocation and use of renewable resources and eliminating unsustainable patterns of mineral production. The use of economic instruments severally as licenses, (for dredging), fees (for land and river use), fees (for environmental management and rehabilitation) and taxing schemes exemplify objectives of the polluter-pays principle, with consequential effects in the direction of sustainable utilisation of natural resources in mining.

Also, as part of the measures required for protecting the social environment, mining leaseholders are required to pay (in addition to the payment of withholding income tax), annual funds for agricultural and community development (ADF & CDF)[16] and rehabilitation.[17] This strategy accords with the innovative mechanisms for directing or achieving the goals of the generational principles in sustainable development, where mining communities can have direct benefit from such activities in the development of their communities and/or other environmental saving content for future generations. The respective funds could allow for alternative uses of land in developing agriculture, which can provide social benefit alongside mineral production; could improve mining communities with reproducible capital and amenities; and could allow for restoration of environmental capacity of degraded lands by reinvesting capital gained from mining in environmental reclamation, restoration and rehabilitation. However, consideration should be given to other methods like environmental cost internalisation in the purchasing of mineral rights, including insurance schemes as environmental and social security.[18]

Furthermore, in specifying mineral rights and surface rights, the act tends to restrict mining and the use of mineral rights in specific areas, including

---

[14]*Ibid* s. 89(4)&(5)

[15]In respect of diamond mining, Artisanal land and river Licenses is estimated at Le 100, 000, per year per acre; Small Scale land and River Licenses-Le 200,000 per year per acre; Licenses to Dredge US$500 per acre per year. (See Mining Policy (supra n. 11) schedule 1)

[16]Minerals Act, (supra n. 6) s.107; the ADF and CDF already created are limited only to mining leases, excluding prospecting, exploration and artisanal mining rights.

[17]Mining Policy (supra n. 11), clause 7(b)

[18]These will redress the gap in the provisions for environmental protection and preventative actions in s. 94(1)&(2)

places of religious or cultural significance.[19] The provisions seem to embody the protection of cultural values, people's welfare, farming and so on. This protection is however watered down by provisions allowing for mining operations in the purported protected areas, upon the written consent of the lawful owner or occupier of land, or his agent.[20] And where the lawful owner or occupier refuses such consent, the act empowers the Minister to authorise the mineral right-holder to exercise all his rights under the licenses. It is untenable that a seeming protection, which might benefit community welfare and interests, is made subject to a determination that does not remotely involve participation of such community.

Another important provision in the act with implications for ensuring sustainability in mining is the issue of compensation. Right-holders must pay fair and reasonable compensation to affected land owners and occupiers 'for any disturbance of [their] rights…and any damage' done by mining operations, to the surface of land, crops, trees, buildings or works.[21] But, factors such as payment of rent by rights-holders or any 'improvement effected' by them on land granted, either offsets the compensation or is discounted from the quantum of compensation that is determined in respect of 'deprivation of use of land'.[22] In my view, the provision does not effect to offset compensation for "disturbance of the rights" and other interests held over land, such as the right to enjoyment of unpolluted water. Strangely however, claims for compensation under the this category must be made within a period of two years from the date when the wrongful act was done; failing which the act renders unenforceable, claims in respect of such compensation both under the act and any other written law.[23] In cases of compulsory acquisition of private land (exclusively for mining lease holders), the rights-holder must pay 'acquisition compensation' before he enters into possession of land to exercise his right.[24] Indeed these provisions seek to direct the sustainability objectives under the intragenerational, participatory and polluter-pays principles, suggesting respectively, fairness and equity; entitlement to claim compensation; and responsibility on

---

[19]Minerals Act, (supra n. 6) s. 23(b)(1-IV) Other protected interests include burial grounds; land set apart for public purpose; land within 50 yards of land cleared for growing agricultural crops, or upon which such crops are growing; or any land 100 yards of any cattle dips, tanks, dam, or other body of water.

[20]Ibid s. 23(1)(b)

[21]Ibid s. 26; Note that the act distinguishes between cases where rights-holders acquire title to land use by agreement with land owner or occupier, and cases of compulsory acquisition of private land for mining purposes. This case represents the former.

[22]Ibid s. 26(1)(i) &(ii)

[23]Ibid s. 26(3); this limitation is quite unreasonable considering that mining leases go on for years and the evidence of destruction remains long after such operations cease.

[24]Ibid s. 28(2); upon such acquisition, compensation issue is to be determined under s. 26 including the claims limitation clause.

developers to assume and meet all costs (social, economic and environmental) generated from mining activities undertaking them.

But the compensation provisions raise difficult questions about their effectiveness in directing mining projects towards social and environmental sustainability. For instance, the goals in the principles are inhibited when compensation is made payable even before the determination of the extent of the disturbance, risk, or damages that the natural, cultural and human environment will be exposed to, or without the effective participation of the persons so affected. Also, it is untenable to have varying standards for compensation, defined by the manner in which access to land use was granted.[25] Further, the imposition of a two-year compensation claims period effects as a denial of, or 'blocking access' to participatory rights.[26] Similarly, the prescribed method of paying compensation completely ignores other environmental assets and materials, emphasising social concerns as farming, peoples' welfare and cultural values. Above all, the act does not seem to regulate the quantity of non-renewable resources that could be exploited so as to leave future population of the country the option of choice to deal with them according to their own developmental needs.

Under the Act, EIA is required as a condition for the grant of mineral rights, specifically in respect of mining leases.[27] The specific use of the term 'EIA', in the minerals act does represent an endorsement of one of the fundamental principles of sustainable development in international law. Specifically, the act requires some form of environmental statements to be prepared in respect of right-holders of exploration and mining leases.[28] Mining lease applicants are further required to submit an approved programme of proposed operations which should be accompanied by an EIA statement.[29]

Similarly, the minerals act covers previously held mineral rights, which may contain unfulfilled environmental conditions. In such cases, the Minister may

---

[25]By compulsory acquisition or local agreements;(see supra n., 18, 20 & 21)

[26]This involves the right to demand and seek compensation for damages or disturbances that might otherwise not be apparent at the time of the agreements for land use.

[27]Ibid s. 92(2); Other forms of mineral rights including mining leases for 'buildings and industrial' minerals are generally excluded from requiring EIA, thus overlooking the environmentally disruptive potential of such activities

[28]Ibid s. s.48 and 59. In respect of exploration licenses, such statement must detail like significant environmental effects of such activities and estimated cost of combating such adverse effects. For mining leases, the statement must include proposals relating to land reclamation and rehabilitation; minimising mining effects on surface and ground waters, on adjoining or neighboring lands, on the local population (particular risk to health), and how they propose to mitigate control or eliminate them. See also s. 67(d), for regulation on wastes and tailings.

[29]Ibid s. 61 (3) (a); see also s. 92(2); this obligation on mining leaseholders extends to cases of renewal of such leases. Note that the limitation of the EIA mechanism to mining leases in the act and the lack of a defined strategy for enforcing it have been addressed by the EPA; relevant EIA requirements in the EPA are examined in chapter 6.

cause the condition to be fulfilled at any cost and must be reimbursed by the responsible party. The cost is deemed a debt owing, and could be recovered in a court of competent jurisdiction.[30] It is also an offence for persons to fail to comply with notices to fulfil prescribed environmental conditions.[31] Both remedies for failing to comply with environmental conditions are concurrent not cumulative and liability can be joint or several. These provisions generally promote use of judicial process to enforce environmental objectives and thereby represent aspects of participatory requirement in sustainable development. It is however not clear from the act whether the provisions could be applied to current or existing right-holders to compel them to fulfil their environmental conditions; or whether the public can rely on the act to institute such actions to compel performance or enforcement of environmental obligations under the specific mandates of mineral rights. Consideration should be given to the use of other flexible processes like tribunals or inquiries which identify among legal processes of directing sustainability.[32]

Finally, the act empowers the minister to make regulations restricting or prohibiting prospecting, exploration or mining operations, for the purpose of giving effect to the environmental provisions within the act.[33] In accordance with the integration principle, the DoE is represented on the MAB, such representation being useful for impressing environmental concerns in mining decision-making.[34] The act also provides for the cancellation of a mineral right 'if the holder grossly violates health and safety standards, or causes environmental harm'.[35] This provision could effect to afford individuals and communities disadvantaged by mining activities or aiming to protect the environment from harm, to seek the cancellation of mineral rights or to check their activities. However, coordination and consultation requirements must be made more inclusive to accommodate developers. It will be very useful for directing sustainable development if future regulations emphasise on cooperation, exchange of information and

---

[30]Ibid s.95 (1), (3) & (4)

[31]Ibid s. 95(1-6). Individuals are made liable on conviction to a fine or imprisonment or both, while liability for corporations is a fine not exceeding five million Leones. This ceiling for corporate liability leaves open a discretionary minimum to be set by the court, which may not always be commensurate with the risk or damage to be prevented by the environmental condition.

[32]This process identifies in the legal character of sustainable development (See supra chapter 2, pp. 57 & 56). Note also that judicial processes are usually very expensive and by Sierra Leone standards, elaborate, time-consuming and in some cases, non-resultant.

[33]Ibid s.123 (3) He must consult with the minister of environment in making such regulations.

[34]The MAB is responsible inter alia, for formulating recommendation of national policy on the exploitation of mineral resources, and monitoring the operation of such policies among other things; see s. 3(1)&(2) Minerals Act (supra n. 6).

[35]Ibid s.31 (1)(b)

participation of identified groups. Above all, future regulations have to address the social impact of mine life and closure, an issue that ultimately defines the sustainability of such operations.

Conclusion

In light of the forgoing, there can be no denial that the environment is effectively made an integral part of the legal regime regulating mining decision-making and processes in Sierra Leone. The evaluation proves the act as entailing some general and specific environmental objectives, which represent aspects of the principles required for sustainable development. These objectives are conveyed mainly through the mechanism of imposing environmental conditions within mineral rights for environmental protection, EIA, use of funds and economic instruments. Within these provisions, the generational, sustainable utilisation, polluter-pays and precautionary principles are given legal effects in regulation of mining for sustainability. Participatory objectives have also been identified in the provisions on compensation including use of judicial means to enforce environmental conditions, and concerns over their effectiveness for directing sustainability were dealt with. There is room for improvement on uniformity of standards on these issues, clearly defined role for the public in mining decision-making, access to justice for compensation and enforcement of environmental obligations, and use of alternatively more flexible dispute resolution mechanisms.

Part B

5:3 Mining Agreements and Environmental Regulation

The Minerals Act empowers the Minister to enter into agreements with any person on behalf of GOSL, for the grant of a mineral right and upon specified conditions not being inconsistent with the parent act.[36] This provides the legal basis upon which agreements for the mining of specified minerals are concluded. It is assumed that such agreements remain bound to the parent agreement in all matters therein stated, including the general and specific environmental provisions discussed in the forgoing part. But there exist a practice to have some mining agreements ratified by Parliament, as part of

---

[36]The minerals Act, (supra n.6) s. 22

the body of statutory laws of Sierra Leone,[37] thereby according them equal status with the minerals act.[38] Examined in this part are two major mining agreements in respect of Rutile and Diamond development activities, to ascertain both their sustainability content and effectiveness for sustainable development.

5:3:1 The Rutile Agreement

The SRA[39] is between the GOSL and SRL,[40] for the development of and processing of rutile and ilmenite. The agreement is distinguished in the sense that it provides that 'the government of the Republic of Sierra Leone will introduce and cause to be passed legislation for the purpose of ratifying and confirming the agreement in all its terms'.[41] The ratification of the SRA validates all its terms, notwithstanding 'any law' that contradicts its provisions, or 'anything contained in any law'.[42] The SRA purports to adopt the environmental provisions in the minerals act relating to mining leases and dredging licences in so far as they are not inconsistent 'with [its] expressed or any implied terms and conditions'.[43] These provisions could also have the effect of limiting application of environmental provisions in the minerals act that are not assumed in the SRA.

Surprisingly, the SRA has neither a specified 'Part' that references protection of the environment, nor does it mention the term 'environmental protection' or even the word 'environment' in any of the provisions in the entire agreement. It seems strange that a mineral development agreement in this twenty-first century of environmental awareness, and one that holds profound implications for environmental issues, can omit any reference to the term. This omission has however been subsequently addressed under the

---

[37]This research could not uncover any legal basis (outside the ratified agreements- see note 41 below) for the ratification of individual mining agreements especially so when they do not fall within the category of international agreements. An interview with the DoM and the Solicitor General revealed that the practice evolved upon insistence of mining companies and this has since become the norm. Examples of previously ratified mining leases are *The Sierra Rutile Agreement 1989 (Ratification) Act, 1989 (Act No.8 of 1989; the Bauxite Mineral Prospecting and Mining Agreement Decree 1992.*

[38]This fact raises some questions of legislative efficiency in sustainable development, which will be discussed under implementation in chapter 7.

[39]The Sierra Rutile Agreement (Ratification) Act 2002, Act No. 4 of 2002.

[40]Sierra Rutile Limited is a Company incorporated and existing under the Companies Act, Cap 249 of the Laws of Sierra Leone.

[41]SRA (supra n.39) preamble;(Cf. Clause 12, *Agreement between the GOSL and SRL, dated 20th November, 2001*

[42]*Ibid* (recital); the reference to 'any law' or 'anything contained in any law' could be interpreted to include the Environmental Provisions in the Minerals Act or the Environmental Protection Act itself.

[43]*Ibid* Clause 2 ; Note that by these provisions, the SRL seeks the benefit of other laws, without the obligations they impose.(see clause 10 and 11(e) on 'limitation of the application of the minerals Act and other acts')

Sysmin agreement.[44] The latter clearly specifies and extends SRL environmental and social obligations beyond the SRA, to include provisions of 'all applicable environmental, health and safety laws... all rules and regulations promulgated thereunder, including GOSL environmental requirements and the World Bank Guidelines'.[45]

The SRA however contains some provisions with environmental objectives as part of the general rights and obligations of the company. The main environmental obligation assumed by SRL is the preparation of a document, (severally termed 'comprehensive master plan', 'detailed Programme') 'that will address the issue of reclamation and rehabilitation of mined out areas'.[46] Some pertinent issues to be addressed in such document relate to replanting, dealing with mining spoils, aquaculture, suitable reforestation, effects of dredging on lakes, and methods of minimising mining effects on adjoining land and water areas.[47] These issues generally serve the purpose of integrating environmental concerns within rutile development planning, in fulfilment of the integration principle. Each of the proposed initiatives seeks to promote environmental protection by recognising the vulnerability of varied components of the environment in the conduct of such operations, and assuming some amount of responsibility for environmental management. However, the prescribed environmental issues to be addressed in SRL plans do not include commitments in respect of damage prevention, nor does it require the exercise of caution in such operations regardless of whether harm is conjectured or perceived.[48]

Also, though a statement of environmental objectives in plans or programmes of SRL could be likened to an environmental statement, which is usually a required component of EIA procedures, it does not explain the omission in the SRA of reference to the term 'EIA'.[49] The logical explanation

---

[44]Loan Agreement between SRL and the GOSL dated 2nd August 2004 (hereinafter Sysmin). Under the terms of this agreement, the EC on behalf of the GOSL will provide a grant of twenty-five million euros to the GOSL which is to be on lent to SRL for the rehabilitation, development and expansion of the latter's rutile and ilmenite mining and processing operations. (See second recital and s.2.01). See also Swarray Dean M. "Private Sector Development in Sierra Leone" at http://www.dse.de/ef/publicbads/deen.htm

[45]Ibid s. 6.04 .The applicable World Bank Guidelines include: the World Bank: - EHSG, including the IFC Policy on Environmental Assessment (OP 4.01) October, 1998; Policy on Involuntary Resettlement (OD 4.30, June 1990; Policy on Management of Cultural Property (OP 11.03), September 1996; EHSG for Mining and Milling -Open Pit, 1995; IFC: Policy on Natural Habitats (OP 4.04) November 1998; Policy on Safety of Dams (OP 4.10), September 1991; EHSG for port and Harbour Facilities, 1998; and the applicable provisions of the World Bank Pollution Prevention and Abatement Handbook, 1998.(see s.1.01 on Definitions)

[46]SRA (supra n.39) clause 10

[47]Ibid clause 10 (k) (i), (ii) &(iii) A 'final report' on these programmes including time frame for their implementation is to be submitted to the government authorities within six months from the ratification date for their approval.

[48]See Minerals Act (supra n.6) s. 93

[49]EIA is a paramount condition mandated by the Minerals act for mining leases, such as the SRA.

for such an omission is a calculated effort to avoid the obligations inherent and commonly implied in a specific use of the term,[50] or to essentially tailor plans or reports, in order to pass the approval stage, with the intention of not adhering to their contents. This scepticism is justified by the fact that, the SRA envisages a likelihood of it not adhering to proposed programmes, after the government approves them.[51]   However, this dilemma has been addressed under Sysmin, requiring SRL to fully implement any mitigation measures, monitoring programs or other actions or activities identified in the ESIA.[52]

Another fundamental sustainability objective which the SRA seeks to address, relates to the utilisation or employment of renewable resources. SRL is accorded wide-ranging rights to use natural resources that occur within or outside its mining lease area, subject to a prohibition on discharge of poisonous or noxious matter therein.[53] It is further restricted from 'altering the water supply of any lands in such a manner as would prejudicially affect water supply enjoyed by any other *persons or land*'. Where SRL employment of water resources is likely to bring about the above conditions, consent for utilisation must be obtained from the DO having jurisdiction over persons or land that would be prejudicially affected.[54]   A third qualification of SRL water rights is an obligation to provide alternative adequate water supply to any village, the adequacy of which is to be determined by the Minister of health.[55] This obligation is not made proactive but reactionary, to be activated only after the DoM certifies that such utilisation is 'likely to pollute, impair, divert or destroy the normal supply of potable water of any village'. The SRA further provides for the obtaining of consent for the destruction of protected forests or forest reserves.[56]

The various provisions clearly set in place standards and channels of controls, in an attempt to effect sustainable utilisation of renewable resources in SRL mining operations. The standards are defined by prohibition on discharge of 'poisonous or noxious' matter in water resources, obtaining consent for utilisation that will have a 'prejudicial' effect on persons or land,

[50]This criticism is justified in light of the fact that the SRA of 2002 succeeds both the Minerals Act of 1994 and the EPA of 2000, both of which effectively incorporate the term EIA.

[51]SRA (supra n. 39) clause 10 (k)(iii); The SRA effectively states that 'should the Programme not be adhered to by the company after it has been approved by the government, the government reserves the right to carry out the Programme on behalf of and at the expense of the company'.

[52]Sysmin (supra n.44) s.6.04 (b); this refers to the ESIA prepared by Knight Piésold & Consultants: *Sierra Rutile Environmental and Social Impact Assessment*, October 2001.

[53]SRA (supra n.39) clause 10(a)(1)(i)&(ii)(A)

[54]*Ibid* Clause10 (a)(1)(ii)(C)

[55]*Ibid* clause 10(a)(2)

[56]Such consent must be obtained from the Forest Officer or upon payment of prescribed royalties and fees pursuant the Forestry Act, 1988, Act No. 7 of 1988.

and the DoM's *perception* of the unsustainability of the said use. However, the SRA does not provide for a determination of responsibility or liability in the event that SRL breaches the prohibition clause. This anomaly leaves the provision very much aspirational. Also the structure of regulation created in a tier of hierarchy and controls at different levels between the DO, DoM and the Minister of health raises questions regarding its efficiency for achieving sustainability. An instant effect of the structure is a situation wherein the DO may give valid consent to SRL to commence adverse use of water resources. Such use could effectively subject the Co-riparian (local communities) to the prejudices of the adverse utilisation by the company, while they await the DoM's determination of whether the use is 'prejudicial' enough to warrant provision of an alternative water supply.[57] By this co-coordinate mechanism, it may take a considerably length of time before the alternative measure is put in place, leaving the poor communities deprived. Furthermore, the provision does not seem to address use that will be prejudicial to the land itself or non-human-species and the marine ecosystem. The emphasis in the SRA is on 'provision of alternative water supply',[58] which does not translate into cleaning up of rivers or maintaining their natural courses. However Sysmin stipulates that SRL shall maintain all required authorisations and licenses relating to air emissions, discharges to surface or ground water, noise emissions, solid or liquid waste disposals and *'other environmental'*, health and safety matters.[59]

Another effort at incorporating sustainability objectives in the SRA relates to social issues of compensation, development funds and community resettlement efforts. SRL shall endeavour to make satisfactory arrangements for payment of a 'fair and reasonable' compensation for any prospective damage to any crops, buildings, trees or works.[60] The act also grants power to the government to assess and negotiate such compensation with SRL, with a right reserved for the landowners to participate in such negotiations.[61] Also, the company must not interfere or disturb the living conditions of the local population settled within its lease area, and must respect their local

---

[57] One would imagine that such a determination would properly rest on an independent body (such as a standards authority or water authority) and an acceptable level of risk or inconvenience must be primarily ascertained before the initial approval of such use is giving by the DO. Note also that the request for 'consent to utilise' is premised on SRL recognition that its proposed employment of those resources will prejudicially affect water supply enjoyed by other persons or lands.(see supra n.52).

[58] Usually exemplifies in construction of water-wells

[59] Sysmin (supra n.44) s.6.04 (a) (emphasis added)

[60] SRA (supra n.39) clause 10 (b) (1); Compare with clause 10(b)(2)(i)).

[61] *Ibid* clause 10 (b) (1) Compensation to be paid based on estimated monetary amount (or fair market value) of damage to be done to buildings trees or works on the land. (clause 10(b)(2)(iii))

customs.[62] Where resettlement of the communities becomes essential, it must be done with consent from the government in consultation with the local authorities, and upon fully adequate resettlement programme.[63] SRL is also required to make annual payments into an ADF,[64] and must set up and manage a non-profit foundation to develop and implement non-mining activities which will further the economic and social development of communities living in the areas of its operations.[65] Above all, it shall fully implement and conduct its business according to its 2001 approved policy statements on environmental, social, health and safety, resettlement and community development.[66] SRL also assumes annual EMR obligations.[67]

The general objective of the compensatory, trust-funds and resettlement provisions contemplate the adverse consequences of mining on the livelihood of the mining communities and attempts to impute some responsibility on the company toward them. These issues, jointly or severally, represent aspects of the integration, intra-generational equity, public participation and the polluter-pays principles in sustainable development. Their full effects in directing sustainable rutile development will ultimately depend on factors like:-

(i)   The technique by which compensable objects are measured since the market value of crops, trees buildings and works are not exactly similar either in their uses or purposes.

(ii)   The reasonableness, adequacy or sufficiency of the actual environment in which the communities are to be resettled as opposed to a descriptive manual of intensions.

(iii)   The scope of freedom left for the affected population to register their dissatisfaction with any unsuitable resettlement conditions.

(iv)   The right not only to participate in the compensation consultations, but also to acquire adequate benefit in the distribution of same.

(v)   And the direction of the ADF and foundations not only toward farming for subsistence, but also in investments on other environmental assets to compensate for nature affected elsewhere by mining, and other reproducible capital.

[62] *Ibid* clause 10(a)(2)(iv)

[63] *Ibid* clause 10(a)(2)(v)

[64] *Ibid* clause 10(j)

[65] Sysmin supra n.44) s.6.04 (d);

[66] Sysmin (supra n.44) s.6.04(c); Note that the World Bank Guidelines (supra n.45) are also applicable

[67] Note however that the durability of company's environmental and social reporting obligation is premised upon the full repayment of the loan, rather than on the completion of the project (Sysmin (*ibid*) s.6.05 and Exhibit A (B))

Finally, it is important to stress here that there is no provision in the SRA that remotely relates to the social impact of mine closure and a strategy to deal with it. This is a fundamental issue in determining the over-all sustainability of mining, and becomes especially relevant where SRL is empowered under the agreement, to remove '*all*' or *any* of its buildings, structures, plants, machinery, equipment *or other effects*' upon surrender, termination or expiration of the lease.[68]

5:3:2 The Diamond Agreement

The KPML[69] is another agreement between the GOSL and KHL,[70] concluded pursuant to the Minerals Act,[71] for the commercial exploitation of diamond resources in kimberlite pipes by open pit and underground mining methods. Like the Rutile Agreement, the KPML was ratified by act of parliament, as part of the laws of Sierra Leone, pursuant to a ratification clause.[72] The company undertakes to comply at all times with provisions of the Minerals Act, other relevant laws and regulations bearing on the conduct of their operations,[73] 'and such rules of international law as may be applicable',[74] and are not inconsistent with the KPML. These provisions leave scope for the adaptability of sustainability objectives in other relevant laws and regulations, (national and international) to the terms of the Diamond agreement. Captioned as 'Protection of the Environment', clause 11 of the KPML makes environmental and social objectives integral to kimberlite mining development goals, and advances the integration principle.

The company assumes the responsibility '*at all times*' to do every thing reasonable in its power to limit damage and disturbance of its mining operations both to the local environment and the populace.[75] In furtherance of this objective to protect the natural and human environment, it proposes to conduct its operations and project activities with a degree of care and

---

[68]*Ibid* clause 2(c)(2); Compare this provision with section 26(1)(i)&(2) Minerals Act (supra n.6) which provides for '*any improvement effected*' on land to offset compensation claims.

[69]*The Koidu Kimberlite Project Mining Lease (Modification and Ratification)* Act (2002), (KPML)

[70]Koidu Holdings Limited (KHL) is a Company incorporated and existing under the Companies Act, Cap 249 of the Laws of Sierra Leone.

[71]Minerals Act (supra n. 36) s.22 (a)(b)&(c)

[72]See Clause 25 of Mining Lease Agreement between the GOSL and Branch Energy Ltd. Dated 22nd July 1995; the agreement (which was originally adopted by military decree) was subsequently ratified by Parliament in 2002. See (supra n. 37) for comments on the ratification of mining agreements.

[73]KPML (supra n. 69), clause 6

[74]*Ibid* clause 21

[75]*Ibid* clause 11:1

professionalism 'that meets or exceeds the best international environmental protection standards',[76] including undertaking of a baseline EIA before the commencement of operations;[77] and to engage an independent environmental consultant to advice upon and monitor procedures set in place for the protection of the environment and rehabilitation.[78] These provisions represent relevant sustainability principles: For instance environmental protection is assured through the company's unequivocal contemplation ('at all times') of the effects of their operations on the natural and community environment, so as to limit disturbance and damage. The precautionary principle is adopted by undertakings to exercise a 'degree of care', institute EIA and set up an EMS that will monitor environmental procedures.[79] Thus, beyond the very general and aspirational connotations of these provisions, and the omission to provide for a well-defined resettlement programme, their broad formulation leaves enough scope for the adoption or interpretation of further sustainability objectives, including the best 'international environmental protection standards'.

The KPML also incorporates the principle of sustainable use or employment of natural resources in mining operations. This is transposed through provisions that prohibit the poisoning of water resources;[80] that mandate the employment of advanced techniques, practice and methods for pollution prevention, limitation and treatment, including the avoidance of unnecessary loss of or damage to natural resources. And in each case, such efforts shall be employed in accordance with environmental standards generally accepted in the international mining industry.[81]

Similarly, the provision requiring the company to prevent, limit and treat pollution translates the objective and responsibility of the polluters' principle, while requirements canvassing protective measures to avoid unnecessary loss or damage to natural resources epitomise facets of environmental protection in mining and sustainable development. However, the provisions do not cover co-riparian interests in those natural resources that the company might interfere with. This condition is socially unsustainable especially since there is bound to be cases where water sources will be polluted or diverted causing deprivation or disturbance to other

---

[76] *Ibid* clause11: 2; (see also schedule 8, para.1)

[77] *Ibid* clause11: 1

[78] *Ibid* schedule 8

[79] *Ibid*

[80] *Ibid* clause 6:3:1

[81] *Ibid* clause 11 .3

users.[82] It may however be possible to redress this anomaly under the general obligations of the company undertaking 'at all times' to 'limit the damage and disturbance of its mining operations both to the local environment and the populace'.[83] So that, where 'damage or disturbance' occurs, it could be deemed a 'material breach' by KHL, warranting remediation of damage or monetary compensation for same.[84] The agreement also provides for annual contributions into an ADF, for the development of agriculture in mining areas. But while these terms may effect to place some responsibility on the company at least for damages and a sustainable alternative land use for local benefits, they however warrant strong criticism for the complete omission of participatory rights including access to justice. Above all the framework addressing breaches would require reliable environmental valuation techniques and mechanisms (including cost–benefit analysis) that would reflect the environment's worth in monetary terms.

Other provisions in the KPML with significant implication for the sustainability of the KPML and its efficiency especially in environmental management, relate to the determination of applicable standards, technology and information. Strangely, the company is protected under the KPML, from the imposition of any further liability in connection with the 'raising or extension of environmental standards', beyond those generally accepted in the international mining industry and prevailing at the commencement of the KPML.[85] It is also exonerated from liability for failing to take action in respect of scientific or technological information, analysis or findings that may indicate preventative or remedial action not existent at the time of coming into force of the agreement.[86] And the government agrees not to impose any additional obligations relating specifically to protection of the environment other than those stated in the set out in schedule 8 of the KPML.[87] The implications of these provisions are far-reaching.

First, the GOSL[88] undertaken not to impose further environmental obligations (regarding standards, use of environmental safe technology and

---

[82]Note that the Minerals Act (supra n. 6) mandates as a condition of mining rights, that compensation be paid for any 'disturbance of rights of land owners or occupiers (s. 26(1).

[83]See supra n.74

[84]KPML, Clause 20:3:3; note that the provisions relating to material breach covers failure to cease using wasteful mining or treatment practices pursuant to section 69 of the Minerals act, and for all other requirements of that act applicable to the KPML.

[85]Ibid Clause 11:4.1(see supra not 82 for comments on international mining standards)

[86]Ibid clause 11:4.2

[87]Ibid clause 11:5; the specific environmental mandates of Schedule 8 include undertaking revegetation to combat erosion, setting aside of top-soil for restoration, minimisation of dust, regulating emissions and disposal of wastes (domestic and industrial) in an environmentally safe way.

[88]This connotation undoubtedly includes the Departments of Mines, Environment, Forestry, Social Welfare, Health, Labour etc

practices) on KHL, is inherently unsustainable in that it purports to foreclose enhancement of the mining environment by restricting the imposition of evolving standards and technology. Similar impression is conveyed by limiting the applicable environmental standards to those existing in the international mining industry at the commencement of the agreement bearing in mind that, international mining industry standards relating to environmental protection are not universal, evolving and not always definitive.[89] The environmental and social effects of mining are real and continuing and so must the information, standards, technology and practices that should direct such activities. Furthermore, it is vital for sustainable development, that new scientific information and technology be applied to prevent, limit or correct environmental harm. The thrust of the limitation clauses could thus effect to undermine the sustainability of all or most of the environmental obligations assumed by KHL under the KPML.

Despite the forgoing concerns, it must be emphasised that the KPML effectively raises the provisions of damage prevention, reclamation and rehabilitation stated in the minerals act in line with international standards. By undertaking to conduct the company's activities with a degree of care and professionalism 'that meets or exceeds the *best international environmental protection standards'*, it is safe to submit that those ones which are applicable could be imposed through the relevant principles of sustainable development to ensure environmentally safe diamond mining practices in Sierra Leone. Also, discounting the limitation clauses and the definitional difficulties in applying environmental standards existing in the international mining industry, it is still helpful to include references to them. The applicable ones could be used as a baseline in the formulation and development of environmental regulations in the minerals sector generally.

Conclusion

The aim of this part was to examine two major mining agreements in respect of rutile and diamond development activities, to ascertain their sustainability content and effectiveness for sustainable development. The forgoing analyses of the SRA and the KPML have revealed a complex effort at incorporating elements of sustainable development in the culture of rutile and diamond development in Sierra Leone. The examination of the SRA identified objectives of sustainable utilisation through user standards and

---

[89]The parties may consider identifying specific environment standards in the Industry that should be adopted for the agreement

controls to regulate use of water resources. Concerns were raised over the structure of coordinative sequences and the mechanisms for assessing standards. These must be made clear, effective and enforceable. Objectives of intragenerational equity, polluter-pays, participation and ESIA were also proved in provisions seeking to promote social sustainability of mining communities, and their efficiency for achieving those goals have been discussed. Omissions of vital and established references like 'environment', 'environmental protection' and 'EIA, have been criticised.

The analysis of the KPML on the other hand, revealed clear appreciation of the principles of environmental protection and precaution through EIA, damage minimisation, control and monitoring obligations. Also uncovered were provisions directing sustainable utilisation of resources by placing responsibility for pollution in the polluter or its user–pay cousin. There is however need to amend the agreement to reflect public participatory rights especially the right of access to justice to enforce both social and environmental obligations under the agreement.

Finally, some of the provisions in both the SRA and the KPML were found to be inherently aspirational, limiting in some cases and neither seemed to address issues relating to transfer of technology or strategy for mine closure. However the adoption in both agreements of general and specific (World Bank) international environmental guidelines and standards will serve to further embellish pertinent principles of sustainable development within these agreements, and they can be used to interpret, modify or adapt the agreements in the general direction of sustainability.

Part C

5:4 The Environment in Petroleum Development

Environmental matters relating to the exploration, development and production of Petroleum in Sierra Leone are to be regulated under PEPA.[90] The Act establishes a Petroleum Resource Unit (PRU), headed by a Director-General (DG), who shall have exclusive jurisdiction in all petroleum matters relating to the environment under PEPA,[91] including power to enter into petroleum agreements with contractors for Petroleum development. Unlike

---

[90]*The Petroleum Exploration and Production Act* (2001), Act. No.11 of 2001 (PEPA) PEPA excludes application of the Minerals Act to petroleum development. Note also that up to the time of writing, Sierra Leone has never effectively commenced development or production of petroleum. PEPA and the MPA are put in place in anticipation of such development.

[91]*Ibid* s. 26 (2) Note that the DG is required to consult with the DoE on all petroleum matters relating to the environment.

the previous agreements in respect of rutile and diamond mining, which had their validation by parliamentary ratification, all agreements relating to petroleum development are made valid and confirmed by PEPA, through a Model Petroleum Agreement (MPA) for all contractors. The latter enhances uniformity and consistency in standards, while maintaining some form of control under the parent act. Both PEPA and the MPA are considered in separate evaluations this part, to ascertain their sustainability content for environmental protection.

5:4:1 The Petroleum Legislation in Sustainability Perspective

The objective of environmental protection in natural resource exploitation as a goal of sustainable development is demonstrated in several provisions of PEPA, which define the responsibilities of the PRU on the one hand, and the obligations of contractors. In relation to the former, the DG/PRU is empowered to make further regulations serving environmental concerns, such as the prevention of pollution and the taking of remedial action in respect of it. Such regulations must also aim at the protection of fishing and other activities carried out within the vicinity of petroleum operations, including conservation of natural resources and must also regulate the avoidance of any form of waste.[92] Where regulations are put in place addressing these various issues, they will serve the purpose of enhancing protection over renewable and non-renewable resources alike, compelling sustainable employment of those resources including conservation, supervision and monitoring of their capacities.[93]

Petroleum contractors are required under the act, to submit their development plans (including long term production programs) to the DG for approval. All such plans must *inter alia;* take account of any regulations relating to the environment and other petroleum matters as may be prescribed.[94] Short of the specific obligation to undertake ESIA *per-se,* information so provided in such plans and production programmes may be used to make a reasonable assessment of the environmental and social impact of proposed petroleum development operation.

Similarly, PEPA imputes on petroleum contractors responsibility for 'any

---

[92]*Ibid* s. 65 (c), (h), & (p)

[93] A contractor, who contravenes any of the provisions of the act, including regulations which shall be put in place, commits an offence for which he can either be fined or imprisoned (s. 64(2)(c)). Note that up to the time of writing however, no regulations have been made by the PRU in respect of the stated mat

[94]*Ibid* s. 26(1) and 27

damage' or 'pollution' consequent upon petroleum development activities,[95] and for non-prevention of waste of petroleum.[96] By distinguishing between 'damage' and 'pollution', the act attempts to afford protection to the generality of the development environment. To achieve this goal, contractors are required to put in place preventative or control mechanisms capable of dealing adequately with fire, oil spills, accidents and emergencies,[97] and must take all necessary measures to minimise loss or damage, and to remedy any pollution or damage.[98] These provisions together, are evidence of sustainability objectives relating to environmental protection, precautionary and polluter- pays principles. Further, the obligation to prevent waste of petroleum which aims at maximizing ultimate recovery of petroleum, has a consequential effect of regulating sustainable employment of natural resources on one hand, and promoting the rational of resource-saving content of intergenerational equity.

PEPA also seeks to address social sustainability issues, particularly those involving the protection of surface rights of land-owners (or occupiers) to information, non-disturbance and compensation. All persons having title or interest in land must be initially notified of the purpose and nature of the proposed operations.[99] This mandate represents the participation principle, to the extent that it accords the targeted public the 'right' to be informed of the nature of petroleum development projects in advance of their commencement, though it fails to place specific responsibility for the duty to notify. The participatory principle is further established through provisions that entitle persons having interests in land, to claim compensation for loss, disturbance or damage suffered (by human beings, nature and other material objects) as a result of petroleum operations.[100] The affected parties are also empowered to determine the quantum of compensation, thus according them the right to participate in a decision-making process that will affect them.[101] However, the act fails to provide a right of access to judicial remedy, or an independent tribunal (other than the PRU), in the event that

---

[95] *Ibid* s. 54; this responsibility extends to include causative and resultant damage from petroleum activities undertaken by contractors, agents, employees and sub-contractors.

[96] *Ibid* s.9 (1)

[97] *Ibid* s. 53; where contractors fail to provide safety measures as required under PEPA or in line with 'best international practice in the industry', the PRU may take all necessary measures to ensure such safety at the costs and expense of the contractors.

[98] *Ibid* s. 54;

[99] *Ibid* s. 18(a)

[100] *Ibid* s. 18(b); applications for compensation must be directed through the PRU (see s. 3(2) (a)). Note also that Compensation can be claimed for purpose ranging from disturbance or loss of owner's or occupiers' surface rights, for any damage to the surface of the land, crops, trees, livestock, buildings, works or improvements on such land (see s. 19.).

[101] *Ibid* s. 20; where parties fail to reach an agreement on the amount of compensation payable, the DG shall determine such amount.

affected persons are dissatisfied with the amount of compensation determined by the DG.

Another important sustainability concern in mining that PEPA seeks to address relate to questions of applicable standards to be employed in enhancing the protection of petroleum development environments. Contractors are required to conduct operations in a safe manner pursuant either to regulations made under PEPA, or 'according to the BIP prevailing in the petroleum industry', or '…in accordance with the BIP in comparable circumstances relating to the exploration, development, or production of petroleum…'[102] Due diligence and 'efficiency' are also required as a standard in line with 'BIP' prevailing in the industry, which such standard includes the use of appropriate and advanced technology, effective equipment, machinery, methods and materials.[103] These provisions suggest possible alternatives in standards for directing sustainability, with significant implications.

First, the combination of local and international standards allows for a degree of flexibility and comparisons in determination of best standard applicable. Second, the reference to 'international best practice' will facilitate the importation of recognised international environmental standards prevailing in the petroleum industry or those that could be applied thereto, to be given effect to by the PRU. Third, the provisions set a baseline standard of the precautionary principle, conveyed by obligation to conduct operations in a 'safe manner', with 'due diligence' and 'efficiency', to 'avoid' damage, pollution and waste including the mandate to use advanced technology and effective methods.[104] These standards should effect to implore consideration and caution towards environmental and social issues irrespective of threat of harm.

Finally and more importantly, PEPA contemplates environmental management upon termination of petroleum development activities or mine closure, and provides for the restoration of the environment in the event. Here the contractor incurs an obligation to restore the affected areas and remove 'all causes of damage or danger to the environment',[105] and the institution of measures for 'the conservation and protection of natural

---

[102] *Ibid* s. 9(1)

[103] *Ibid* s. 45; for other references of 'BIP' (in the context of standards) see ss. 3(2)(f) & 55. '*Best Practice*' is defined as including all reasonable steps to secure the safety, health and welfare of persons; but subject to 'any directions given, restrictions imposed or requirements made by the DG/PRU to ensure compliance with prescribed regulations. (See s.9 (2))

[104] *Ibid* s. 45

[105] *Ibid* s. 62(1)

resources in the area concerned.'[106] Equally vital is the provision requiring contractors to prepare and implement plans for the transfer to the state, of technological know-how and skills relating to petroleum operations.[107] The fulfilment of these undertakings could ensure protection of the natural, human and capital environment, which could enhance future populations' right to 'access', 'quality' and 'option'.

5:4:2 The Model Petroleum Agreement of Sierra Leone

The MPA is a standard form agreement between the GOSL and contractors wishing to explore, develop and produce petroleum in the country.[108] In terms of the environment, petroleum agreements are to be regulated through the PRU, pursuant to the terms of their agreement, PEPA and any environmental regulations prescribed there under,[109] laws and regulations of Sierra Leone (unless otherwise provided under the MPA),[110] and good international petroleum industry practice.[111] Most of the environmental dictates of the MPA have been drawn from the mandates in PEPA, and for these (as are identified hereunder) the same sustainability arguments developed in the forgoing discourse under PEPA applies. Some warranted observations and clarifications will also be made.

(i) Modelling Sustainable Development

The MPA describes main environmental undertakings under a separate article captioned 'Inspection, Safety and Environmental Protection'.[112] This identifies the signature principle of sustainable development, recognising the importance of the environment and integrating such concerns into petroleum development documents and processes. Some of the sustainability obligations under PEPA modelled in the MPA include: the preparation and submission of development plans detailing measures for environmental protection;[113] the conduct of operations with utmost diligence, use of

---

[106] *Ibid* s. 62 (2); these must be effected in a manner provided for by the act or the prescribed regulation; see also supra ns. 92 & 93

[107] *Ibid* s. 52

[108] *The Model Petroleum Agreement of Sierra Leone* (MPA), preamble 2 and 3

[109] PEPA (supra n.90) s.26 (1) and 27

[110] MPA (supra n. 108) article 2:4

[111] *Ibid*, article 6:1 Note however that regulation of this agreement falls outside Environmental Protection Act, its rules, regulations and procedures. (see PEPA, (supra n.) s.26(2)

[112] *Ibid* article 16. There are other related provisions identified in other articles of the MPA that are included in the analysis

[113] The MPA (supra n. 108) article 8:10(g); also s. (article 8:9)

appropriate technology, effective equipment, and methods;[114] to ensure maximum conservation of petroleum;[115] provide an effective system of waste management[116] and an environmental restoration strategy after operations.[117] The identified sustainability objectives transposed by these obligations are EIA, the precautionary and sustainable utilisation principles, including conservation as an environmental saving content for fulfilment of intergenerational equity.

Contractors further assume other specific environmental protection responsibilities in the exercise of rights acquired under the agreement, to ensure minimum ecological damage or destruction, employ preventive measures to protect onshore lands, trees, crops, buildings (or other structures), marine life and fishing activities in offshore operations; and must avoid actions that would endanger the health and safety of persons.[118] These obligations suggest strong emphasis on protection, of various components, materials and species of the environment, including human beings, their properties and means of livelihood. The MPA thus effectively promotes objectives of ecological, social and environmental sustainability by insisting on preventive measures to either avoid or minimise the damage potential to these.

Further, where as a result of non-compliance with the above requirements, the sea, seabed, land, fresh water, marine, plant or animal life are polluted by release of petroleum or any other form of pollution, the contractor shall be liable.[119] He must take prompt and necessary measures to control or clean up the pollution or repair to the maximum extent feasible, damage resulting from any such circumstances.[120] The MPA distinguishes the forgoing from situations where releases and pollution results directly from gross negligence or wilful misconduct of the contractor. In this case, the cost of clean-up and repair activities shall be borne by him.[121] It is however not clear from the agreement the purpose sought to be served by this distinction, because in my view, to be non-compliant with a preventative requirement resulting in harm is not exactly very dissimilar with 'negligence' or wilful misconduct either as to their cause and effect. Also, setting a degree of standard in this situation

[114] *Ibid* article 6:1(a).
[115] *Ibid* article 6:1(b)
[116] *Ibid* article 16:3
[117] *Ibid*
[118] *Ibid* article 16:4(a)-(g).
[119] *Ibid* article 16:5
[120] *Ibid*
[121] *Ibid*

has little beneficial relevance to environmental enhancement. The situation will probably be different where pollution or damage results with the contractor having fully complied with the requirements, including the exercise of due care and attention.

In spite of the forgoing criticism, the value in the provisions for the polluter-pays principle is unequivocal. The contractor is made to bear the cost (whether in reparation or otherwise) of any pollution or damage that results from his activities, though the particular cost in each case will depend on whether the pollution or damage results from 'non-compliance' or from direct and gross negligence.[122] The principle is further represented through the mechanism of cost internalisation in respect of 'ecological and environmental charges'.[123] This provision illustrates a fundament of more modern strategies advocated under sustainable development, ensuring that environmental costs are met when properly internalised.

Finally, there is a resounding undertaking by contractors to observe '*accepted petroleum industry practice*' in conduct of petroleum development activities.[124] This commitment makes possible the employment by contractors of similar (and stricter) international standards in their business, over any lower or relaxed local standards. However, the omission in the MPA of the adjective 'best', which is employed in PEPA to qualify the applicable international standards, does provoke scepticism. It could however be possible to correct this anomaly under the provision requiring that petroleum agreements shall be 'governed by and construed in accordance with the laws of the Republic of Sierra Leone, and consistent with such rules of international law as may be applicable, including rules and principles as have been applied by international tribunals'.[125] This broad formulation affords scope and opportunity to adopt the principles of sustainable development as evolved under these mechanisms to regulate petroleum development environments in Sierra Leone.

Conclusion

The investigations into the petroleum legislation and its model agreement revealed a well-structured and environmentally focused regime. There is

---

[122]It is reasonable to assume the inclusion in such cost analysis compensation issues in order to address any disturbances, damages or losses suffered by owners and occupiers affected by the consequences of noncompliance or negligence of petroleum contractors or their agents.

[123]*Ibid* Annex 2, section 3(n)

[124]*Ibid* article 16:2; relates to flexibility in the choice of, and application of the most appropriate standards to regulate such developments.

[125]*Ibid* article 26:1

clear hierarchical relationship between the parent act and the agreement in terms of environmental obligations and regulation. Relevant principles of sustainable development have been identified either directly or by implication, and the extent of their effectiveness for environmental and social sustainability in petroleum development discussed. Both documents sufficiently integrate wide-ranging protection efforts over varied environmental components, materials and beings, through objectives of precaution, sustainable resource employment (including conservation), generational equity and polluter responsibilities, and applicable international petroleum industry standards relating to these. More attention however needs to be paid to the assessment of environmental impacts of such operations, through a well-defined EIA procedure and to improve on the access to justice component of participatory rights.

Thus far, this chapter has proved the sustainability content of mining specific laws and agreements and has suggested ways in which they could be further enhanced. The next chapter will seek to identify sustainability objectives in non-mining mandates and apply their legal controls to the regulation of sustainable mining in Sierra Leone.

6 PROMOTING SUSTAINABLE DEVELOPMENT IN MINING THROUGH OTHER LEGAL CONTROLS

6:1 Introduction

In the previous chapter, principles of sustainable development were identified within mining laws and agreements of Sierra Leone, and their efficiency for effecting sustainable mining plans and activities was examined. The controls of the extractive-specific rules tended generally, towards maintaining the balance between the respective development instruments, and their proscribed environmental objectives, though some of the provisions were found to be broad, aspirational and limiting in some respects. This chapter extends the search for sustainability objectives outside mining laws, to other legal regimes in Sierra Leone. The reasons for this extension are twofold: First, mining operations affect all environmental media and the interrelationship that exists between them.[1] Second, some of the mining-specific laws do include as necessary for their regulation, 'applicable' laws and regulations of Sierra Leone.[2] These concerns call in the direct relevance to mining, of several pieces of legislations that seek to regulate natural resources and the physical environment, including those directly affected by conduct of such operations.

It is appreciated that there are seamless strands of laws regulating natural resources and the environment in the country. This chapter is however constrained to an examination of selected legal regimes for environmental protection, nature conservation and forestry, town and country planning, public health and water control, specifically because of their environmental and social relevance for mining and sustainable development. Legislations regulating these broad fields will be examined in two parts. The first part

---

[1] See supra chapter 1, pp. 33-37 for illustration of some social and environmental effects

[2] See the SRA, KPML and the MPA (supra chapter 5, p.135, n.45; p.139, ns. 73 & 74; and p. 147, ns. 109-111) respectively

will consider legal regimes that have specific design in environmental protection, like the EPA, WCA and Forestry Act. Part B will entail analyses of the TCPA, PHA and the Water Act, which, though not of environmental orientation are considered to serve environmental objectives canvassed by the principles of sustainable development in international law. The overall aim of the chapter is to determine the sustainability content of the selected regimes, and establish the context in which they can be used as direct or alternative legal controls over mining operations, including their capacity to promote one or more of the relevant principles of sustainable development in Sierra Leone's mining culture.

Part A: Laws Specially Designed in Environmental Protection

6:2 The EPA: Structure and Nature of Environmental Protection

In the context of sustainable development and mining in Sierra Leone, the EPA,[3] seeks to provide for 'the effective protection of the environment'[4] and the institutional machinery to ensure such protection.[5] The pertinent protective provisions of the EPA stipulate measures requiring the licensing of mining projects, including their assessment by a process of EIA.[6] The EPA prohibits the undertaking of certain projects within 'extractive industries' (including mining operations) without first obtaining 'valid licenses' in respect of such projects, notwithstanding the provisions of any other law.[7]

It requires that before the commencement of mining operations under any mining right, an application must be submitted to the DoE,[8] for him to decide whether the proposed project requires EIA.[9]

---

[3]*The Environmental Protection Act* (2000), Act No. 14 of 2000 (EPA)

[4]*Ibid.* EPA defines the environment to 'include land, air, water and all plants, animal and human beings, living therein and the interrelationships which exists among these or any of them'. (see Part 1 on interpretations)

[5]*Ibid.* ss. 2, 3, 11, 12 and 13 of Part 11.The NEPB and the ED are the structures established to oversee environmental affairs in Sierra Leone including the EIA process. The institutional aspects relating to the regulation of mining under the EPA, and the interrelationships with other sectors are addressed under the framework of implementation in chapter 7; only the protective provisions, are analysed hereunder.

[6]References will also be made to the EIA Procedural rules; (Sierra Leone: *EIAP*, MLHCPE: July, 1999 (EIAP).

[7]EPA (supra n. 3) ss. 14(1) and 15(2); it is made an offence to undertake any of the prohibited activities (without a valid license), such offence punishable by fine, imprisonment or both (s. 14(2)). See also EIAP, (*Ibid.*) clause 4.4.; See also First Schedule for categories of 'Projects requiring EIA Licenses'.

[8]All such applications must be accompanied by a description of the proposed mining project. Note that references to DoE, includes EB, with whom it must consult on almost all matters under the EPA

[9]EPA (*ibid*) s. 16(1) (see also EIAP (supra n. 6) clause 3.1). Note that the EPA does not provide a formal definition of what an EIA is. The term is employed in the act in a dual capacity: in one respect, it is used in reference to an ES prepared and submitted by a mining applicant, and to describe the process by which the ES is assessed for environmental impacts.

In making such decision he must give due consideration to the following specified factors: -

(i) The environmental impact of the prospective mining activity on the community.

(ii) The location of the project.

(iii) Whether the project will transform its locality or is likely to have substantial impact on the ecosystem of that locality.

(iv) The likelihood of such projects endangering species of flora, fauna or their habitat.

(v) The scale of the project; the extent of the degradation that may be caused to the quality of the environment, including the resultant diminution of aesthetic, recreational, scientific, historical, cultural or other environmental quality of that locality.

(vi) Whether, embarking upon such mining venture will result in an increase in demand for natural resources in the environment.

(vii) And the cumulative impact of the proposed activity together with other activities or projects in the locality, on the environment.[10]

A 'PCEC' have been established, as a guide for such decision-making, and for ensuring a fair and consistent review of all proposed projects at the screening stage based on the information provided by the developer.[11] Where a decision is taken that the relevant project does not require EIA, the DoE shall issue a 'valid license' to the applicant to proceed with such mining activity without more.[12]

At this point, it is necessary to clarify some of the immediate consequences that flow from the issue of valid licences to commence mining operations pursuant to the decision that the relevant projects do not require EIA. First, the EPA includes mining activities within the category of 'extractive industries', amongst projects 'requiring EIA licenses' before their commencement.[13] But the substantive provisions in sections 14 and 15 (on which the First Schedule gives guidance), effectively allows for mining

---

[10]*Ibid*, Second Schedule; this stage of the procedure is described as the screening process. Screening is done with the aid of EIA 'Screening Forms' which are available at government departments. (EIAP (supra n. 6) clause 3)

[11]Projects are classified as- Class A, requiring full EIA; Class B, requiring additional information (which may determine whether the project falls into class A or C); and Class C, usually Projects with no significant impact on the environment (EIAP (*ibid*)).

[12]EPA (supra n. 3) s. 17; note that the EB is also empowered to direct that the DoE issue licenses to an applicant in respect of the undertaken of a project (s. 21).

[13]*Ibid* (see First Schedule)

operations to take place on 'a valid license' acquired after the initial assessment (screening). This is clearly distinguished from a formal 'EIA licence' that is obtainable after going through a formal EIA process provided for under the act.[14] Within this framework of protection therefore, only some, not *all* mining projects will undergo the formal EIA contemplated by the Act, or as advocated for under the principle of sustainable development. Consequently, a legal complication is engendered by this formulation whereby there is no mandatory requirement under the provisions for all mining projects and activities to subject to 'EIA licence' procedure.

This is rather a determination to be made by the DoE, on an assessment of limited descriptive information on the proposed project that is submitted by the applicant and within the ambit of the specified factors.[15] The DoE is thus given wide discretion to choose which mining activities are likely to cause harm to the environment. He is also not bound under the EPA to reach a conclusion requiring formal EIA procedure in any event.[16] This discretion which perhaps is necessary to be maintained in relation to other activities under the EPA,[17] does not agree with the common perception that mining activities are inherently damaging to the environment in diverse ways. Such a state of affairs does not only create uncertainty in the application of the provision but is likely to defeat the whole purpose of specifying mining projects under the first schedule, as requiring EIA licenses.

In spite of the forgoing concern, one can still discern sustainability objectives in the formulation of this initial protective mechanism. The EPA does establish the need for consideration of information relating to environmental effects of mining projects, as a mandatory component of the decision making process. Also, the prescribed factors that are material in determining the need for an EIA contemplate the inter-relationships that exist between the exploitation of mineral resources for economic development on the one hand, and the consequences they wrought for the environment. The objective of environmental protection is discerned from the material specifications to the extent that cognisance is given to the effects of mining on the values of the ecosystem and its organisms, species, flora and fauna, natural resource

---

[14]*Ibid* ss. 18 -24

[15]Note that the factors stated in the second schedule are not for the guidance of applicants seeking a valid licence, but for the DoE; therefore the brief descriptive information on applicants' projects may not be sufficient in their content of the material facts, or the highly technical or specialised environmental analysis necessary for such determination. (See also EIAP, (supra n. 6), Clause 3:1).

[16]Note that the EPA does not specify any of the determining factors in any preferential order nor does it require that the DoE ought to be satisfied of the likelihood of all the factors occurring in order to recommend EIA.

[17]Such as industrial, waste management and housing construction activities; (see EPA (supra n.3) First Schedule)

conservation, the quality of the environment including the anthropocentric relationships and social conditions. These are value precepts necessary for maintaining sustainability of mining activities.

6:2:1 Protection through Formal EIA Procedure

Where the DoE decides from the initial assessment that a mining applicant requires EIA licences, the protective mechanism is triggered in various procedural stages commencing with the requirement to submit an ES, public participation and a determination of the ES by the Board.

(i) The EIA Statement

An applicant caught by the assessment process must prepare and submit to the DoE, an EIA of his proposed project.[18] The reference to EIA in this context is to the applicant's document which is generally informative in manner but highly specific as to its contents.[19] Going by the prescription of the third schedule of the EPA, the applicant's ES must contain statements or descriptions of the following: -

(i)   A description of the location of the project and its surroundings; its principle, concept and purpose must be clearly established.

(ii)   A perception of any effects, whether direct or indirect, social, economic or cultural, that the project is likely to have on the people, society or the environment. It must further be indicative of any actions or measures that may avoid, prevent, change, mitigate or remedy the likely effects on people and society and must be suggestive of alternatives to the proposed project.

(iii) Information must be given about natural resources in the locality that are anticipated to be used in the project.

(iv)   Plans for the decommissioning of the project must also be submitted.

(v)   The ES must generally, be informative on all other matters that the applicant might consider necessary for the proper review of the

---

[18] *Ibid.* s. 18(1)

[19] *Ibid.* s.18(2); note that the use of 'EIA' here, is in reference to the environmental statement (see supra n. 8 for variant of EIA). The EIAP (supra n.6) distinguishes between Draft Environmental Impact Statement (Draft Statement) containing study of the developer on the one hand, and the Final Environmental Statement that will contain approvals and/or conditions recommended with the Process. But to effect clarity, whenever the term EIA is used in references to the environmental statement, the words Statement, Document or Assessment Information are used interchangeably to convey that meaning.

environmental impact of his project.[20]

An important addition to these criteria is a requirement that the contents of the ES must also include an assessment of legal impacts of the project, in the sense that it must make reference to the relevant national and or international laws, treaties and conventions that are likely to be affected by the impacts.[21] Also required is a description of the methodology used for collecting and generating the information on impacts.[22] Upon inclusion of all these facts, the applicant's document is submitted for assessment, and a 'scoping meeting' is convened to review the draft statement.[23]

From the forgoing it could be observed that the facts that must make up the applicants assessment document are largely of an environmentally protective purpose- relating to the effects of projects on the legal, social, cultural and natural environment, anticipated use of natural resources including preventative, mitigating and restorative measures. One could argue that a developer who successfully captures all these environmental considerations is a developer that is made aware of the environmental consequences of his operations and his responsibility in respect thereof. Instilling this environmental consciousness both in developers and in the decision-making process, is one of the objectives of sustainable development promoted through the EIA mechanism.[24]

Similarly, there is for the first time, mention of the economic effects of the proposed mining project on mining communities and on society as a whole. The inclusion of economic considerations in the ES is useful in that it portrays the balance advocated by the integration principle, in encouraging developmental goals and environmental objectives to go hand in hand. In other words, the design of an ES can trigger the discourse on sustainable development.[25] Even where economic considerations are likely to overshadow wholly environmental ones, depending on the manner in which they are canvassed, environmental concerns would still have gained a place in mine development thinking, discussions, decision-making and practice.

---

[20]*Ibid* (Third Schedule)

[21]EIAP (*ibid*) clause 3.3.1(VI)

[22]*Ibid* This same methodology will typically be used in auditing and monitoring exercises (Clause 3.3.1(VIII))

[23]EPA (supra n. 3) s. 20; EIAP (*ibid*) clause 3.2.1

[24]See the views of Gray and Sadler, on the merits of EIA (supra chapter 3, p.98, ns. 158 &159 respectively. See also summary on EIA (supra chapter 4, p.138-139)

[25]This makes an important contrast to the largely economic connotation often underlying conduct of mining in Sierra Leone (see supra chapter 1, pp 28-32).

(ii) Requirements for Public Participation

The EPA requires the DoE to circulate copies of the ES to government ministries, professional bodies, associations and non-governmental organisations (NGOs) for their comments.[26] He must thereafter, open the assessment information for public inspection and comment, and must give notice to that effect in two consecutive issues of the Sierra Leone *gazette* and news paper publication.[27] The EPA does not specify arrangements for this public consultation, but according to the EIAP, all the recipients of the draft statement and members of the public who consulted the document should forward their comments to the DoE.[28] The draft statement will then be revised to incorporate all comments engendered by the assessment information, and will be submitted to members of a Working Group.[29] A public hearing may only be desirable where there is sufficient public opposition to a proposed project.[30]

From the perspective of sustainable development, the provisions of s.19 (1) & S.20 of the EPA (and endorsed by EIAP), signal an unequivocal intention to provide at the *national level*, for a cross section of the public to have access to environmental information and to participate in the decision-making process pertaining to the conduct of mining activities.[31] The relevant public authority is mandated to make available to the public environmental information generally concerning mining activities, to be conducted in particular local communities;[32] and has extended the right of participation to departments, groups and associations.[33] Within this framework both public and private bodies regulating various interests likely to be affected by the proposed activity will be consulted.

More importantly, the specific reference to NGO participation identifies with recent trends in using this category to promote and enforce sustainability principles.[34] The general assumption is that they often possess the required expertise and financial capacity to take on mining companies in furtherance

---

[26]EPA (supra n.3) s.19 (1)

[27]*Ibid* s. 19(2) &(3)

[28]This should effect within 30 days from the date of distribution

[29]EIAP (supra n. 6) clause 2; This is a technical/working group composed of representatives from the private sector, NGOs, Community Groups, as well as a wide range of governmental entities (see also clause 3.4)

[30]*Ibid*; a developer may also choose to convene a public hearing. Here the Board will appoint a mediator, and the commenting period may be extended beyond the standard 90 days.

[31]This is a prerequisite for effective environmental decision making under Principle 10 Rio Declaration (see supra chapter 3, pp.99 & 100)

[32]Rio Declaration *ibid*

[33]*Ibid*, p.111, n. 171 -173

[34]See WCED (supra chapter 2, p.63 n.131)

of environmental objectives.

However, the participatory provisions are restrictive and limited in some respects. The EPA seems to have provided for 'wide availability' of the assessment information but limited in granting accessibility to it.[35] Also, the prescribed method by which the publics' involvement is canvassed is likely to delimit the bulk of the rural masses, most of whom are either incapable of reading publications, or understanding the technical debates that usually surround environmental and mining discourses.[36] Efforts, which emphasise dissemination of information, must also include mechanisms for its appreciation at the 'grassroots' level.[37] A public that is aware, is one that is educated enough to understand the implications of the issues upon which they are expected to comment. A further diminution in the transposition of the participatory principle by the act, relates to the omission to provide for the 'access to justice' component. Nowhere in the EPA or the EIAP, are the specified public given the right to compel authorities to make environmental information more accessible, or to seek an injunction either in judicial or administrative capacity for non-compliance with the requirements.[38] Overall, the nature of public participation employed under the EPA is more akin to the model of a process-based goal objective, seeking to achieve *inter alia*, public awareness, the opportunity to express concerns, increased acceptance of the public of decisions reached, and conferring legitimacy to the decisions.[39] It falls short of the primary motive for requiring participatory rights for sustainable development, namely to influence economic activities through effective contribution of the public, and prescriptions which effectively cater for victims of development activities to have some form of redress.

---

[35]It omits in the specified category of consultees Paramount Chiefs, or Chiefdom counsellors who have primary jurisdiction over the local lands and communities where most mining operations are carried out.

[36]Bell & Macgillivray have suggested that EIA process will only operate satisfactorily if information is disseminated in 'intelligible terms', to enable the public to play a more effective and vital role in these consultations. (see Bell & Macgillavray: *Environmental Law* , (fifth edition), Blackstone Press Ltd, 2000, p.352)

[37]Note that under the participatory principle, officials also incur the responsibility (as part of the duty to inform) to *facilitate* effective participation by for example, educating the public (see Malanczuk.P, (Supra chapter 3, p.102 n. 190)

[38]Citizens are encouraged to inform the ED of any suspected breach of EIA standards and provisions and it is the responsibility of the ED to investigate and take action. This explains as a role of the public in environmental auditing. EIA Appeals could also be made in respect of any of the various stages in the process including developer/government disputes, internal government disputes, international disputes, public disputes, and stakeholder disputes; and the stipulated means of resolution is through negotiation.(EIAP (supra n.6) clauses 3.8.3; 4.3.1-4 and 4.2)

[39]For the distinction between public participation as a 'process-based goal' and 'substantive- based goal' objectives, see Pring & Noe, (supra chapter 3, p.95 n.137) p.23

(iii) Determination of the Environmental Statement

The public's involvement in the EIA procedure ends with the submission of their comments on the assessment information to the DoE, for the consideration of the EB.[40] Three possible decisions could be recommended, each with a separate consequence.[41] It could disapprove of the ES, if it is satisfied that the project and the alternatives suggested in it will have adverse effect on the environment, people or society.[42] Alternatively, the EB could request for further information on the impact of the proposed activity;[43] or it could approve the draft statement with or without conditions.[44] Where environmental approval is granted on specified conditions, the approval and the specified conditions will be incorporated into the draft statement.[45] An EIA licence is then issued to the applicant for a fee, and on such terms and conditions as may be considered appropriate and necessary for the protection of the environment.[46]

These provisions which allow for environmental disapprovals or imposition of environmental conditions on mining projects could prove a very valuable alternative legal control mechanism (outside mining laws) for promoting or enforcing principles of sustainable development in mining culture in Sierra Leone. The EPA is not explicit on the ultimate effect of a disproval where the applicant chose not to go to court, but arguably, there is no reason why a decision disapproving an environmental statement should not effectively prevent or halt existing or new mining activities. Also, although ultimate, decision to approve a proposed project for implementation and overall operations is determined by the MMR, owing to their responsibility for granting mineral rights, licences and other permits, they are nonetheless obligated to take into consideration the decisions of the DoE on EIA results.

However, the legislation seems to confer unrestricted powers on the decision-maker in determination of the assessment information. Nowhere in the provisions is the DoE or EB *mandated* to refuse a proposed project or impose conditions because negative environmental impacts are envisaged.

---

[40]EPA (supra n. 3) s.20(1) In practice, the DoE will study all the comments received and prepare a Review Report which will be sent to the EIA Working Group for consideration. In any case, the entire review process may not exceed 90 days (EIAP (supra n. 6) clause 3.4). See supra n. 38 above, for further possible public involvement in Environmental Auditing or EIA Appeals.

[41]EPA (supra n. 3) s. 20 (2) (a), (b) & (c)

[42]*Ibid* s. 20 (3) & (4). Note that the grounds for disapproval are not conjunctive, and could be warranted for any envisaged impact, whether on the natural, social, or cultural environment. And any person aggrieved by the rejection of his application may appeal to the High court.

[43]*Ibid* s. 20(3); any new information must be submitted within 21 days of the date the request was made, failing which the application lapses.

[44]EIAP (supra n. 6) clause 3.5; if the Draft Statement is considered environmentally sound, the proposed project is accepted without conditions.

[45]*Ibid* The Public will be informed of the final decision through public notice such as local newspaper

[46]EPA (supra n. 3) s. 20(2) (a)

Also, they do not bear any responsibility or accountability for the decisions that they make.[47] While these wide discretionary powers may be necessary to afford them absolute control over the process, it may regrettably also allow for political and other factors to defeat environmental concerns, or breed a system that is devoid of coherency. To cub this wide discretion will in my view make for a more detailed regulation and coherency in standard setting efforts.

The forgoing concern could find possible solution in the provisions requiring the ED to keep a register of all EIA statements for public scrutiny and reference, such register to include all related comments, reasons and decisions of the Board.[48] If this practice is followed meticulously, it may gradually form the basis for precedents on what are tolerable and intolerable limits of adverse environmental effects of mining. It may further, go a long way at eliminating potentially significant inconsistencies that are likely to arise between various mining companies, thereby making the EIA process and the whole regime, credible in the eyes of all parties concerned. Above all, the specific provision for EIA by the EPA represents an endorsement of principle 17 of the Rio Declaration on sustainable development, as a national mandate for regulating domestic developmental activities including mining.[49]

(iv) 'EIA Licences' As Mechanism for Environmental Regulation

Where an EIA license is issued, it remains valid for the period of 12 months from date of issue, or such other period as the DoE may determine.[50] This provision is very vital in that it allows for a reassessment of the environmental responsibilities that may have been undertaken by developers. To further enhance control of licensed projects, EIA licenses are made not transferable, except in cases where ownership of the project or its management changes.[51] Also, the requirement to register all EIA statements and licenses is without doubt, tied up with the ED obligation to monitor all projects in respect of which licenses have been issued. This is made necessary in order to assess their effect on the environment or to ascertain

---

[47]Note the submission that the mechanism can be more valuable if the legal mandate among other things, holds authorities accountable for taking its results into consideration. (see supra Chapter 3, p. 98)

[48]EPA (supra n. 3) s. 28; see also EIAP (supra n. 6) clauses 3:6 and 3:7

[49]Rio Declaration (supra chapter 2, p.43, n.12)

[50]EPA (supra n. 3) s. 23

[51]Ibid s. 27 (1)-(5) The DoE must be notified of such occurrence, in order to endorse the license and validate its transfer. It is an offence to fail to submit notification of transfer (s. 27(6)).

compliance with the provisions of the act.[52]

This monitoring responsibility makes it entirely possible to integrate new environmental information into projects while the licenses remain valid. Such a practice will accord with judge Weeramantry's assessment of the EIA principle in the *Gabcikovo-Nagymaros case*, in line with international standards.[53]

Furthermore, the EPA reserves a right in the DoE to cancel, suspend, or modify any conditions in licences, where there has been a contravention or non-compliance with any stipulated conditions; or where a substantial change has occurred in the operations of the project resulting in an adverse effect on the environment.[54] The DoE is given further powers to prescribe measures to be taken by the project owner to abate any such adverse effects or remedy any damage done to the environment.[55]

The foregoing provisions clearly establish a formidable legal mechanism of licences to help prevent, control or regulate adverse environmental consequences of mining activities. Through the various regulatory powers, principles of sustainable development can be employed severally and managed effectively within one umbrella regulatory instrument, with possibility to integrate continuing environmental concerns within the framework. Mining operations can thus be directed toward true sustainability through this environmental management mechanism.

6:2:2 Protective Provisions outside the EIA Process

There are several other mandates in the EPA that are designed to afford further protection of the environment from the potential and actual damages of mining activities. For instance, the Minister is empowered to make regulations establishing national environmental standards for various purposes including water quality, waste and effluent limitation.[56] Where such standards are formulated, they will not only serve as further protective measures, but could also be sown seeds for harmonisation of environmental

---

[52]*Ibid* s. 29(1); for the effective exercise of this monitoring responsibility, the authorised officer, is given powers including the right to access any mining facility or premises) including immunity from legal action for exercise of these powers (s. 29(3)-(4) and s. 32)

[53]Judge Weeramantry (supra chapter 3, p.98, n.161); He recognises that 'continuing EIA' of development projects is an element of sustainable development, thus warranting continuous monitoring of projects for their environmental impact.

[54]EPA (supra n. 3) s. 26(1) Note also that any person aggrieved by the decision may appeal to the High Court within fourteen days of the notification of such cancellation or suspension (s. 26(5))

[55]*Ibid* s.26 (3)

[56]*Ibid* s.34 (i)-(ix); Up to the time of writing however no such regulations relating to standards settings have been promulgated.

standards for mineral extraction. Similarly they can help regulate unsustainable utilisation of environmental resources and thereby gradually promote sustainable patterns of mineral production.[57]

Furthermore, the act provides for regulations to be made requiring persons responsible for specified projects to maintain insurance or other appropriate financial security, to guarantee payment of compensation for damage resulting from development activities; or for such funds to be used for preventive measures or restorative action where necessary.[58] The introduction of insurance schemes under the EPA must be commended. It defines one of the innovative techniques of use of economic instruments and 'cost internalisation' for environmental protection advocated through the integration principle. The broad formulation of the provision allows scope for integration of both social and environmental concerns through compensatory schemes and preventative measures, in furtherance of intra-generational equity and polluter-pays objectives.[59] Finally, the act also establishes a NEF for specified environmental objectives, including the carrying out of programmes to prevent or reduce pollution, promote environmental education and research, to encourage local environmental initiatives, environmental reporting and support.[60] Thus the proper direction and control of the NEF for these specified objectives in the context of mining could help forge environmental awareness, protection and consequently sustainability.

6:3 Environmental Protection through Conservation: The WCA

The WCA[61] is another enactment among the laws of Sierra Leone, considered relevant to the environmental protection discourse in sustainable development. It is environmental in context of both its evolution and the goals it seeks to achieve.[62] Generally, it aims to preserve and protect ecology and animal species while also taking account of aesthetic and recreational

---

[57]See Rio Declaration (supra n.49) Principle 8; note also that standard setting and harmonisation are regarded as high priority in environmental regulation in Agenda 21(Agenda 21, (supra chapter 2, p.43, n.13) Chapter 8:32

[58]EPA (supra n.3) s. 33(1)

[59]see Rio Declaration (supran.49) Principle 13; requires states to develop national laws regarding liability and compensation for the victims of pollution and other environmental damage

[60]The EPA (supra n. 3) s. 39(a)-(g)

[61]*The Wild Life Conservation Act* (1972), Act No. 27 of 1972 (WCA); This Act represents one of the very few legislations implementing an international environmental convention.

[62]*Ibid*; the long title describes it as making further and better provision for the continued protection of flora and fauna of Sierra Leone; and to give effect to the 'international convention relating to the protection of fauna and flora in such national state - 1933' as amended by the 'International Convention For The Protection of Fauna and Flora Of Africa, 1953'.

requirements. It is therefore important to establish the context in which its provisions can be employed to prevent, minimise or control the effect of mining on nature for sustainable development.

6:3:1 The Nature of Protection

The legislation makes provision allowing for the establishment of National Parks, Strict Natural Reserves (SNR) or Game Reserves on any area of land.[63] The various Reserves could be declared only for certain specified purposes. National Parks shall be maintained for the 'purposes of propagating, conserving and managing wild animal life and wild vegetation and protecting sites, landscapes or geological formations of scientific or aesthetic value, for the benefit and enjoyment of the public'.[64] SNR shall be kept for the 'purpose of protecting the land, flora and fauna therein from any kind of injury or destruction'.[65] And Game Reserves shall serve the objective of preserving and protecting animals, prohibiting the hunting of specified animals, while also regulating the hunting of game animals within seasons.[66] Having clearly defined the purposes for which the various reserves shall be established, the act specifically and directly prohibits the carrying out of any act connected with mining, excavation or prospecting on those lands. It further forbids acts of drilling, levelling the ground, construction or any work involving the alteration or configuration of the soil, or the character of the vegetation thereon.[67] Similarly, it prohibits any activities likely to injure or destroy flora and fauna, or otherwise to obstruct the channel of any river or stream.[68]

These provisions represent a clear intention to secure land for the pursuit of wholly environmental objectives as opposed to development goals. Mining activities that are traditionally development imperatives are for the first time expressly prohibited on constituted Reserves regardless of their economic benefits. The WCA thus promotes the practice of rational allocation of land uses by allowing for parts of the country and its nature to be conserved to compensate for the destruction of the rest of nature through the conduct of mining activities. Its emphasis is on the benefits that such establishments can

---

[63] *Ibid.* s. 3; note however that where the land in question is situated in the provinces, the power must only be exercised after consultation with the Chiefdom Council.

[64] *Ibid* s.6

[65] *Ibid* s.4

[66] The afforded restrictions, prohibitions, protection and preservation measures are itemised under schedules 1-8, in Part VII of the WCA

[67] *Ibid.* s. 7(f)

[68] *Ibid.* s. 7(g) & (l)

have primarily in maintaining nature's capacity and life support systems, with consequential benefits for humans to enjoy a healthy environment.[69] By this emphasis, WCA 'steers' the course between the needs of mining and the necessity to protect the environment and harmonises both needs in the sense that, mining gains can be pursued and enjoyed in mining areas; while environmental objectives are pursued and enjoyed in nature reserves. This is what according to Judge Weeramantry, aptly expresses the concept of sustainable development.[70]

A further element of sustainability mirrored in the specified objectives of Nature Reserves is the protection of interests of present and future generations, the former identified also as 'national interests'. In line with weak sustainability, both generations will, through this conservation mechanism, be able to enjoy aesthetic interests from undegraded landscapes and eco-systems (including the biotic and abiotic),[71] and could also boast of species, scientific and geological resources in their bank of environmental equity of natural wealth, in addition to other manmade capital.[72]

6:3:2 Mechanism of Control

WCA designates a category of officers with authority and specific responsibility to execute it provisions.[73] RSO is accorded powers of a magistrate under the act to inquire into claims that may be brought by persons having interest (including mineral right-holders) over lands designated as Parks or Reserves. He must then submit a report on any such enquiry to the Minster.[74] In considering the report, the Minister may choose either: to extinguish any rights or claims with appropriate monetary compensation, confine or restrict the rights or claims to certain areas, or adopt wholly or in part any one or any combination of the above positions. The act however stresses that what ever position the minister chooses to adopt, must either have the end result of enhancing the purposes of SNR, National Park or Game Reserve, or must not seriously hinder their efficient

---

[69]See Rio Declaration (supra n.49) Principle 1

[70]Judge Weeramantry (supra chapter 2, p. 49, n. 47)

[71]Rio Declaration (supra n.49) Principle 7 requires states to conserve, protect, and restore the health and integrity of the earth's ecosystem.

[72]See ILA (supra chapter 3, p.86, n.45) Also note thesis submission that the principle of Intragenerational equity can only gain its full compliment if environmental capacity is maintained, its resources efficiently managed and its components sufficiently guarded through effective environmental controls like conservation. (See supra chapter 3, p. 90)

[73]WCA (supra n. 61) s. 66; these include CCF, Officers of the Forestry Division, (have primary and general responsibility), Officers and employees of the WCB (see Preliminary of the Act). For the various powers conferred on these category to enforce the act see, ss. 67-71

[74]Ibid s.12 (1) (b) & (3) and s. 12(b)

working.[75] This control mechanism asserts the primacy of establishing reserves over other interest. It is safe to assume that it could be used when necessary and appropriate over lands set for mining and thereby indirectly to restrict, control or minimise such operations and avoid further depletion or exhaustion of renewable and non-renewable resources alike.[76]

There is however, provision for any persons or interests affected by the minister's decision to appeal to the High Court in the first instance, and in the Court of Appeal.[77] The exercise of such options would have profound consequences for the objectives of environmental protection in sustainable development. While developers and ordinary persons enjoy 'access to justice' in environmental decision-making, (as oppose to development decisions), both objectives will be pitched against each other, weighed in court and a balance maintained. It may also present an opportunity for environmental law and policy, to be brought to the core of the country's legal system and jurisprudence- an area of law in Sierra Leone that still awaits judicial intervention.[78] In further consequence, sustainability principles could be judicially validated through this mechanism, which represents an important aspect of the legal character of sustainable development.[79]

Finally, nature is not conserved under the Act for a purpose limited to its inherent value, but also for the benefit and enjoyment of human kind in line with the intra-generational principle. Thus, WCA provides for protected forests and non-hunting forest reserves, affords protection to certain species and animals, while allowing for the hunt of others.[80] These are generally regulated by licences and permit systems, while reserving rights in the responsible authorities with minimum discretion, to make variations and allowances for the enjoyment by humans of the benefits of nature where necessary. The objectives of sustainable utilisation, the polluter-pays and its user-pay cousin are well established thereby.

---

[75] *Ibid* s.15

[76] It is not clear how far this provision may be used to impose over economically biased mining activities in Sierra Leone. There is however, nothing stopping the responsible authority under the act, where they so desire, to restrict or limit practices in the name of nature conserva- tion.

[77] *Ibid*. s. 14; there is nothing in the act that forbids the process of constituting Reserves and Parks, while a claimant seeks redress in court, and it is not clear whether the courts may direct injunctions against the continuation of the process pending judicial determination of the matter.

[78] Up to the time of writing, environmental issues have not been tested in the superior Courts of judicature in Sierra Leone pursuant to any legislation, environmental or otherwise.

[79] Note Lowe's, suggestion that the concept can properly claim a Legal status as an element of the process of judicial reasoning and the application of the concept to resolve disputes in which environmental objectives and developmental goals conflict (See supra chapter 2, p. 56, n. 84)

[80] WCA (supra n. 61)Part VII

6:4 Forest Protection Efforts and Mining

There are several pieces of legislations, rules and orders regulating Forestry in Sierra Leone, but the parent enactment is the Forestry Act.[81] A large part of the forestry laws represents the economic aspects of forestry concerned with the regulation of the exploitation of forest produce, especially timber, and other purposes connected with the utilisation of forest products.[82] The act is also designed with an environmental component, in context of regulating 'forest protection' and 'non-forest uses'. Through 'forest protection' objectives, the act seeks the preservation of the forest environment, protection of soil, water, flora and fauna,[83] the efficient management and rational utilisation of the country's forest resources,[84] the regulation of afforestation[85] and to 'preserve the environmental role of forest lands'.[86] It is in context of these environmentally oriented protection efforts that the act is analysed to illustrate its relevance and applicability to the regulation or control of mining activities within the perspective of sustainable development.

6:4:1 Protection Objectives and Management Controls

Within the framework of the act, environmental protection objectives are assured through provisions for the constitution of 'National' and 'community' forests[87], including 'special' provisions for Protected Areas and Protected Trees.[88] A Production Forest or National Protection Forest (NPF) is constituted pursuant to notice in the *gazette* declaring it as such.[89] A freehold or lease of any land can be obtained in the western area, for this purpose subject to the right of any persons to apply to the court in respect of the adequacy of compensation. But where the proposal relates to provincial

---

[81] *The Forestry Act*, (1988) Act No.7 of 1988. Note that the relationship between the Forestry Act and the WCA, is not specified and there is evidently marked areas of overlap and complications in their applications. This anomaly will not be addressed in this study.

[82] *Ibid* The primary management objective is the production and sale of forest produce, regulating forest utilisation, concessions for production of forestry and so on.(See ss. 12-17)

[83] The Forestry Act (supra n. 81) Preliminary

[84] *Ibid* s. 3(a)

[85] *Ibid* s. 3(f)

[86] *Ibid* s. 3(b); the responsible officials are required to manage and implement the act to give effect to these purposes including other duties pursuant to any other law. Note that the act generally requires every classified forest – forest production, forest protection and non-forest uses - to be regulate through a management plan to achieve the greatest combination of economic, social and environmental benefits that they can be made to provide within their respective objectives. (See ss. 5 & 7 respectively).

[87] *Ibid* Parts IV & V respectively

[88] *Ibid* Part VI ss. 21 and 22 respectively; the Minister may by declaration in the *gazette* determine any area to be a protected area for purposes of the conservation of soil, water, flora and fauna; or declare any specie or other description of tree as protected.

[89] *Ibid* s.10; Note that the CCF prepares the proposal for such constitution which said proposal must contain certain matters specified under

lands,[90] the minister may have to acquire lease of such lands for a term not exceeding 99 years.[91] Any existing land use rights before the acquisition (including mineral rights), shall be confirmed in so far as they are consistent with the main objective of the proposed forest.[92] The chiefdom council constitutes community forests over any area in the particular chiefdom subject to the approval of the DO.[93] The Minister may then constitute any such land (including state land) by Notice in the gazette to be a community forest for the specified purpose.[94]

What emerges from the foregoing is the possibility for National and Community Forest protection efforts to clash with mining activities especially where such declarations are made in respect of lands over which mineral rights may already exist.[95] And since the act clearly specifies that only those activities that are compatible with the objectives of forest protection will be 'confirmed usage rights', mining operations will have to be subject to the control mechanism of the forestry act in certain respects. For instance, the legislation prohibits the carrying out of certain specified acts in any protected forest, whether 'national' or 'community', without 'lawful authority'. Such prohibited acts include the cutting, burning, uprooting, damaging or destroying any tree, removal of timber or any other forest produce. It is further prohibited to clear any land, build any road or structure, take any earth, clay, sand, gravel or stone, except pursuant to a concession agreement, contract of sale, licences, confirmed usage right or other authority under the act.[96] The undertaking of any of the above stated prohibited acts without lawful authority is deemed an offence punishable by fine or imprisonment.[97]

It will be observed that most of the prohibited conducts outlined in the act are those necessary to be undertaken within forests or elsewhere for the

---

[90] Ibid s. 10(2) (viii). Tenure and interest in Provincial lands, are generally subject to customary law and jurisdiction, and are presumed to be inalienable by way of freehold interest. ((Ref. Provinces Land Act Cap. 122, *Laws of Sierra Leone*; see also Renner-Thomas (supra chapter 1, p. 28, n.48)

[91] Ibid s. 10(2)(b)(i) In respect of part of the land that is constituted a forest reserve, no compensation shall be paid to land users whose use contravene the provision of the forestry act (section 10(2)(b)(v)

[92] Ibid s. 2(a)

[93] Ibid s. 18(1). National and community forest are distinguished by the manner and location in which they are constituted including their management authority. They do not differ much as to their purposes since both forest utilisation and environmental objectives can be pursued under each category.

[94] Ibid s. 18(3). The required specifications are set out in section 18(2) (a)-(f); compensation could be given for suppressed rights, either in money or alternative land use. See further s.19 (1) & (2), for management of community forest that are not on state lands.

[95] Note that, under the Minerals act, this is possible through land-use agreement for mining with Landowners or land compulsorily acquired for such purpose (see supra Chapter 5, p.132, n. 25). The act only requires forest management plans to 'take due account to national and regional land use plans prepared by other agencies of government (s. 7)

[96] *The Forestry Act* (supra n. 81) s. 9; (See also ss. 21(1)&(2)& 22(2))

[97] Ibid. Part VIII on offences and enforcement; see also the *Penalties (Amendments) of specified fines Act* (1993) Act No. 9 of 1993.

commencement of mining operations. So that miners are almost always likely to be in breach of the act, unless they can show lawful authorisation to carry out such acts within protected forests, protected areas, or deal with protected trees. Where such authority is proved, it may warrant some form of resource development alongside environmental protection objectives. But in order to maintain the required balance between both objectives as an indication of the integration principle, miners will have to operate under prescribed licensing system.[98] One may however want to doubt the purpose of constituting 'protected' forests or prohibiting activities in protected areas only to have them overridden by permission through the licences mechanism. There is also a temptation to conclude that due to the licensing regime, the effect of the forestry laws generally appear to have no direct environmental beneficial pertinence, either by way of imposing restrictions or prohibitions on mining operations. But it should be borne in mind that the prohibition adopted under the act is not absolute in context of 'strong' sustainability, but rather of its 'weak' alternative, thus according with the logic of the integration principle in sustainable development. Where miners fail to obtain licenses for operating in protected forests and are convicted of an offence under the act (or any regulations made there under), they shall incur the penalty provided for under both. In addition, the judge may order a convicted person to pay a sum equal to the value of any damage to forest produce or land caused by the offence. He could also cancel any license that had been previously obtained.[99]

The use of Licences could help in directing sustainable utilisation of forest resources in mining operations especially since the act provides for environmental conditions to be included in them.[100] For instance one of the prescribed conditions in respect of 'land clearing' requires that the land in question be restocked with approved forest vegetation within the period specified in the licensed.[101] Also, fees are payable in respect of any licences that is obtained, including the payment of further fees into a reforestation fund as security for reforestation works.[102] Also licences can be cancelled or suspended for non-compliance with either the provisions of the forestry act

---

[98] *Ibid* supra n. 88 Compare with the provision in the SRA providing for the obtaining of consent from the forest officer for the destruction of forests for mining purposes (supra chapter 5, p. 153, n.56). Miners may also be obliged to fulfil 'confirmed usage' rights in relation to fulfilling environmental conditions already acquired under their respective mining agreements, where these fall within the specified protection objectives.

[99] *Ibid.* s.30(b); the yard-stick for assessing damage to forest or land value is not provided for in the act.

[100] *Ibid* s.11 (2); a licence issued under the act is generally valid for one year

[101] *Ibid* s. 11(4) note that in this case the licences validity extends beyond the general one year period, to such longer period as is necessary for the maturation and harvesting of the crops or tree products to be planted.

[102] *Ibid* s. 4(1) & (2); see also s. 17

or any prescribed environmental conditions.[103] There are further provisions for inspection of licensed area, supervision of reforestation works and enforcement procedures.

In light of these provisions, it is safe to suggest that the mechanism of control reflects a dimension of sustainable development that allows for competing uses of forests to be balanced by rational land use management albeit through the licensing scheme. The approach recognises the state's right to utilise forests to meet developmental needs, while using the licensing control mechanism for reducing the effect of over-exploitation of soil, deforestation and pollution in furtherance of environmental protection.[104] If the discretion given to the forestry authorities to allow mining activities within protected areas is used judiciously, and within the terms of the forest protection objectives provided for under the act, it could prove useful in minimising some of the adverse environmental consequences of mining and gradually promote sustainability.[105] By regulating forest uses, mine operators will be forced to integrate environmental conditions (reforestation, soil treatment, prevention of pollution of forest waters) into their processes. The licensing scheme is the legal standard of precaution that is developed under the act to achieve this.

Conclusion

The aim of this part was to evaluate the EPA, the WCA and the Forestry Act as legal regimes with environmental design and establish the context in which they could be used as direct or alternative legal controls for regulating environmentally adverse mining and promote the principles of sustainable development. Various aspects of sustainability principles have been identified in the objectives of these legislations, that could in my view assist in directing mineral resource development to sustainability. Some of the shortcomings of the enactments have also been highlighted. More specifically, the EIA principle is proved in primary legislation (the EPA) as a national mandate for regulating domestic developmental activities including

---

[103] *Ibid* s. 23

[104] See Rio (supra n. 49) Principle 3; Forest Principles (supra chapter 3, p. 84 n. 72) (Principle 2 (a)). See also Liobl's suggestion that, regulations for environmental protection are not to be seen as limitations for utilisation, but rather as 'the right to utilise the resource environment' in a certain manner (supra chapter 3, p. 74, n. 14)

[105] Note that the MPSL (supra chapter 1, p.27, n.10) indicate the discovery of minerals in areas some of which have been already designated as Forest Reserves by Orders made under Cap. 189, of *Laws of Sierra Leone*– such as Kangari Hills, Gori Hills, Loma Mountains, Nimini Hills (North & South) and Kambui Hills. The effect of the strength that the forestry laws will have in regulating or limiting mining activities in preservation of the environment will therefore hinge on how the discretionary powers of the responsible authorities are used.

mining, in fulfilment of Rio principle 17, even though some and not all mining projects are likely to be tested.

The objective of public participation was also uncovered in provisions for access to information and participation in environmental decision-making though it fails to provide a mechanism that will facilitate participation, especially public education and 'access to justice' compliment of the principle, to challenge decisions or seek redress. Various other legal controls are proved to exist through EIA licences, standards setting, environmental monitoring and auditing, insurance schemes, environmental funds and offences, which could promote principles of environmental protection, sustainable employment of natural resources, intragenerational equity and the polluter-pays principle in sustainable development.

Similarly, through the provisions of the WCA which emphasise primacy in establishing nature reserves, conservation, management of wildlife and vegetation and protection of land, flora and fauna from injury or destruction, the environmental interest of future generations could be secured in conduct of mining activities. Further environmental protection objectives were identified in the Forestry Act, through provisions that cater for the constitution of forests, protected areas and trees. The regulation of these by a conditioned licensing mechanism has also been proved as vital for directing sustainable utilisation of forest resources in mining.

Part B: Other Sectoral Regimes and Sustainability Issues in Mining

6:5 Environmental Protection through the Law of Planning

Principally, the TCPA[106] and the Amending Act[107] regulate the planning system. The former act was designed to regulate and control land use relating to development, through the preparation of planned development schemes that would integrate both social and economic needs.[108] Under the provisions of the TCPA, the Minister may, after consultation with the appropriate authorities, and upon hearing the views of the public,[109] make an

---

[106]*Town and Country Planning Act* (1946), Cap.81, Act No. 19 of 1946 (TCPA)

[107]*Town and Country Planning (Amendment) Act*, (2001), Act No. 3 of 2001(the Amending Act).

[108]The 1946 Planning Law (TCPA) was originally not applicable to the whole of Sierra Leone. Its application was limited to the municipality of Freetown, the immediate surrounding townships and the Bonthe sherbro district, all of which were at the time subject to British rule. The bulk of the rural provinces where almost all the mining activities took place since the 1930s, were therefore excluded from constructive planning. There was an amendment to the TCPA in 1967-*The Town and Country Planning Act (Amendment) Decree, 1967*, which sought to extend the scope of application throughout Sierra Leone, but its legal effect at the time is uncertain. The Amending act of 2001, effectively gave statutory recognition of the application of planning law to the whole of Sierra Leone; (see s. 6(a)).

[109]*The Amending Act* (supra n 110) s. 6

order declaring any part of Sierra Leone specified by a survey plan to be a planning area.[110] Where any such order has been published, all persons are prohibited from carrying out 'any development of land'[111] in the specified area without permission, until a detail scheme in respect of all designated planning lands, is prepared and approved.[112] The planning board has authority to grant such permission and with it could impose any conditions deemed necessary to control and regulate such development. Thus, the commencement of mining operations (including constructions necessary to enhance operations) would be appropriately considered to be development within the meaning of the act, where they are undertaken on any new plot of land (that was not subject to mining) before a planning order; and not necessarily to imply the conduct of new or expanded ventures. Therefore all mining projects that are to be conducted in specified planning areas, (before a scheme is approved for those areas), will require planning permission and will be subject to the control of relevant planning conditions in the first instance.

An outline-planning scheme must then be prepared in respect of all lands within a planning area, with the general objective of securing proper health conditions, sanitation, convenience and amenities in connection with the laying out and use of land.[113] The scheme must include amongst other things, provisions regarding delimitation of zones within which *special trades and industry* may be carried out, or for other purposes.[114] In addition, the scheme may provide for matters relating to the prevention of pollution of streams, rivers, lagoons and other watercourses, preservation of views and amenities, natural beauty or interest, protection of forests, trees, woods, flowers and shrubs. It may further cater for the prevention, remediation or removal of injury to amenity arising from neglected conditions of any land situated in the planning area and for the prohibition, regulation and control of the deposits of waste material.[115] The planning authorities are also empowered to prohibit or restrict the use of land where they consider such use likely to involve danger, injury or detriment.[116] And where any of such

---

[110]*Ibid* s. 6(3); Note that any order so made shall come into operation through a prescribed method (pursuant to s. 170 (7) of the Constitution (supra chapter 5, p.127, n.4)) but shall cease to have effect if within three years from the date of its coming into operation, no scheme has been approved.

[111]"Development' means 'any use' that is made of land (including buildings and alterations), which is different from the purpose for which the land was being used immediate before such land was declared a planning area; (see TCPA (supra n. 106) s. 2).

[112]*Ibid* s.7; It is deemed an offence under the Act to undertake any development of land on specified planning land without such permission.

[113]*Ibid* s. 12(1)(a)

[114]*Ibid* s.12 (2)(d) emphasis added

[115]*Ibid* schedule 1, (Part III-Amenities) of the TCPA; the schedule also provides for additional matters to be included in a scheme.

[116]*Ibid* s. 26(3). No compensation shall be payable on the enforcement of such restrictions or prohibitions so imposed

matters as listed above, are laid out in a scheme planned for any area, it shall affect the application of '*any law* relating to development', where such law appear to be either inconsistent with the above matters, or where its application would tend to hinder the proper operation of the scheme.[117]

The scheme is then to be deposited at an appropriate place for public inspection and the public must be notified thereof, for their comments and recommendations. Any challenges to the scheme must be made within two months of the date of the notice being published, failing which, the scheme and all recommendations thereon are forwarded to the minister for his approval. Once approved, the board assumes the responsibility of executing and enforcing the scheme through powers vested in it under Part V of the TCPA.[118] The various issues outlined in this general perspective are no doubt relevant for enhancing some form of environmental effectiveness in mining operations in the context of sustainable development.

For instance, the use of schemes to provide severally for the zoning of areas for special industrial land uses like mining, protection of forests and amenities, prevention of pollution of natural resources and the prohibition of likely injurious activities among other things, reflects the element of integration. In other words, planning orders and schemes seek to ensure that development activities such as mining are designed and conducted with due consideration to the economic, environmental and social issues engendered by them.[119] Also the principle of sustainable employment of natural resources is advanced through provisions that cater for pollution prevention and prohibitions on injurious activities. An improvement on the general quality of the environment is also contemplated. It may thus be possible to use the general planning system to exercise some form of control over mining. A more direct regulation may exist through the licensing system, by the obligation to seek permission before undertaking such development projects in declared planning areas.

Also, the planning system may become invaluable especially where properly directed planning schemes will be relied on to determine areas in which mining operations will be undertaken including the stipulation of environmental conditions over permitted developments especially in respect of shared natural resources. Under the current Minerals Act, mining areas

---

[117]*Ibid* s. 12(5) and 13(6); emphasis added

[118]This is a general legal picture of the development planning strategy in Sierra Leone.

[119]See Principle 13 Stockholm (supra chapter 2, p.43, n.3) requiring States to adopt an '*integrated*' approach to their development planning so as to ensure that development is compatible with the need to protect and improve the human environment for the benefit of their population'.

are determined (especially for artisanal mining) on the basis that the Minister of mines considers that it is in the public interest to encourage such activity in 'any area', where the methods to be used do not involve 'substantial expenditure' or use of 'specialised technology'.[120] The use of the standards of 'public interest', the mining method and the quantum of investment to designate mining areas has left most of the rural areas of the country dug-up in patches in a disorderly and uncoordinated manner, leaving appalling visual effects.[121]

Another important sustainability objective represented in the TCPA is the involvement of the public at the initial stages of determining which developments should be where, and under what conditions. This provision will create an opportunity for the public to be able to express their concerns over mining projects long before they are to be assessed (if at all), by formal EIA procedure under the EPA. The value held in this stipulation extends also to amend the anomaly evidenced in the fact that the publics' participation is in practice not sought in all cases requiring approval for the commencement of mining operations.[122] The opportunity to participate may also, within the objective of the precautionary principle, encourage decision-makers, developers and the public to consult, cooperate, exchange information, demand modern or safe practice with a flexibility that will appreciate the particular type of mining activity in the giving environment.

It must however be mentioned that development planning schemes only lay down objectives that are envisaged by planners to obtain in planning areas. They are permissive or desirable objectives that are subject to modifications, alterations or cancellation.[123] Second, both the TCPA and the Amending Act do not specifically mandate a central role for planning authorities for enhancing environmental protection through the imposition of development conditions. Environmental concerns are thus likely to be given secondary consideration where the competing economic imperatives of mining come to the fore of the planners' schemes. Similarly, it seems that only a one off permission is required to undertake mining within a designated planning area with no review or monitoring capacity. It is therefore important that environmental goals be made central to planning by clear statutory mandate, and further to allow by legal requirement, for the specific objectives of

---

[120]Minerals Act, (supra chapter 5, p.127, n.6); s. 20(2).

[121]Researcher's visit to artisanal mining areas in Tongo field of eastern Sierra Leone

[122]Under the EPA the publics' involvement in decision making is limited to particular cases that the Board considers should require EIA. All Cases of mining projects which obtain a 'valid License' exclude the involvement of the public. (See supra n.25)

[123]TCPA (supra n. 106) s.17

sustainable development, so as to afford environmental enhancement of areas that are zoned out for mining purposes.

Despite the forgoing hiccups, it may still be possible to employ the mechanism for directing mining toward sustainability, in the least by determining which type of mining should be carried out and where.[124] What is required is a willingness on the part of the policy makers to seek to regulate mining activities through direction and control of planning with as much emphasis on environmental protection as its economic implications. Where development planners choose to interpret all such proscribed objectives in defined programs for implementation and enforcement, the planning regime can become a very important and necessary authority for promoting economic, social and environmentally sustainable minerals development.

6:6 Public Health in the Mining Environment

The Public Health Act of 1960 regulates general public health and safety in Sierra Leone.[125] This act is not ecologically orientated, but designed to protect the public by ensuring that certain basic health standards are met so as to assure a quality of health mainly to human beings. It seeks to maintain environmental quality by stressing on sanitation, proper water supply, housing and food safety in declared 'Health areas', and proscribes all actions and omissions likely to endanger public health and safety involving those issues as statutory nuisances. Though the adverse consequences of mining on human health is not usually direct, yet such activities still bear an unquestionable relationship with those adverse health effects.[126] Therefore, where by the conduct of mining operations there is brought about results that are, 'prejudicial to health', such acts or omissions may be regulated under the provisions of the Act;[127] and where health is protected and improved in mining areas, the natural quality of the environment including air quality will also be enhanced. The Public Health provisions are therefore invaluable to the environmental and social sustainability challenges in

---

[124]It is appreciated that minerals are location specific, and therefore planning may not determine where they may be mined before they are discovered. But it is untenable in any country, to permit mining wherever and whenever the need arise as is the case with Sierra Leone's artisanal mining activities.

[125]*Public Health Act (1960), Act No. 23, 1960* (PHA)

[126]Some of the adverse effects of mining on the social and natural environment have been illustrated in chapter 1; Examples include incidence of pollution of shared natural resources; the likely deterioration in health conditions that emanate from polluted resources; the practice of relocating whole communities without proper housing and sanitation facilities; and overcrowding mainly in artisanal mining areas.

[127]'Prejudicial to health' means 'injurious or likely to cause injury to health' (interpretative part)

mining communities from their own peculiar stand point and strategy.

Specifically, the act creates a statutory nuisance on the occurrence of any of the following conditions: -

(i) Where any 'premise' is in a state as to be prejudicial to health or a nuisance.[128]

(ii) The bringing up of dust or effluvia in the conduct of any business or process that is prejudicial to the health of the inhabitants of any neighborhood.

(iii) The use of any watercourse and leaving it in a state that is prejudicial to health.

(iv) The collection of water on land on which conditions, whether natural or artificial are likely to cause the propagation of mosquitoes.[129]

These stipulated nuisance-generating conditions are amongst the common incidences of mining activities that have often questioned their sustainability. Generally, they seek to direct social sustainability, enhance environmental quality, prevent pollution, and promote sustainable utilisation of water resources. Liability for the occurrence of all the above circumstances, whether by act, omission, default or sufferance is strict.

The health authority is empowered to serve a notice on any person whose acts default or sufferance causes any statutory nuisance, requiring him to abate such nuisance. The PHA requires the perpetrator to execute any measures necessary for abating the nuisance, unless the nuisance is believed to arise from any defect of structural character.[130] And where the abatement notice is not complied with, an abatement order can be obtained from the courts of summary jurisdiction;[131] or where the health authority is of the opinion that summary proceedings would afford an inadequate remedy either for securing the abatement of a nuisance or prohibiting it, he can seek an abatement order from the High Court.[132] The officer can also endeavour to abate the nuisance or prevent a recurrence of it at the expense of the creator.[133] This provision is illustrative of the polluter-pays principle for

---

[128]'Premises' is defined to include lands, hereditaments of any tenure, whether open or enclosed, built or not, whether public, tribal or private. This description places all forms of mining activities on land under the ambit of the public health controls.

[129]PHA (supra n. 125) s. 23(a), (d), (e) and (f) respectively

[130]Ibid s. 25.

[131]Ibid s. 26. Failure to comply with any pollution abatement order under this Act is deemed an offence (s. 28).

[132]Ibid s. 32. Note that the Health Authority shall have this power irrespective of whether he has suffered no damage from the nuisance.

[133]Ibid s. 29

sustainable development, which advocates among other things, polluting and cleaning up, remediation of environmental harm and conferring environmental responsibility regardless of the legitimacy of the economic activity. It also imputes on the health authorities the responsibility to ensure that the polluter meets all cost of nuisance abatement or prevention.[134]

More importantly, the act further seeks to protect the public from polluted water even where such water is not vested under the public health authority. It is enough that the authority considers it likely that use may be made of such waters by the public for domestic purposes or consumption, and that such pollution is likely to prejudice health.[135] So that, where mining companies and local miners utilise streams and rivers for operations and render them polluted for the co-riparian, the health authority could seek a court order against them either as owners or controllers of land on which polluted water source exists. The authority may even impose user conditions that are necessary to prevent injury or danger to the health of other persons using the water. He may also declare any area from which water is gathered, as a 'water gathering area' and subject it to protection from any form of pollution.[136] This protection mechanism echoes the objectives of the principle of intragenerational equity, to the extent that they seek to protect the interests of present population in the midst of mineral development activities, even securing their health. The mandate does represent a more direct legal control or regulation of pollution of water resources in mining than that catered for by the Minerals Act or the related mining agreements, in the sense that liability hereunder, is strict.[137]

A symbolic achievement under the act is the power given to individuals who may be exposed to pollution, to seek an abatement or prevention of it.[138] In this regard, the right of access to justice as a participatory component of sustainable development is hereby effectively guaranteed.[139] They are empowered to make complaints about a statutory nuisance to any magistrate's or local courts having jurisdiction in the area, and demand an

---

[134]See Rio Declaration (supra n. 49) Principle 16, suggesting that the polluter bears the environmental and social costs of his activities in the 'public interest'; see further De Sadeleer, on the 'preventative' and 'curative' functions of the polluter-pays principle (supra chapter 3, p.88, n. 90)

[135]PHA (supra n. 125) s.93 (1)

[136]Ibid s. 96

[137]For the provisions in mining laws against pollution of water sources, see supra chapter 5: p. 128, n.10; p.136, n.53; p.140, n.80; and p.145, n.96 respectively.

[138]PHA (supra n. 125) s. 31

[139]Rio Declaration (supra n.49) Principle 10, lays emphasis on citizens right of effective access to institutions, for redress or remediation of environmental wrong, damage or threat of harm; This is the first time throughout this work that individuals are empowered directly to seek redress for pollution through judicial means.

order for abatement or remediation of the nuisance.[140] This participatory component is further embellished through provisions requiring that the party said to have committed the nuisance meet all expenses and costs incurred in instituting such actions.[141] This provision promotes the polluter-pays principle, and could effect to ease the usual contention that locals cannot afford cost of litigation against mining companies for pollution abatement.[142] The PHA even specifies a general procedure to be used in conduct of such proceedings, which could prove vital for the integration of sustainability objectives, and for removing some of the difficulties relating to expense and delays generally, associated with private actions.[143]

Further, the PHA could be useful in addressing a fundamental social effect of mining in Sierra Leone, relating to over-crowding of artisanal mining environments, usually with poor facilities.[144] The act provides for inspections to be carried out in declared 'labour health' areas to ascertain whether there is over crowding.[145] Where it is ascertained that such conditions exists the Minister may make an order declaring such environments to be an overcrowded area and steps shall be taken to abate the overcrowding.[146] The minister may also make rules (generally of a social nature), for the better carrying out of the 'purposes' or 'provisions' of the act.[147] The value of this provision for social sustainability and the consequential enhancement of environmental quality in mining areas cannot be over emphasised, especially since this peculiar effect of mining has not been contemplated in any of the legal mandates that have been analysed so far.

However, in relation to its adequacy for directing mining activities towards sustainability, the PHA is criticised mainly for its compartmentalisation of environmental issues. It limits environmental concerns to endeavours of human welfare, subtracting from it fundamental issues like land degradation, ecological stability, and nature conservation.[148] In spite of this

---

[140]*Ibid*. In all such cases, there is no requirement for the individuals to prove that the have suffered damage by the nuisance; it is enough if they are aggrieved by it.

[141]Such expenses and costs shall be recovered, (if not paid) by distress or sale of his property.

[142]Ibid s. 127; the *Statutory Nuisances (Summary Punishment) Act, of 1968* specifies the penalty to be incurred in the event of breach of the Nuisance provisions in the Public Health regulations, including powers of arrest.

[143]*Ibid* s. 128

[144]See supra chapter 1, p.32, ns. 70-72

[145]PHA (supra n.125) s.98 (1)

[146]*Ibid* s. 100-103

[147]*Ibid* s. 107(a)-(o)

[148]Note that the Public Health act was designed to address the desperations of the 1960s - the human environment - providing for housing, good sanitary conditions, disease free, food safety and health standards for human beings. But present day efforts in my view must emphasis the importance of the environment as one big entity, with several parts; and demanding a protection of each component as much as is desirable or possible for the continued enhancement of the interrelationships that exist amongst the whole.

criticism, it is hard to deny that there are some consequential benefits to be gained to the natural environment by enforcing the PHA to regulate mining activities. Such benefits include the protection of living organisms in rivers, streams and lakes and the overall improvement of air quality. The social and environmental solutions presented by it are necessary for sustainability of mining in Sierra Leone, especially since human beings are the 'center' of concern for sustainable development; and could prove useful in assuring the entitlement *'to a healthy [environment] and productive life in harmony with nature';[149] or otherwise guarantee their rights 'to …adequate conditions of life, in an environment of a quality that permits a life of dignity and well being.'[150]*

6:7 Regulating Water Resources in Mining for sustainability

Current mining operations conducted in Sierra Leone, especially those in respect of winning diamonds (or Kimberlite), gold, rutile and bauxite, are all water-based operations. The importance of water to these operations is as peculiar as it is for ecological and human sustenance, not to mention the need to conserve the earth's water resources.[151] It is with this eye of concern that it is deemed relevant to examine controls under water resources legislations for directing sustainable mineral developments.

The two major enactments dealing with control and supply of water resources are the Water (control and supply) Act (the Water Act)[152] and the Guma Valley Water Act.[153] The latter legislation is less relevant to this work.[154] Its only relevance lie in a specific prohibition on all persons, including GOSL, from working any mines or minerals lying under a building or reservoir belonging to it, or within such distance as would result in injury or damage to its properties. Where, however persons desire to work mines within forty yards from the mains, pipes or other company's works and apparatus, notice must be given to the company, and any expenses incurred

[149]Rio (supra n.49) Principle 1

[150]Stockholm (supra chapter 2, p. 43, n.3) Principle 21

[151]Rio (supra n.49) Principles 3 & 4; impress this concern by requiring sustainable utilisation of natural resources so as to equitably meet the 'developmental and environmental needs' of present and future generations. Similar concern is implied in the Watercourse Convention, through the requirement for 'co-riparian' to use and share the waters on an equitable, sustainable and rational manner; (Suebedi, (supra chapter 3, p.85, ns.76 & 77)). Also, UNEP water policy aims at assisting governments in establishing integrated water management plans, programs for the aquatic environmental hot spots, application of preventive, precautionary and anticipatory approaches, for environmental protection in harmony with economic and social development; (see "UNEP Water Strategy and Policy (Draft): Statement of Key and Emerging Issues related to Water" in EPL, Vol.29 1999, pp. 279-80).

[152]Act. No. 16 of 1963 (the Water Act)

[153]Act. No. 3 of 1961 (GVWA)

[154]*Ibid* the act sets up the GVWC, with responsibility for the supply of water protection of water-works assets, natural and built, and matters incidental to its supply efficiency. The scope of authority is mainly in the Western Area, excluding most major rural mining areas

by the company from such interference shall be compensated.[155]

The Water Act on the other hand, provides for the control and regulation of natural water supplies to the public in all Sierra Leone.[156] The Minister is empowered to declare water supply areas. Upon any such declaration, all natural waters within such areas shall become the property of the GOSL, and control of it shall vest in the minister pursuant to the Water Act.[157] So that, where mining areas become designated as water supply areas, then water resources in those areas may fall directly under the regulation of the water authority. In such situations, unless use is made of water for domestic purposes',[158] (for which license is usually obtainable), the Water Act forbids 'persons'[159] from doing 'any act' which shall have the effect of increasing or diminishing, diverting or interfering with any natural water supply in any water supply area in Sierra Leone.[160] If properly enforced, the provision could aid a vital cause in the conservation and sustainable utilisation of water resources, in face of the challenges that are presented by its categorisation as an exhaustible natural resource.[161] Other pertinent provisions of the water Act are those creating offences for nuisance, misuse, pollution, waste, diversion and injury in the use of such resources.[162] The penalties in respect of such breaches shall be in addition to other penalties and remedies, thus allowing for enforcement of these provisions concurrent with other legal controls including those which are mining specific.[163]

One could however question provisions in the act suggesting that a person is not required to obtain a license for water resource use, where the manner and extent of the use is the same as that before the date that the area would have been declared a water supply area.[164] But while this provision may effect to exclude certain mining projects that may have commenced use of water sources or supplies prior to a declaration and control of the water

---

[155]*Ibid* s. 114

[156]The Water Act (supra n. 152) s.1; its scope is limited only from operation in GVWC supply areas.

[157]*Ibid* ss.3-4

[158]*Ibid* s. 2; the definition of 'domestic purposes' excludes *inter alia*, use of water for any trade, business, or manufacture; or for supply of tanks, ponds, or machinery.

[159]*Ibid*. 'Persons' include any company, association, body cooperate or incorporate, as well as individuals; (see s. 4 Interpretation Act No. 46 1961).

[160]*Ibid* s. 5(1) The act also provides for medical examinations to prevent contamination of water supply (s. 17)

[161]Note that 'externalities' usually suggested in development economics applies to Sierra Leone's mining ventures; wherein the prices of mineral rights and products have never been determined to capture the full price of water pollution in such operations. A contemplation of value (in monetary and prohibitory terms) for these resources within mineral rights and products will help bolster their environmental significance for present and future generations.

[162]The Water Act (supra n. 152) ss. 49 and 50 of Part V

[163]*Ibid* s. 62

[164]*Ibid* s.5 (2)

authority, the act empowers the Authority to grant licenses for the regulation of use or supply of the resources. In doing do, he could impose terms and conditions as he thinks fit. This power could therefore be used to impose conditions on miners against wasteful usage, pollution, diversion, impairment and so on, within the objectives of environmental protection and sustainable utilisation of water resources.

In consideration of the forgoing therefore, it is safe to impress the value of the water regime for sustainable development. With effective water management and monitoring capacity, setting of acceptable user and pollution standards, use of economic instruments, (taxes, charges and permits) and the pinning of liability and responsibility for harmful utilisation, all of which are catered for under the act, this regime could aid sustainable development of mining in Sierra Leone. It could even become more effective if the regime be distinguished by legal mandate, from that which regulates pipe-borne water supplies.

Conclusion

The discourse in this Part sought to illustrate how other none environmentally orientated sectoral mandates could be used to regulate or control certain mine-borne impacts for sustainable development. The forgoing evaluation of the Planning, Health and Water laws have revealed that the goals pursued by these regimes are not completely devoid of the relevant sustainability principles underlying the protection of the human and natural environment; and that it is possible to exert some form of control over mining operations under their provisions. The analyses proves that these sectoral legislation, though disparate from their standpoint of application and enforcement, could each contribute to the enhancement of the mining environment in their own unique way, if, and more hopefully, when effective use is made of them.

Specifically, planning law is revealed as a more effective mechanism in the prevention of harm to the environment with an emphasis on precaution, while also allowing for mineral development and environmental protection to go together, weighing each for its own value to the society. The capacity of the planning regime to enhance objectives of public participation and the precautionary principle in mine development decision-making have been proved in the sense that it could encourage decision-makers, developers and the public to consult, cooperate, exchange information and demand modern safe practices with a flexibility that will appreciate the particular type of mining activity in the given environment.

The relevance of the Public Health dictates for addressing aspects of pollution prevention and control in line with objectives of the polluter-pays principle have been demonstrated. Its relative value for dealing with mining and social sustainability concerns for intragenerational equity have been established especially in the context of regulating overcrowding, protecting labour and community health, ensuring safe relocation practices and for guaranteeing the rights of individuals to access justice and seek prevention or remediation of environmental harm. Further, the consequential benefits to be gained to the natural environment by effect of all these objectives have been represented as environmental solutions for assuring the entitlement '*to a healthy [environment] and productive life in harmony with nature*'

Finally, the Water Act has been exposed as having the capacity to enhance the conservation and sustainable utilisation of water resources through provisions that forbid conduct which shall have certain prescribed effects on natural water supply or water gathering areas. Its sustainability contents for regulating mining have been illustrated through water management and monitoring strategies. These are conveyed through acceptable user and pollution standards, use of economic instruments and the pinning of liability and responsibility for harmful utilisation in furtherance of the polluter-pays, precautionary, integration and participation principles. The value of the water regime for promotion of sustainable patterns of mineral production is further revealed in provisions which allow for enforcement of its penalties and other remedies for breach to run concurrent with (or in addition to) other legal controls including those which are mining specific.

The chapter has thus demonstrated the capacity of sectoral regimes to advance the goals of sustainable development in Sierra Leone's mining, as direct or alternative legal controls to those catered for under the extractive-specific regimes. The next chapter will examine the methods of implementation of the relevant sustainability principles, including those identified in the selected legislations already discussed.

7 IMPLEMENTATION OF SUSTAINABLE DEVELOPMENT IN MINING

7:1 Introduction

In earlier chapters of this book, some relevant principles of sustainable development in international law and mining were identified. The principles of Environmental Protection, Integration, Inter and Intra-generational Equity, Sustainable Utilisation, Polluter-pays and Precaution, EIA and Public Participation were established including the parameters within which their respective objectives could address environmental issues in mineral resource developments. A method was also designed for their adaptation and implementation within national environments, as a process by which domestic development activities generally and mining in particular, could be steered toward sustainability. Chapters 5 and 6 entailed an evaluation of legislations of Sierra Leone (minerals specific laws, agreements and other sectoral legal controls), to ascertain the extent to which their individual mandates represent the relevant principles of sustainable development for regulating the country's mining activities. The exercise revealed the presence of sustainability principles (implicit or explicit) in all the legislations scrutinised and it illustrated various ways in which the objectives of the respective legal regimes could assist either directly, alternatively or as concerted controls, to regulate the social and environmentally adverse effects of mining.

This chapter will examine the methods of implementation of the relevant principles of sustainable development in international law in Sierra Leone's mining, including those identified in selected legislations and agreements already discussed. One basic mechanism for implementing sustainable development at the national level in order to achieve environmentally safe development activities is the integration of environmental objectives and development goals as a national strategy. It was generally established that an enabling national environment is required for better appreciation of the principles of sustainable development, such environment enabled by implementation processes of 'localisation', 'legalisation' and 'institutionalisation'.[1] In other words, if the various principles of the concept (as identified in several legal rules) were to effectively control or direct environmentally sound mining, they have to be reflected in national policy and initiatives, legalised within the nation's legal system and managed within an integrative institutional framework. The chapter will therefore evaluate the extent to which environment and mineral development concerns have been integrated as a national strategy at policy, planning and management levels, and how this bears on mining. It will further assess the efficiency of the legalisation and institutionalisation methods of implementation of the sustainability principles identified in the selected legislations, while noting how much use is actually made of innovative strategies as compliment to those legislation.[2] The ultimate objective is to ascertain whether there is a relationship between the adverse effects of mining in Sierra Leone[3] and the manner of implementing the relevant principles in regulating such developments.

7:2 Localisation of Sustainable Development

Sustainable development in international law requires that the concept of integrating environmental considerations into development activities be implemented at the national level.[4] It will be recalled that relevant principles of the concept were revealed within mineral laws, agreements and other sectoral legislation. But these are neither sufficient to warrant a determination that the concept does not sit well in Sierra Leone, nor are they enough to infer from, a national or political commitment to ensure social and environmentally sustainable mining.[5] Given the high political and economic imperative of mining in this country, coupled with the social and environmental implications, national commitment to ensure sustainable minerals development is of vital importance, and must be transposed into concrete policies, improved institutional arrangements and reflected in the

---

[1] See supra chapter 2, pp. 63-70.

[2] Such strategies would include use of economic instruments, and voluntary initiatives, environmental agreements and corporate responsibility. Note that this discourse omits the implementation of Petroleum laws because such activities have not effectively commenced.

[3] See supra chapter 1, (pp. 33-37) for highlights of social and environmental effects of mining and the overall implication for the country's economic growth and development.

[4] See generally, WCED, Rio Declaration, Agenda 21, Johannesburg Declaration & POI; (supra, Chapter 2, p. 62 ns. 121-125 respectively)

[5] Note WCED recommendation that 'Sustainable development must rest on political will'; (WCED (supra chapter 2, p. 43, n.10), p.9

decision-making process. Thus, a comprehensive localisation effort must primarily include a review of all mining, environmental and related sectoral policies; an assessment of progressive implementation of objectives and goals of sustainable development; and an evaluation of the extent of institutional strengthening for addressing mine-related social and environmental issues.[6] These conditions will mark the parameters for determining whether the principles have been effectively implemented as a national endeavour, and in a manner that ensures environmental protection in mineral development in Sierra Leone.

7:2:1 Review and Analyses of Policy Frameworks

The notion of 'sustainable development policy' has been defined as a policy requiring that development be addressed within an integrated policy framework'.[7] The inference is that policies that direct economic activities for development purposes must also integrate environmental concerns and management objectives at all levels.[8] Thus, the test of the extent of localisation of sustainable development begins with the recognition of the integration principle within state policies and decision-making processes. Sierra Leone's economic policies and planning strategies pursued until the 1980's did not contain incentives for the proper management of the environment and were best described as negative.[9] Since 1990 however, policies and other measures have been instituted that are likely to enhance proper management of the environment.[10] Economic policies have been formulated for the mining sector and various other sectors that are usually impacted by mining activities, such policies generally recognising environmental objectives and responsibilities.

(i) 'Environment' in Mining Policy

The 1990s mining policies were very general in their environmental objectives aiming among other things to ensure that adverse social and

---

[6]For a detailed specifications for nationalising sustainable development, see Agenda 21(supra chapter 2, p. 43, n.13) Chapter 8

[7]UN/CSD- "Industry and Sustainable Development Meeting" in *EPL* 28/2 1998, p. 61 (citing UN Secretary Generals Report E/CN.17/1998/4 and Adds.1-3)

[8]Handl has argued that a nation's failure to follow sustainable development policies imposes 'value deprivations' on members of the present generation; (Handl G. "Environmental Security and Global Change: The Challenge to International Law" (1990) in *1 Yearbook of International Environmental Law 3*. Note also French D., (supra chapter 1, p.33, n.59) p.56; suggesting that sustainability relies on the organisational ability of the state to manage change, and to promote a particular vision of public policy

[9]Sierra Leone: *National Environmental Action Plan* (NEAP/SL) Vol.1, 1995, MLHCPE, p. 10.

[10]*Ibid*

environmental impacts of existing mineral activities are minimised.[11] The recently adopted 'Core Mineral Policy'[12] is an improvement on earlier ones in the sense that it does not only integrate economic, social and environmental concerns in minerals development as broad statement of objectives, but explains the principles behind those objectives and describes measures by which government aims to institute and enforce them. Generally the environmental commitments in the CMP deal with four important environments – the legal, social, natural and corporate- and truly reflect the objectives of sustainable development in these, thereby effectively localising them.

In defining the statement of its legal obligation to protect the mining environment, GOSL will enforce all existing laws designed to provide such protection. In addition, it 'will develop and review existing environmental legislation in particular the law relating to the rehabilitation of abandoned mine workings'; and ensure that current rights and agreements made with exploration mining and investment companies are enforced and protected in accordance with the laws of Sierra Leone. Above all, it will protect the rights of citizens, communities, investors according to laws of Sierra Leone and international law where applicable. On its social objective, which seeks to ensure that mineral wealth supports social and economic development of mining communities, the GOSL will return some of the mineral wealth to the communities. It shall further ensure that they are protected where their livelihood, infrastructures or housing is being affected by mining and will develop and enforce measures to reduce social problems in mining communities.

In respect of its specific environmental commitments, the GOSL in a historic statement acknowledges that it 'has the duty of care to protect the environment in the national interest' and aims to institute and enforce measures to protect the environment, minimise and mitigate the adverse impact of mining on health and environment of communities. To enhance this duty of care, two further important commitments are made regarding the promotion of institutional and corporate responsibility.[13]

On its institutional responsibility, the government undertakes to:

(a)   Monitor the duration of mining and environmental licences and ensure

---

[11]Sierra Leone, Mining Policies of 1995 and 1998, (supra chapter 1, p. 30, n.46); see also 2002 Policy (supra chapter 5, p. 128, n. 11)

[12]MMR: "Core Mineral Policy", September 2003, Freetown (hereinafter CMP); also at <http://www.minmines-sl.org/>

[13]Note that institutional and corporate responsibility identifies as fundamental ingredients for implementing sustainable development at the domestic level. (See supra chapter 2, pp. 66, 68 & 69)

that they are concurrent; and will improve, monitor and enforce laws relating to closure, reclamation and rehabilitation of mines.

(b) Promote use of process methods that will reduce environmental impacts; and will improve public knowledge on the environmental consequences of mining including processing methods used at present.

(c) Review the requirements for the preparation and monitoring of procedures and conditions in EIA; and will develop methods for the enforcement of environmental conditions in approved EIA.[14]

In respect of corporate responsibility, the government aims to encourage medium and large-scale miners to operate in safe and environmentally responsible manner in accordance with approved EMP, and will strive to effect the following: -

(a) Encourage industrial mining companies to be responsible cooperate citizens, by investing in the development of communities in which they live.[15]

(b) Review and make recommendations on charges made to cover the cost of environmental compensation and rehabilitation of former mine (artisanal, small/scale and industrial) workings.

(c) Ensure all mining companies contribute to agricultural development funds and encourage them to institute welfare benefits to participants and victims of mining.

And in respect of petroleum mining, exploration and production, the government will adopt and implement international standards and codes of practice (including environmental ones) within the industry.[16]

One can safely conclude from the forgoing summary, that the prevailing mining policy does recognise environmental concerns as part of the challenge of achieving sustainable economic development through mining. Such Policy acknowledgements localise the integration principle as a basis

[14]The objective is to ensure that such methods clearly state any exemptions from EIA reporting requirements.

[15]Such commitments will generally relate to developing and maintaining infrastructure that benefits local communities, support for healthcare facilities, dispensaries and HIV/AIDS programs in areas in which they operate.

[16]GOSL: *The Energy Policy for Sierra Leone* (Draft), MEP, UNECA sponsored study undertaken by Cemmats Group Ltd) May, 2004, p.54 (hereinafter Energy Policy). Note that Policy commitment to adoption of international environmental standards and practices is an attribute of localising sustainability objectives, through national implementation. (supra chapter 2, p.63, n.127)

for any constructive implementation of sustainable development, in the sense that it generally supports mining that is ecologically, socially as well as economically sustainable. It also represents as policy restatement of the relevant principles of sustainable development already identified in national legal requirements, and effectively fulfils a fundamental recommendation of WCED for localising sustainable development as a national strategy.[17]

(ii) Environmental Policies

Achieving sustainable environmentally sound development would need a national environmental policy that is built on existing precautionary principle. This is deemed a prerequisite, especially if such policy must carry out its far-reaching task of integrating environmental objectives into other areas.[18]

Sierra Leone can boast of a National Environmental Policy (NEP),[19] with its goal stated as a desire 'to achieve sustainable development in Sierra Leone through sound environmental management'.[20] The term is not defined other than stating it as an outcome of a *process* that is attainable through sound environmental management.[21] But its precautionary underpinning cannot be missed and is portrayed as a necessary component in a catalogue of environmental management objectives.[22] Also, the environmental policy goal in relation to the mining sector is to ensure that prospecting, exploration, mining and processing of mineral resources on land and water proceed in an environmentally sound manner; ensuring among other things the restoration of land and vegetation, the prudent exploitation of all mineral resources and the prevention, control and treatment of pollution.[23]

These statements of general and specific objectives are in my view, representative of the principles that this work considered relevant for

---

[17] It recommends that sectoral ministries must assume responsibility for preventing environmental damage caused by their policies and be made accountable for ensuring environmentally sustainable economic activities; see WCED (supra n.5) pp.39 & 314.

[18] GCEA Report: "In pursuit of Sustainable Environmentally Sound Development" in *EPL*, vol.25/3 1995 p.92

[19] "NEP" in *NEAP/SL* Vol.1 (supra n.9) p. 36

[20] *Ibid.* Note that this perspective represents the instrumental and process-based interpretation of sustainable development canvassed in this thesis, as to both its meaning and legal character. (See: - Gaines, Lindner, Weeramantry (supra chapter 2, pp.48-49, n.45-47); see also De Sadeleer, Higgins, Fitzmaurice, and Lowe (supra chapter 2, pp.55-56, ns. 79-84) respectively).

[21] *Ibid.*

[22] These objectives include: efforts to secure a quality of environment adequate for the health and well-being of Sierra Leoneans; conservation and sustainable use of the environment and natural resources for benefit of present and future generations; to restore, maintain and enhance the ecosystems and ecological processes; to raise public awareness on environment and development issues and to encourage individual and community participation in environmental improvement efforts (NEP (supra n. 19) p. 36.)

[23] NEAP/SL (supra n.9) chapter 5, pp. 62-64

sustainable mineral development activities, and which are made tangible objectives of national endeavour. Other aspects of national policy concerning resource management and environmental protection with implications for mining operations can be sourced from the EPA,[24] the NEAP/SL[25] and the Constitution of Sierra Leone.[26]

(iii) The Constitution and Sustainability

Constitutional safeguards have been deemed necessary in terms of fulfilling the domestic policy function of sustainable development, in order to realise the principle of intra and intergenerational equity under international law.[27] The Constitution of Sierra Leone does not make direct or explicit reference to the concept of sustainable development or 'protection of the environment for present and future generations',[28] as an objective of the states economic or social policy.[29]

However, some social and environmental objectives can be discerned from the provisions as an exception to the guarantees of fundamental rights and freedom. For instance any person may be restrained by authority of any law in the interest of 'public health or conservation of natural resources, such as minerals, marine, forest and other resources of sierra Leone', or for the acquisition or use by any person of land or other property in Sierra Leone.[30] The constitution thus places limitations on private property holders in the interest of the conservation of natural resources. In effect, persons may be deprived of protection of property or any interest in or right over land (including mining rights in this case), for the purposes of 'work of soil conservation or the conservation of other natural resources;[31]...or improvement which the owner or occupier of land has been required and

---

[24]EPA (supra chapter 6, p. 152, n. 3); the pertinent issues relating to the localisation of sustainability objectives under the act have been addressed under EIA procedure, licensing and monitoring requirements (see pp. 171-183)

[25]NEAP/SL (supra n. 9); it contains detailed analysis of the country's environmental trend and impact from various economic activities, including specific policies on sectors like; water resources; forestry and wildlife; biological diversity, and so on. Note that the formulation of national sustainable development strategies and action plans is recommended as the first step in its domestic implementation; (see supra chapter 2, p. 63)

[26]*The Constitution of Sierra Leone, 1991*, Act No. 6 of 1991 (the Constitution)

[27]ILA, 66th Conference 1994, (Buenos Aries), 1994, p.133

[28]Most National Constitutions today reflect this trend; for examples, see Weiss E.B (supra chapter 3, p.78, n.40)

[29]The Constitution (supra n. 26); its economic objective is to 'harness all the natural resources of they nation to promote national prosperity, and an efficient, dynamic, and self-reliant economy'; it's social policy proposes to recognise, maintain and enhance the sanctity of the human persons and human dignity. (See s. 7(a) and 8(b) respectively).

[30]*Ibid* chapter 18(3)(a) &(b); (see chapter 18(4) &(5) for the processes giving effect to the provision).

[31]*Ibid* Note the observation that localising sustainable development could raise questions of the limits of private property, particularly in terms of what governments can do to restrict or allow the use of resources; (see Boer B., (supra chapter 2, p.63, n. 130)

has without reasonable or lawful excuses refused or failed to carryout'.[32]

Of immediate relevance, these provisions could be used to forge conservation objectives, rational allocation of land uses, management of protected areas, and enforcement of land rehabilitation or treatment of pollution obligations. In effect, while the country still remains to include unequivocal admissions of its commitment to sustainable development in constitutional terms, the cited references could at least form a basis for interpreting and adapting objectives of the concept in impressing environmental concerns in mining at both administrative and judicial levels. As has been suggested, constitutional provisions could be implemented to enhance mining sustainability either by application of the general environmental law applicable to every productive activity ('central approach') or by the enactment of specific sectoral provisions ('sectoral approach').[33] Thus, being the supreme authority of the land, these constitutional provisions can be used both as a 'shield and sword' in promoting and enforcing social and environmental goals in mining.

(iv) Other Sectoral Environmental Policy Commitments

There are also various sectoral policy commitments to environmental objectives. For example, Development policy seeks to ensure sustainable exploitation and effective utilisation of environmental and natural resources, while maintaining a healthy environment (SL Vision 2025).[34] The forestry objective is stated as including protection of flora and fauna, forest and wildlife conservation, including biodiversity action plan,[35] while the health policy emphasises a clean environment for all Sierra Leoneans through actions against 'environmental Pollution'.[36] Planning policy recognises the need for plans to forge land distribution and the responsibility to enforce planning through court actions.[37] Water policy recognises the need for water supply on a 'sustainable basis' and the responsibility for 'protection and

---

[32]Ibid s. 21(2) (h)(i) & (ii). Note that these provisions are justiceable and the Supreme Court has original jurisdiction to determine any of these issues without prejudice to any other action with respect to the same matter which is lawfully available to that person, and may issue orders for the purpose of enforcing, or securing the enforcement of any of the provisions (s. 28(1)&(2))

[33]Bastida E.; "Integrating Sustainability into Mining Law: The Experience of Some Latin American Countries" in *International Law and Sustainable Development*, Schrijver & Weiss (eds.) 2004, Koninklijke Brill NV., The Netherlands p.589. Note also that this is made possible through the flexible legal character of the concept which allows its true content to be sourced from any context in which its objectives are applied (see supra Chapter 2 p.56, n.85)

[34]*Final Report on Poverty and the Environment* (Environmental Contribution to the PRSP of Sierra Leone) MDEP, Bomah & Bassir; Freetown, April, 2004 p.114 (hereinafter PRSP Environmental Report)

[35]"Assignment Of Responsibilities to Ministers" in *The Sierra Leone Gazette* Vol. CXXXIII, No.47 of 30th July, 2002;

[36]Ibid.

[37]Ibid.

management of water resources'.[38]

The forgoing reflects a general recognition of environmental objectives as part of sectoral responsibilities as a national endeavour. It also represents the advocated integrative approach to the extent that environmental protection and resource management goals are made the business of other sectors. The effect is that these policy commitments help to interpret and emphasise the various elements of the concept identified in laws and agreements already discussed, and provides these sectors with reason to take appropriate action in protection of the mining environment.

7:2:2 Ensuring Progressive Implementations of Policy and Legal Objectives of Sustainable Development

So far, the policy reviews and legal evaluations have generally represented sustainable development beyond an ideological concept to instruments that advance the integration of environment and development. But sustainable development also requires measurable outcomes of implementation of the various policy and legal objectives and to this, the subsequent discourse is devoted. The findings should also reflect the extent of implementation of the legal requirements of the objectives of sustainability already discussed in earlier chapters.[39]

7:2:3 Measurable Outcomes

From a practical appreciation, the broader objectives of the above mentioned policy commitments on the one hand, and sustainability objectives identified in selected legislations, are being implemented in some measure in decision-making processes relating to mining operations. Foremost, it was uncovered that in practice, some mining companies assume some EIA, responsibility, warranted in most cases not out of compliance with legal requirements, but rather by the vastness of projects, social sensitivity and above all, a desire on the part of companies to get the environmental certificate in compliance with other international demands.[40] In such cases, the decision-making body has

---

[38]*Ibid.* (see also Energy Policy (supra n. 16) p.42. In respect of marine resource, activities will be undertaken in furtherance of marine environmental protection.

[39]Part of findings of this review was achieved through individual interviews held with the policy and decision-makers of the departments of the Mines, Environment, Forestry, Planning and Health (environmental health Unit), mineral right holders, Paramount Chiefs and other interest groups including NGO representatives. Note also that some of the interviewees wished to remain anonymous, and this will be indicated where necessary.

[40]Sellu A., (DoE), MLHCPE, Freetown; Only few industrial mining companies submit to EIA procedure; a small portion of small scale mining companies have submitted a preliminary environmental report

in keeping with the precautionary and inter-generational principles, considered the extent of impact that those projects will have on ecological integrity in environmental statements. Measures to minimise or avoid environmental impacts have also been documented in few cases.

Also, where the above circumstances exist, companies bear the costs of employing environmental consultants, undertake research and prepare own ES in keeping with the polluter-pays objective.[41] Similarly, monies are paid by miners and companies into specified categories of funds – ADF and CDF -, including rehabilitation and monitoring fees, as required under the Minerals and environmental policies, legislations, and agreements.[42] Also set up is the NEF, to fulfil specific objectives including social ones.[43] However, there is no insurance fund or scheme maintained by developers, specifically for environmental damage; or the regulations requiring them pursuant to the EPA.[44]

About 40 per cent of KHL profits – in the form of corporation tax ($200,000 per annum), annual surface rent (of $25 per acre), royalties totalling five per cent of diamond sales and four per cent of precious metal sales – ultimately go to the state[45] to address intragenerational equity concerns. Further revealed is the practice of deducting a portion of the government's three percent diamond export tax that is being put into a DACDF, earmarked for small-scale development in diamond communities.[46] The practice is however not applied uniformly to all diamond exports. Some major mining companies exempt themselves from making such payments.[47] There is also evidence of employment of locals in mining activities, symbolising an aspect of social ethos of the intra-generational principle.[48] Some form of environmental management is promoted through the issue of permits and

---

[41]SRL had its ESIA Report prepared by Knight-Piésold Consultants pursuant to SRA and Sysmin (supra chapter 5, p.136, n.52) (see "Sierra Rutile Environmental and Social Assessment at< http://www.knightpiesold.com/downloads/pdf/MineEnviro_SierraRutileLtd.pdf ; KHL also engaged services of Cemmats Consultants to undertake an EIA study on its behalf, pursuant to the KPML (supra chapter 5, p.140, ns. 77 & 78). See also Cemmats Consultants at, cemmats@sierratel.sl

[42]See supra chapter 5, (Part A) pp. 128-129, ns.12 & 16; and (Part B) p. 138 ns. 64 & 65; and see CMP, (supra n.1) above.

[43]This fund is under the budgetary control of the MoM and MLHCPE respectively.

[44]EPA (supra chapter 6, p.162, n. 58)

[45]PAC & NMJM Sierra Leone Diamond Annual Review, 2005 - (Diamonds and Human Security Project,) Gberie, Ahmimed & Smillie (Eds.) February, 2005

[46]Leahy S., "Sierra Leone: Global Aid Needed to Make Diamond Trade Sparkle" http://ipsnews.net/interna.asp?idnews=22946 This fund is said to have nearly totaled 800,000 dollars (USD)

[47]An Official from the GGDO, Freetown; Note that this claim in respect of KHL has been justified by a company representative, in reliance on a clause in KPML, exempting it from further liabilities in respect of the environment other than those stipulated in KPML;(See supra chapter 5, p.141, n.87ff for the relevant clause and critic on it).

[48]KHL is noted as having reasonably well-paid staff of about 400, mainly comprising of Sierra Leoneans (see PAC & NMJM (supra n. 45)

licenses for dredging lakes and other river uses,[49] and contracts are being awarded for the rehabilitation of mined out areas.[50] These efforts signify aspects of implementation of the principle of 'sustainable utilisation' or 'wise use' of natural resources in mining.

At another level, the provisions concerning conservation of nature and forest protection are being implemented mainly over areas designated for protection. Conservation is effected through the management of protected areas where in-situ conservation takes place. It was emphasised that these efforts are never over-ridden by mining pressures, but always remain strict reserves in protected areas.[51] The regulatory mechanism of licences and permits are also enforced to forge the objectives of sustainable use. Mining could be allowed, subject to requisite environmental conditions that are suitable for the type of land use to be made in a protected forest.[52] This is ensured through consultations between the Forestry division, the department of Surveys and Lands, and the ED.[53] Also, there are several on-going natural resource management projects and several more have been proposed, but most of these are directed towards policy-oriented studies.

7:2:4 Some General Policy, Decision-Making and Sectoral Concerns

In spite of the efforts acknowledged in the forgoing discourse, several problems still remain which need to be addressed in order to ensure efficient implementation of law and policy including decision-making processes that would promote sustainable mining. Firstly, despite the integration of social and environmental protection objectives in the NEP, the policy is regrettably not incorporated as a substantive part of the EPA. Its incorporation into an act would have served as a direct legal guidance or coercion, for implementation and enforcement of sustainability objectives while coordinating the activities of all environmental sectors, including mining.

[49]Kamara O.B. (DDoM) MoM, Freetown; Élan H.; representative of Magna Egoli Mining Company

[50]PRSP Environmental Report (supra n.34) p.30

[51]Garnett K., (Assistant Conservator of Forests) MAFFS, Freetown

[52]Ibid Note that these efforts are, to some extent in line with WCPA 'best practice' standard in respect of mining in protected areas. (See IUCN/WCPA 'Position Statement on Mining in protected Areas' and 'IUCN Guidelines for Protected Area Management Categories'-(in respect of the management of Strict Nature Reserves; Natural Parks, National Monuments, Habitat/Species Protected area; Protected landscape/seascape/conservation) (supra chapter 4, p.121, n.20)

[53]Garnett, ibid. For some orders reserving forests see-: The Forestry Amendment Order 1981 and the Forest Reserve Orders Cap 189; P.N No. 25 of 1982 – (also of The Forestry Act Cap 189); P.N No. 26 of 1982 – (Gafele Forest Reserve Order); P.N No. 26 of 1982 (Woa forest reserves) Order (Kenema district); P.N No. 27 of 1982 (Tajayei Forest Reserve) Order (Kenema district); P.N No. 28 of 1982 (Mansayei Forest Reserve) Order – (Kono District). These orders categorically specify that mining is not a 'beneficial use' permitted thereon; P.N No. 148 of 1961 allows for temporary buildings to be set up by Mines monitors in Forest Reserves pursuant to Rule 12 (a) of the Alluvial Diamond Mining Rules 1956; but all such buildings must be destroyed when use of them is ceased.

Also there is no law, policy or a system of national environmental accounting, as part of the national accounting indicators, such as would include the trend of natural resource depletion, the environment and social effects of mineral resource developments. These together could secure constructive and proper implementation of sectoral laws that have significance for controlling environmentally adverse consequences of mining, through conservation, forest management, planning, water security and public health.

The second problem relates to the lack of definition of 'sustainable development' in all the legal and policy prescripts analysed in this work. This lack of explicit reference leaves decision-makers confused as to its true content. During interviews with officials of both the mines and environmental departments, each placed emphasis on particular components of the concept as reflecting their respective mandates,[54] though all connected it directly with EIA. While it might not be prudent to suggest a strict definition of the concept, there is need to restate its objectives (probably in constitutional terms), bringing out the inter-linkages between, environment and development.

There is clear appreciation of the EIA process as reflective of sustainability considerations. But according to the DoE, these considerations will only be applied to mining applications 'that find their way to us'.[55] The insinuation is that MoM has responsibility to refer all mining applications to the ED for the EIA process, but is not always doing so. While government might be committed to the objective of considering environmental impact of mining activities before making a decision on project implementation, and has localised this objective by legal and institutional arrangements evidence in the EIA procedure, the process remains to be implemented systematically. It seems to have been reduced mainly to the production of EIA plans and statements by applicants.

Also, mining policy, laws and agreements contain provisions for environmental management and rehabilitation of mined out areas. But the process of reclamation and rehabilitation of mined out land is said to be very slow and unsystematic. Reportedly, funds collected by the GOSL for reclamation have not been used to encourage responsible environmental management especially of artisanal diamond mining areas.[56] Persistent social

---

[54]The ED official emphasised strictly environmental concerns, while Mines official stressed economic components of the concept.

[55]Sellu A., (supra n.40)

[56]The MoM has only recently started contracting for reclamation of an extremely contentious mining site in central Koidu- the 'Kaisambo site' (see Peace Diamond Alliance: (funded by USAID/ PDA)"The problem to be addressed" at < http://www.peacediamonds.org/>

problems still plague mineral development activities, attributable to the fact that the respective capacities of MoM and ED in regulating mining-related social issues are not well defined. It appears that the responsibility of the ED to consider social aspects ends with the granting of a 'valid' or 'EIA' licenses. Social disputes arising from mining operations are raised with the MoM, which approves project implementation, though the ED still retains responsibility to monitor the environmental soundness of such projects. It is also common practice for persons affected by mining operations to make representation to the DoM. Not only is the legal basis for such representations unclear, there is no mechanism in place for addressing such complaints. However, mines officials are known to hold meetings at the local level to discuss environmental and social issues arising from mining disputes but with limited achievements in particular cases, due to lack of information, co-ordination and chiefly, 'unfounded' suspicions of government-company collusion.[57] This uncertainty poses difficulty for the effective implementation of social sustainability objectives in mining.

In the realm of planning, there is widespread concern over the continued lack of land use plans to guide or regulate resource use and exploitation in the entire country.[58] According to the Director of Planning, the practical application of the planning legislation has little implication for effects of mining on the environment. One reason proffered for this anomaly is that planning is not done according to either 'scales of planning' or 'planning schemes' with detail plans for development control; this makes the direction of planning 'more attitudinal than legal'.[59] Thus, implementation of the planning legislation such as would control mining according to the principles of sustainable development identified under the TCPA, can at best be described as nil. There is need for reorientation to development planning, pursuant to legislation.

Another area of inefficiency relates to the implementation of the water regulations for sustainable utilisation in mining. The responsibility to provide, supervise, conserve and manage water resources (including control of water quality) is spread among the DWRD, the GVWC, and SALWACO. The institutional framework has been described as weak and structurally inadequate for effective sector management of water resources in Sierra

---

[57]Wurie (DoM) MoM, Freetown; Note that in most cases mining leases are premised on the compulsory acquisition of land and upon pre-determined compensation before operations commence; (see supra chapter 5, p.130, n.24).

[58]PRSP Environmental Report (supra n. 34) p. 6

[59]Johnson M. A.O. (Director of Country Planning) MLHCPE, Freetown, Sierra Leone

Leone.[60] In fact, there is no unifying code of practice and standards as each agency set their own standards and policy to satisfy their needs.[61] It appears that the mining sector has never been fully incorporated into overall water resources planning despite its water-based method of extraction. Earlier critics blame the situation on the fact that most of the country's water policy and legislation evolved around the mining industry, with mining agreements according companies wide-ranging rights to consume as much water needed for their operations, including rights over rivers, streams and swamps in their lease area.[62] Effective localisation of the principle of sustainable utilisation would require a national regulatory authority and standard for rational management of all water resources. This will ensure that water resources in mining operations are exploited within the model of natural resource valuation and pricing.

Forest protection and conservation objectives were identified in mining and sectoral policies and laws, including the constitution of Sierra Leone; and were represented as having the propensity to direct intra, and intergenerational equity in mining principally, through the constitution of reserves and parks. However, as at time of writing, only one of the various reserves has been gazetted, while many remain as 'proposed' or notified.[63] This situation cannot be divorced from a recent observation, suggesting that the implementing sector lacks coherent strategies and well-coordinated policies for creation and management of nature and wildlife.[64] The policy objectives and legal requirements will only be met if the pertinent decisions to constitute reserves are taken, and are followed through by clearly defined management strategy that is enforced indiscriminately.

Similarly, the public health policy and regulation still remains to be utilised in regulating mining operations, especially in relation to pollution control. There is considerable attention paid by health officials towards curative strategy, without addressing the cause of the mosquito-infested mining ponds. Also, concerns with blame shifting on mines officials for not enforcing rehabilitation and reclamation provisions seem to overshadow the obligation to enforce statutory nuisances. A refocus of strategy is strongly

---

[60]MDEP/SL: "Draft Water Sector Review for the PRSP, May, 2004 p.2 (hereinafter Water Sector Review) also at http://www.daco-sl.org/encyclopedia2004/

[61]*Ibid*

[62]Akiwumi F. A., "Roots of Conflict: water, world View and sustainability in a West African Environment at <http://www.ucowr.siu.edu/proc/W4D.pdf>. Note that even today, compensations (monetary) and provision of alternative water supply (wells) are relied on in agreements for regulating water uses by mining companies

[63]CCSL; *Wild Life and Nature Reserves in Sierra Leone* (GTZ funded) 1993, Freetown. The 'Tiwai Island' is gazetted as a community reserve for protection of flora and fauna.

[64]PRSP Environmental Report (supra n. 34) p.41

recommended, coupled with the need to educate the public on their collective and integrated responsibility to use the PHA for controlling mine pollution.

Finally, localising sustainable development requires funding for implementing the several legal and policy goals aimed at promoting sustainable mining. There is evidence of donor and agency support for the preparation of the NEAP/SL and the National Action Plan to combat desertification.[65] Also, donor funds and GOSL budgetary support has been allocated to hosting various sectoral workshops, which include mining and environmental issues.[66] However, there is hardly any support either for implementation of recommendations from these workshops, proposed environmental projects, or for enhancing institutional capacity whether by expertise, logistics or necessary technology for environmental management in face of mining.[67]

7:2:5 Facilitating Participation of Interest Groups

Another important aspect in ensuring progressive implementations of Sierra Leone's law and policy objectives in context of mining and sustainable development relates to the facilitation of stakeholder participation in the decision-making process, benefits-sharing and ensuring transparency in their outcome. The concept of 'participants' have been defined *inter alia*, as 'those who have the responsibility for, depend on, live within, or otherwise care for the variety of life and living resources'.[68] This definition accords with the broadly established participatory categories, amongst which are sectoral administrations,[69] local communities,[70] NGOs,[71] and corporate entities.[72]

---

[65]NEAP was funded by GEF, through the enabling activities Programme, which was established specifically to provide funding for National Biodiversity Strategies and Action plans (NBSAP) and National Reports under the CBD. See the Biodiversity support Programme at < http://www.undp.org/bpsp> and also http://www.gefweb.org. The UNCCD Secretariat funded the preparation of the report on the desertification action plan.

[66]Sellu (supra n.40); other efforts include support from the World Bank, UNDP, DFID, and USAID/OTI. For instance, DFID is providing expert advice to the government on the management of its diamond resources and has been working with the government to develop a diamond sector strategy that includes establishing an appropriate legal and regulatory framework and strengthening the capacity of relevant government departments and supporting NGOs. Also, convention institutions like Ramsar have been known to fund wetlands activities. (see Sierra Leone Wetlands Day Celebration, 2002 at http://www.ramsar.org/wwd2002_rpt_sierraleone1.htm

[67]A senior Environmental Officer remarked on the lack of donor support for several projects drawn up by the ED.

[68]Herkenrath P., (citing miller and Lanou) "The Implementation of the Convention on Biological Diversity-A Non-Governmental Perspective Ten Years On" in *Reciel* 11 (1) 2002 p.35

[69]WCED (see supra chapter 2, p.63, n. 128)

[70]Rio Declaration (supra chapter 2 p.43, n.12) Principle 22; Other identified groups include women, youth and indigenous people, are addressed as part of local communities; (Principles 20 & 21)

[71]WECD (supra chapter 2, p.63 n.131)

[72]See Johannesburg Declaration & POI (supra chapter 2, p.61 n.112)

These stated categories have been deemed important for implementation of sustainable development objectives, and therefore mark a perfect boundary for assessing the participation of interest groups in environment and mining issues in practice.

(i) Sectoral Administrations

The laws and policies of various sectors including mining, recognise sustainability objectives especially the responsibility to take actions to protect the environment. Apart from other implementation efforts and concerns described above, the common evidence of sectoral participation relates to their consultative role in the EIA process, membership and participation on environmental and/or mining committees,[73] and organising workshops to encourage dialogue on strategic environmental and social policy objectives.[74] These representations would influence policy and decision-making at various levels. However, less use is made of the precautionary elements, such as exchange of information, co-operation and coordination. Sectors have to employ these precautionary measures in an integrated manner, and upon a well-structured framework of coordinative sequences.

(ii) Local Communities

The extent of community participation in mining decision-making process in practice is not clear. The pertinent requirements for public participation relate the EIA procedure,[75] the benefits that must accrue them from mining principally through the setting up of various funds,[76] and compensation. On the implementation of the access to information and participation components of sustainable development, the public's participation is solicited mainly through adverts (news-paper and radio), which are designed to attract response from interested groups, including local communities. However, none of the solicited responses so far, revealed by EIA records of the ED, were from representations of local communities in mining areas. One implementing official, remarked that the public are not usually interested, and do not respond to adverts. According to him, those

[73]The DoE is a member of the MAB (see supra chapter 5, p.132, n.34)

[74]Such objectives include the minimisation and mitigation of the adverse impact of mining operations on health, communities and the environment; see Report of Workshop on Policy Support Planning for Mining Sector held on January 28th and 29th, 2004, MoM, Freetown, and (PSPMS Report).

[75]The NEB has responsibility to inform the public of environmental statements, consult and solicit their comments thereon; (EPA supra n.24) s.19; EIAP (supra chapter 6, p.152 n.6) (clauses 2 & 3).

[76]See supra ns. 41 -43 for evidence of applicable funds

who manage to send comments will have their comments noted.[77] Whether this justifies the lack of instituting constructive dialogue with local communities is not certain. What is clear is that such perceptions breed chaos, instability, and leave communities in substantial opposition to developers. There should be clear procedure and guidelines for public consultation.

Equally so, the extent of their actual participation is controversial. For instance, some form of community participation was allegedly solicited in one case, by consultants acting on behalf of KHL.[78] But interestingly, at the time when consultants may have been seeking public involvement in the decision-making process, pre-production construction activities had already begun before the acquisition of environmental approval or EIA Licences.[79] The picture painted of the EIA process by this order of events is not clear. It will appear that the company assumed the EIA process at best as 'a matter of course', needed only to validate its operations, but with no real commitment to incorporating the public's views within the outcome of the seeming consultative meetings.

Similarly, in respect of SRL, there is no record in the ED, of when, how, or where 'public consultation' or the local communities' involvement were solicited. Consultants, on behalf of the company, undertook a 'fast track' assessment project,[80] and the findings were disclosed to the World Bank information shop.[81] While the assessment is stated to have involved some form of environmental and social impact assessment, including *inter alia*, 'public consultation disclosure' the report admits to have relied heavily on 'recall by SRL site personnel' in some respects and on independent profiling of site conditions, both of which hardly suggest community involvement at any stage.[82] It must be emphasised that an important aspect of the legal character of sustainable development in international law, is 'deliberative processes' (on a case by case basis), in order to solve today's problems and achieving sustainable outcomes.[83]

---

[77] Bah S.A (Senior Environmental Officer) MLHCPE, Youyi Building, Freetown.

[78] See Cemmats Consultants, (supra n.41) "Notification of the Development of a Diamond Mine in koidu, Sierra Leone, by Branch Energy", 2003. The meetings were held in the Freetown as part of a Public consultation and disclosure process. It included minimal representations from some ruling houses in the immediate operational township mining areas. The results were incorporated into the Draft EIA. (Note under the EIAP, Developers could convene public hearings (see supra chapter 6, p.157, n.30))

[79] *Ibid*; for instance, production sites had been established, pipelines, haul and access roads, accommodation and site offices including water storage dams had already been constructed.

[80] See Knight Piésold Consultants (supra n.41) emphasis added.

[81] *Ibid*. According to the Consultants, their findings were to provide 'a gauge for lenders to assess the project relative to established environmental and social policies guidelines'. Note that the relevant SRL/ ESIA Report (supra, chapter 5, p.136, n.52) is akin to an Environmental plan, program or Statement, which SRL is obligated to submit to national authorities. But by this method of publication, it will hardly be accessible by members of the local communities in the company's mining area.

[82] *Ibid*.

[83] See Higgins and Fitzmaurice respectively (supra chapter 2, pp. 55-56, ns. 80-82)

Nowhere else is this attribute more useful than in engaging communities in decision-making processes relating to mining. Effective public consultation leads to better community development programs, fewer complaints about projects and better sponsor-community relationship generally.[84] Recent events in Sierra Leone involving confrontations between local communities, NGO representatives and KHL, leading to the withholding of MIGA approval of proposed guarantees and halting the companies mining activities, justifies this suggestion.[85] It also raises questions about the adequacy of any alleged access to information and community participation in the EIA process, and confirms the significance and necessity of instituting actual and proper community dialogue for sustainable development.

There is no legal or policy requirement holding officials accountable for marginalizing whole communities in the decision-making process. Similarly, there is no constituted right or forum to challenge the refusal of access to information or participation. For instance, it took the withholding of MIGA approval, for official attention and reaction to communities concerns to be considered.[86] These rights have yet to be directly and specifically secured through legislation. Some have relied on the protection of rights clauses in the constitution to enforce these participatory rights against 'the government'.[87] But it will be difficult to establish or claim social and environmental rights under the applicable provisions where most of the exceptions apply.[88] Recourse could immediately be had to the provisions under the EPA relating to cancellation or modification of licences where it is established that a company has breached environmental conditions or varied its operation substantially at the expense of the environment.[89]

---

[84]See CAO "A Review of IFC's Safeguard Policies" January 2003, (CAO Report); available at http://www.ifc.org/ifcext/policyreview p.74

[85]Allegedly the local communities were not properly or sufficiently informed about the impact of mining activities, never made an input on the EIA and were completely ignorant of any agreement made between the company and the GOSL. (See Kamara A., (Research and Legal Adviser of NMJM)), "Human Rights, Mining and the People of Kono" at <http://www.minesandcommunities.org/ >

Other concerns relate to the impacts of blasting on communities; inadequacy of resettlement action plan for the more than 5000 people affected; and the need for a local grievance mechanism to resolve outstanding disputes between the community and the company. (See BIC: USA) - "Civil Society Groups in Sierra Leone Voice Concerns About Proposed MIGA Project" at <http://www.bicusa.org/>

[86]One official reaction involved consultations with Kono District and Chiefdom authorities of the affected area, and company officials at the office of the Vice President ;(Interview with the Hon. S.E Berewa, V.P. Republic of Sierra Leone, Freetown, June, 2004.) This 'quasi and bottom up' consultation aimed at reassuring the MIGA Board and hopefully weaken their resolve. An agreement was signed in September 2004, between one hundred and twelve property owners in the 'blast zones' and KHL representatives in which KHL had agreed to pay for the relocation of their houses. (See PAC & NMJM Diamond Annual Review (supra n.45))

[87]Kamara A (supra n.85); relies specifically s. 23 of the constitution (supra n.26), relating to provision to secure protection of law in the determination of the existence or extent of civil rights or obligations before any court or authority in public.

[88]For instance, in respect of the deprivation of property, mining companies or government can justify their actions as an incidence of a mining lease (see the Constitution (supra n.26) s. 21(2)(c))

[89]EPA (supra n.24) s. 26(1)

However the full legal effect of this provision could only be attained if it is established first, that the EB did issue an 'EIA licence' for the relevant project; whether the legal mandates in mineral specific laws make such allowances for cancellation;[90] and the extent to which individuals (or communities) could use the provision to force official action to implement the legislation. It will be a plus on all sides if communities in which all forms of mining activities take place are made to have sufficient and constant flow of information and knowledge of mining projects, (before, during and after EIA), including an input into the activities that have so much potential to affect their lives in a positive or negative way.

Also, outside participation in the EIA procedure, intra-generational equity considerations have not been found forthright in some areas. In respect of benefits sharing, the ADF and CDF do not appear to have a well-structured mechanism for distribution of their respective proceeds. This has affected the even distribution of benefits amongst inhabitants of particular mining communities, creating further scope for social discord.[91] Reportedly, 'local communities get very little direct benefits from mining revenue earned by central government', and there is often wide divergence of views and open conflict between national government and local communities over how such revenue is shared. Communities are often pitched in direct conflict with mining companies demanding solutions to environmental and development issues.[92] Other pressing issues warranting special implementation attention relate to the lack of established criteria and mechanism for assessment and distribution of compensation, including provision of infrastructural and social amenities and post-mining developments.[93] Overall, too much emphasis seems to be placed on economic (monetary) benefits as opposed to environmental health and wealth.

(iii) NGOs and Other Interest Groups

The call for inclusion of NGO or interest group participation is firmly entrenched as an objective of sustainable development though the limits of 'permitted' participation or involvement are not certain. Domestic law and policy acknowledge their right of access to development-oriented

---

[90]For instance SRL and KHL agreements provides for arbitration in case of breach.

[91]See PSPMS Report (supra n. 74)

[92]*Ibid.* Para.5: 5ff

[93]*Ibid.* Para.4: 2

information and, participation in environmental decision-making.[94] Other identified NGO participatory rights relate to environmental management and social issues,[95] including their entitlement to judicial and administrative access in so far as they seek to enforce or ensure the sustainable use of natural resources and the protection of the environment.[96] The extent to which NGOs and Groups have exercised participatory privileges in the various fields in sierra Leone to direct sustainable mining have been mixed.

Generally, NGOs are increasingly participating in environmental concerns both in a proactive and reactive capacity, acting in most cases as a pressure group on government and mining companies to implement legal and policy objectives for sustainable mining practices. In the field of access to information, it is official view that the public advertising of draft EIA statements is enough to inform any interested NGO, though effort is always made by the ED to address specific requests for information.[97] In other quarters however questions were being raised by NGOs regarding the inaccessibility to EIA information,[98] coupled with proactive campaigns both national and international, to enforce the right to availability and access to information.[99] Officials however blame the gap in the systematic implementation of the access to information requirements on the lack of modern information systems, such as websites.[100]

NGO participation in relation to formulation of policy and decision-making in mining in the country is mainly through their representation on workshops, conferences, and official meetings;[101] and in some cases, even on national committees.[102] Similarly, policies have been influenced through NGO reports and recommendations.[103] Also NGOs have been instrumental in bringing environmental and social mining issues to the public domain

---

[94]See EPA (supra chapter 6, p. 157, n.26) Note that Rio (supra n.70); Principle 10 advocates appropriate access to information, for 'each individual' at the 'national level'; and Agenda 21 extends participatory rights to 'groups' and 'organisations' (see supra chapter 3, p.100, n.172).

[95]WCED (supra n. 5) pp. 310-319

[96]Pring and Noe (supra chapter 3, p. 99, n.166)

[97]Sellu (supra n.40)

[98]NMJD (Press Statement) "The Koidu Kimberlite Project - Is Koidu Holdings Ltd. above the Law?" 11th February, 2004 at <http://www.minesandcommunities.org/Action/press263.htm>

[99]See supra n.85 above.

[100]Sellu (supra n.40)

[101]Sometimes in an organiser capacity; e.g. CHECSIL hosted the workshop and seminar, which gave birth to the NEAP/SL.

[102]CSSL is a member of the National wetlands Committee (see Fofanah A. S., "Proceedings of A One-day Inaugural Seminar for Members of the National Wetlands Committee - Sierra Leone"), MAFFS, February 2002- <http://www.ramsar.org/mtg_sierraleone>
CBAN, another NGO, has membership on the National Biodiversity Project Planning Committee; (see Prof. Cole N.H.A., "Profile of Community Biodiversity Action Network" (CBAN), Freetown, Sierra Leone), also at < http://www.cbdcprogram.org/>

[103]USAID funded an environmental report on artisanal mining and recommended to GOSL certain environmental regulatory reforms; (see PDA (supra n.56))

through media coverage and educational activities,[104] and community action groups.[105] Similar NGO involvement has also been notable in environmental management,[106] Conservation[107] and intra-generational issues;[108] and recently in conflict mediation between companies and the local people.[109] It should be pointed out that these references are just examples and indications of areas in which NGO participation is dominant in relation to mining and sustainability issues, and do not represent a limited category of participants.

However, the nature and extent of NGO participation in mine-related concerns is not without questions. A common criticism often levied against them, and one that is adopted in this case study, relates to the lack of transparency in the selection of their agendas,[110] proper governance and external accountability.[111] The lack of an effective integrated networking and transparency in NGO operations have allowed for convergence in the mandates of most NGOs dealing with environmental issues and thus an overlap in functions and activities. This takes away much needed resources from other areas. Another difficulty relates to the fact that they are often, so concerned with implementing their individual mandates at all cost without consideration to other stakeholders, and even at the expense of meaningful dialogue.[112] NGOs have also been known to blur genuine social and environmental issues with political critique. The notable practice is to engage the mass media for dramatic reporting and publication of inaccurate, often exaggerated and politically biased claims.[113] More importantly, it was

[104] CHECSL, promotes ecology through mass media environmental information; (see PRSP Environmental Report (supra n.34) p. 30)

[105] For instance, the 'Talking drum', (an NGO operated Radio Station), airs out mining related issues; see http://www.usaid.gov/gn/sierraleone/sl_democracy/news/031001_pda_launch/; Also, the EFA, is involved in raising awareness on environmental issues in communities and schools; see < http://www.efasl.org.uk/>

[106] EFA reclaimed and rehabilitated 20 acres of agricultural swampland, which was degraded by diamond mining, and also spearheads community work in conservation (see EFA, at <http://easyweb.easynet.co.uk/efa/general/enfosal.htm>); also dominant in conservation and natural resource protection activities: CSSL, in collaboration with the RSPB, obtained an agreement with GOSL for the protection of 75,000 hectares of the Gola forest. (See CSSL, at <http://www.birdlife.net/worldwide/national/sierra_leone/index.html>)

[107] CSSL campaigns for protection of wildlife, parks and sanctuaries through education, advocacy and research ;(CCSL, ibid; see also PRSP Environmental Report (supra n.53) p. 30.)

[108] Such as caving pressure on GOSL to return some of the mining proceeds back to mining communities; see PDA (supra n. 56)

[109] Koenen-Grant J., "USAID's PDA Mediates Community Dispute in Kono" March 30, 2004 (see PDA Ibid.); PDA brought together community representatives and the mining company to promote greater understanding about the mining process, and to help negotiate a compromise agreement for those being displaced by the mining. (see supra n.85 for the related dispute).

[110] Ximena F., "International Law-making in the Field of Sustainable development: The Unequal Competition Between Development and Environment" in International Law and Sustainable Development, Schrijver & Weiss (Eds.), 2004 Koninklijke Brill NV., The Netherlands, p.17

[111] Walde T.W., "Natural Resources and Sustainable Development: From "Good Intentions" to "Good Consequences"" in Schrijver & Weiss (Eds.), 2004 (ibid) p.149-50

[112] Keillie A., (Cemmats Consultant)(supra n. 41)

[113] For instance, some NGOs are alleged to have 'fanned' community unrest in Kono mining areas by 'irresponsible press statements and provocative news captions'; (see Koenen-Grant (supra n. 109);

uncovered that credits usually assumed by NGOs were acquired through efforts of civil society organisations.[114]

It must be impressed that sustainability demands dialogue and deliberative processes as a way forward especially in mining related cases where environmental, social and economic interests are interlocked. Implementation process will benefit more, from NGO participation, if environmental NGOs 'demystify', their participation as representing democracy,[115] take a more integrative, co-coordinative and co-operative approach in cognisance of the interrelatedness of mining and sustainable development goals.

(iv) Corporate Entities

The companies Act present three capacities in which corporate entities could operate in Sierra Leone.[116] First, companies can be incorporated in Sierra Leone under the Act.[117] They can also be incorporated outside Sierra Leone.[118] Third, international companies (principally with foreign investment) can choose to be incorporated under the laws of Sierra Leone as limited companies and be subject to the company's regulation. This later category defines the major mining companies operating in Sierra Leone, such as SRL and KHL, which are subject to the laws and jurisdiction of Sierra Leone in the first instance.[119]

But the legal regime of these companies is made complex by other international connections, involvements or obligations in various respects, and has enormous implications primarily, for determining the scope of their environmental responsibility and accountability. For instance both companies are essentially TNEs,[120] operating in the country on foreign direct investments, and as subsidiaries or affiliates of companies based or operating

---

[114]Representatives of both the 'Grass Roots Movement' and the 'Peace Diamond Alliance' in Sierra Leone

[115]Ximena F., (supra n.110) p.17

[116]The Companies Act of Sierra Leone, chapter 249 of the Laws of Sierra Leone.

[117]Ibid; under ss. 3 & 4

[118]In this case, they must have an established place of business within that country, and must deposit the Memorandum and Articles and other instruments of the company (including information on their principal offices abroad and locally) with the registrar of companies.

[119]See supra chapter 5, pp.135 & 139, ns.45 & 73 respectively.

[120]The term 'TNE' is used here (as opposed to MNC or MNEs) in relation to mining entities and companies owning or controlling production, sale or services, or otherwise engaged in direct investments internationally, and includes domestic firms that export part of their output but is not limited to incorporated business entities based on parent subsidy relations alone. For other categories of definition of TNC, MNC, or MNE, see Mulinchksy P.T., *Multinational Corporations and the Law*, Blackwell, Oxford 2003 pp12-15.

in other countries.[121] Also, ushered into their regulation, are interests of foreign lenders or guarantors, including their respective environmental policies and regulations.[122]

But while the term 'corporate' generally refers to strict legal personalities of companies, its meaning adopted for purposes of 'implementation' of sustainable development, will also include mining entities which are not incorporated under the categorisation in the Sierra Leone Companies legislation, though their respective obligations will vary.[123]

(iv)(a) Corporate Participation as Responsibility

The concept of participation of corporate entities generally, (including mining companies) has gained momentum since the WSSD, and is commonly connoted as 'Corporate Responsibility' (CR).[124] What defines the term is not certain.[125] But suggestions have been made on the subject, which generally interprets into the several challenges facing the mining industry. For some, it translates into the practice of effectively applying sustainable development principles, into everyday operations and decision-making of a

---

[121]SRL is owned by MIL Investments SA based in Luxemburg (owned by Jean-Raymond Boulle a British national) and U.S Titanium of Texas, USA; Clause 22 of the KPML invokes the multinational character of the company for purposes of ICSID arbitration. KHL is joint venture owner-ship by Energem Resources Inc.,(a South-African based company) previously known as Diamond Works), BSG Resources Ltd (Geneva-based and owned by Benny Steinmetz), West Africa Trade House and Gem Fields Resources Limited (controlled by John Boulle); and Magma Diamond Resources Limited (Magma) see Energem Resources Inc. - *Mining Division - Update* October 28, 2004; <http://news.surfwax.com/worldcities/files/Koidu_Sierra_Leone.html> Note also that there are several other companies with international affiliations involved in mining, prospecting or exploration activities in Sierra Leone - the Toronto Stock Exchange are involved in diamond pros-pecting and exploration; Magna Egoli controlled by Fauvilla Ltd.(Israeli-based); Africa Diamond Holdings (Calgary-based); Sierra Leone Diamond (part of Timis Diamond) owned by De Beers and Rapaport Group etc;- (see PAC-NMJD *Diamond Industry Annual Review Sierra Leone*, 2004(Diamonds and Human Security Project) Gberie, Isaac & Smillie (Eds.) Freetown).

[122]Note that SRL obtained $25 (USD) loan from OPIC, an independent profit-seeking US Government Agency, that provides loans, guarantees and insurance for US private investment in mining projects in developing countries and emerging economies around the world. It has stringent environmental policies and is required by the United States *Foreign Assistance Act* (22 U.S.C. § 231(n)) to perform EIAs on any Programme or project 'significantly affecting the environment of any foreign country'. Where OPIC feels World Bank mining guidelines may not be sufficient, it will consider other standards such as international mining industry standards, and United States NEPA standards; (<http://www.opic.gov>). Also under the Sysmin agreement, the European Union loaned SRL, (technically made in favour of GOSL) and made applicable to SRL specified World Bank Guidelines. (see supra, chapter 5, p.135, ns.44 &45)

Similarly, KHL obtained political risk guarantee from MIGA, the chief insurance entity within the World Bank Group. MIGA generally adopts the IFC's environmental policies and Guidelines but improves the operational aspects of it (<http://www.miga.org>).

[123]Note that this hybrid and extended meaning has been adopted so as to reflect the general but varying scope of responsibilities of mining entities in sierra Leone, though emphasis will be placed at present on the companies whose mining agreements and implementation thereof form subject of this thesis

[124]The more prevalent terminology that defines the concept is 'Corporate Social Responsibility' (CSR), and in some cases 'Corporate Accountabil-ity'. I omit the inclusion of 'Social' in my particular reference, so as to avoid any delimiting conception of the varied responsibilities (including social, economic, environmental, accounting etc.) that defines one way or another CR.

[125]Mullerat R., (OBE) "The Still Vague and Imprecise Notion of Corporate Social Responsibility" in *International Business Lawyer*, Vol. 32 No 5 October 2004, p.236; According to him 'CSR' is susceptible to be portrayed at least in priorities of some of its aspects according to individual backgrounds and views: as an ethical aspiration; a legal corporate regulation; a market tool; or a management risk instrument.

responsible company.[126] Others view it as a 'continuing commitment by businesses to behave ethically...'[127] CSR is taken to also extends beyond compliance with legal expectations to investing into human capital, the environment and relations with stakeholders.[128] It has also been portrayed as a 'concept whereby companies voluntarily decide to respect and protect the interests of a broad range of stakeholders while contributing to a cleaner environment and a better society through the active interaction of all'.[129] Further, CR has been identified as a 'duty on companies to find sustainable solutions' for their relationship to people, the external environment, and to the economy.[130]

These various perceptions on what entails company participation seem to relate to two main categories of responsibilities - Legal and Voluntary initiatives (VIs). The legal responsibility represents in companies fulfilment of legal mandates or compliance with negotiated or voluntary agreements.[131] The Voluntary responsibility connotes company initiatives and 'industry activity potentially covering all actions not required by legislation',[132] including *inter alia* statements of 'best Practice,[133] or the incorporation of industry specific environmental and social guidelines or principles.[134]

---

[126] Lord Holmes, "Sustainable Development: Most Effective Way to Put Principles into Practice" Geneva, 28 July 2004 WBCSD, available at <http://www.wbcsd.ch/plugins/DocSearch/details>

[127] Renner D., "Mining Companies Are Socially Responsible" *Africa News*, 14 September 2004 – (- Speaking on "CSR and Capacity Building")

[128] Bergkamp, Hunton & Williams, (Brussels), "Corporate Governance and Social Responsibility: A New Sustainability Paradigm" in *European Environmental Law Review*, May, 2002, p. 138 (citing CEC/GP on promoting European framework for CSR.)

[129] Mullerat, (supra n.125), p.236

[130] Thorsen and Oury, "Corporate Social Responsibility and Lawyers" in *Human Rights Law*, Newsletter (IBA Section on Legal Practice) No.7 October 2004 p.10 This model is derived from the 'triple bottom line' formula -people, planet and profit-, of how businesses can contribute to sustainable development. (See article for illustration on how solutions for CSR can be extrapolated from international human-rights values as an international frame of reference).

[131] MMSD (supra chapter 2, p.,47 n.33) p. 337 ff

[132] Walker & Howard; "Finding the Way Forwards: How Voluntary Action Move Mining towards Sustainable Development" (ERM, IIED WBCSD) London, 2002. Note also that the requirements of VIs could in some cases, be binding on those who voluntarily subscribe to it; (MMSD *ibid*) p.349).

[133] MMSD (*ibid*)

[134] On CSR and national implementation, see generally (supra chapter 2, p.70). Some examples of industry specific guidelines of international orientation designed to improve industry performance include: - ICMM- *Sustainable Development Charter* - an international code of conduct for the mining and metals industry, with 32 management principles covering environmental management, product stewardship, community responsibility, ethical business practices, and public reporting; UNEP, series of guidelines relevant to the mining sector: include *Monitoring Industrial Emissions and Wastes, Environmental Management of Nickel Production, and Environmental Aspects of Selected Non-Ferrous Metals Ore Mining; the UN Global Compact* (includes Rio Principles on Environment & Development) and ISO 1400; Berlin II Guidelines (supra, chapter 4, p.107, n.12) (See generally Walker & Howard, supra n. 128). See also 'World Bank Guidelines' which is directly applicable to SRL, pursuant to its adoption under Sysmin (supra chapter 5, p.135, n.45).

It will also require the emulation of guidelines established on 'IBP' for corporate regulation generally.[135] Some writers have, expressed the need to strictly distinguish between the legal responsibilities that is binding and enforceable law - 'corporate governance', and VIs, which are ethical, voluntary, non-enforceable rules.[136] Others have advocated caution and the desirability for convergence in environmental standards and practice between the regulated (legal) and unregulated (voluntary) divide.[137] But as has been suggested, what is crucial to CR, especially for implementation of sustainable development, is the importance of identifying the limits of what companies can reasonably do.[138] It is only when such limits are accepted that one can come closer to reasonable expectations over their possible contribution to sustainable development.[139] Implementation of companies', participation responsibilities, particularly SRL and KHL, will be examined in this case study, based on legal requirements, and including VIs that are assumed.

The principal legal requirements for mining entities generally includes undertaking EIA, minimisation of mining impacts on the natural and human environment, rehabilitation of mined-out areas, polluter-pays responsibilities relating to funds, compensations, resettlement, adopting 'best practice' and international environmental protection standards.[140] The stated mining policy goals of GOSL[141] also impress these legal objectives including a new emphasis on promoting and ensuring corporate responsibility. Companies could therefore implement related objectives as legal and/or VIs.

General evidence suggests that companies are meeting their responsibilities relating to payments of fees and development funds, though the same cannot

---

[135]For example, the *OECD Guidelines for Multinational Enterprises* (http://www.oecd.org/) These Guidelines are recommendations by governments to MNEs operating in or from the 33 countries that adhere to the Guidelines. Its specific application to enhancing CR in the mining sector is expressed in provisions relating to:- contributions to economic, social and environmental progress (II 1); respect for Human Rights (II, 2); refrain from seeking exemptions not contemplated in statutory framework (II, 5); consult with directly affected communities (V, 2b); maintain contingency mitigation plans (V 5); ensure occupational health and safety in operations (IV 4b); behave in competitive manner (I X); and Taxation – contribute to public finances (X). The guidelines have been analysed as especially relevant for regulating corporate behaviour in the mining sector. For instance, the reference to the 'international legal and policy framework in which business is conducted' in the preface of the Guidelines is interpreted to represent an explicit recognition of the application of overarching supranational obligations as relevant for corporate conduct. (See Feeney P., "The Relevance of the OECD Guidelines for Multinational Enterprises the Mining Sector and the Promotion of Sustainable Development" Oxford January 2002; also at < http://www.oecd.org/dataoecd/>
see also Draft *UN Code of Conduct of Transnational Corporations* (1990) UN Doc.E/1990/94 of 12 June, 1990
[136]Mullerat (supra n.125) p.237
[137]Ewing, Hutt & Petersen "Corporate Environmental Disclosures: Old Complaints, New Expectations" in *Business Law International*, Vol. 5 No 3, (IBA) September, 2004 pp.461-466 See article for an in-depth analysis of the US Sarbanes-Oxley Act designed to regulate corporate behaviour.
[138]Wälde (supra n.111) p.147
[139]*Ibid*
[140]See generally, supra chapter 5.
[141]CMP, (supra n. 12)

be said for artisanal miners, probably because of the difficulty to regulate them.[142] The government itself is reported to derive little revenue from the mining industry and the thousands of men, women and children who get down on their hands and knees to find the gems still lead a difficult life.[143] Usually, compensations are negotiated before commencement of operations, with enormous amount of government pressure on what is acceptable compensation.[144] Diamond companies participate in the Kimberley process, an international diamond certification scheme, though it does not symbolise a verification of environmental management. Also, Company reaction has not been prominent in responsibility for management of the natural environment, especially the systematic reclamation of land as mining progresses, and support for conservation activities.[145] They tend to limit these obligations to monetary payments as opposed to preventative and protective measures.

In respect of the undertaking of EIA, the determination is not as conclusive.[146] Official position is that SRL has proven record of compliance with legal EIA requirements, in accordance with 'government laws and regulations, and the policies and guidelines of international lending institutions'.[147] This conclusion is based on the preparation of two consecutive environmental programmes by SRL for its mining area in 1990 - the ECDP,[148] and recently in 2001, - an ESIA.[149] It seems that the interrelationship that must exist between the legal obligation to prepare environmental and social programmes (or ES), and that requiring assessment or implementation of its contents may have been confused or officially over-sighted.[150] The implementation aspects of both sets of programmes have not overcome scrutiny. In respect of the previous ECDP, SRL had allegedly failed in its responsibility to rehabilitate and reclaim mined-out land and had turned arable agricultural lands into 'lakes and ponds', and had severely impacted local people.[151] Similar accusation has been levied elsewhere.[152]

[142] See supra ns. 46 and 49; Inspection of records of fees, for dredging and rehabilitation

[143] UN Integrated Regional Information Networks: "Sierra Leone: Diamonds Shine Brighter, But remain Dull" February 24, 2005

[144] A traditional Chief (Kono District)

[145] GOSL contractors, civil society organisations and NGOs generally discharge this responsibility.

[146] See critic in respect of Community participation in EIA; (supra n. 78-85 & 98)

[147] Kamara, Mansaray & Wright in *Mining Annual Review Sierra Leone* - 2003

[148] Creamer & Warner: *ECDP for SRL*, Rep. No. 92040, July 1990; see notes 151 &152 below for criticisms on the implementation of the 1990 ECDP.

[149] See SRL ESIA, by Knight Piésold Consultants, (supra n. 41)

[150] Note that in relation to mining, these are conjunctive obligations under the Minerals Act and the EPA, both of which apply.

[151] "Sierra Leone: Another Round of Mining Difficulties?" at <http://www.wbcsd.ch/plugins/DocSearch/> Note that visit by the writer, to SRL mining areas revealed appalling visual effects of lands that had not been rehabilitated.

[152] NGOs claimed that SRL has violated Bank (IFC, OPIC, the Export-Import Bank and Common Wealth Development Cooperation) resettlement and environmental guidelines, by the flooding of 6,400 acres of land, displacing 5300 people and dumping 7.4 million tons of mining waste in the local region every month; (Friends of the Earth (US) *Review for Sierra Rutile Limited*, July 20, 1997; also at

As regards the recent ESIA, SRL acquired the official EIA License after publication of the assessment report (in news papers, internet resources and library of university institution), as evidence of the public disclosure and consultation process.[153] There is however no record within the ED, of any challenges or comments levied against the programme by any sector of government, member of the public or local communities. Also, no public hearings or consultations were held on the documents. But upon acquisition of official 'EIA license', the ESIA document was 'valid' enough to secure for SRL, loans from its international sponsors.[154] While strict interpretation of the SRA and the EPA would suggest the fulfilment of the EIA requirements through the preparation of the assessment information and its publication, it is expected as an aspect of CR, for companies not to rely on 'compliance with domestic rules' as an excuse for failing to perform at least to standards of home state or accepted international standards where these exist. They should not exploit institutional weakness but compensate such by extra efforts to apply modern environmental standards.[155] SRL's adoption of the 'World Bank Guidelines'[156] under Sysmin would have necessitated actual (grassroots - intelligible disclosure of information) and physical involvement of the public (in the lease area) in consultative hearings. This will ensure that the ESIA is not only represented as a one-sided aspirational document, but also reflective of an agreement in which the publics' actual concerns are noted. A representative of the company however denies that SRL had behaved irresponsibly in the past, or that it will ignore its environmental obligations 'now', and also promises company strict adherence to global environmental regulations.[157]

The Kimberlite miners have also been on the down side of community relationship, not only in respect of its EIA, but failing in its obligations to minimise impact of its activities on the human environment. KHL had reportedly carried out 'blasting' activities close to homes of local residents, without first taking steps to finish the construction of resettlement facilities. But according to KHL environmental consultants, the affected people were squatters on KHL lease areas, who had deliberately trespassed thereon in

---

[153]Sisay J. (Director of Operations, SRL) Guma Building, Lamina Sankoh Street, Freetown. SRL has only officially recommenced operations in April 2005.

[154]An official of the NEB contends that the process was 'as a matter of course' caving to government pressure over the economic importance of recommencing operations of the rutile mines. The EISA document was only submitted to the ED in the last quarter of 2004, to authenticate it for the Sysmin agreement.(supra chapter 5, p.135, n.44). Note also that the ESIA was prepared in 2001 by a 'fast-track' process for the lenders reaction (supra n. 81)

[155]Wälde (supra n.111) p.147

[156]See supra chapter 5, p.135, n.45

[157]Sisay J., (supra n. 153)

order to acquire new homes through the process of relocation.[158] Such implementation controversies are what Weeramantry's concept of 'continuous EIA' is meant to address.[159] However, KHL may have shown 'best practice' in some measure when it submitted to dialogue and voluntarily agreed to construct additional homes, and to include community participation in the planning, layout and design of the dwellings yet to be built.[160]

Overall, the extent to which companies adopt 'IBP' in their operations before and after the scrutiny of environmental plans and statements is not clear. What is clear is that IBP is expected to be the hallmark of most international investment organizations including those that have provided loans and guarantees to SRL and KHL.[161] These Organisations have acknowledged, and well documented environmental and social guidelines, and possess enough leverage over companies to promote implementation of CR,[162] especially in undertaking ESIA, detailing of plans and programmes on environmental protection, management measures, resettlement, conservation, public disclosure and consultation processes and so on. Mining is a specified category under these international institutions requiring ESIA, failing which assistance could be declined. Environmental factors have been integrated as part of normal work of the World Bank structure, and environmental decisions have real bearing on international decision-making and policy dialogue of its partners.[163] In fact the environmental-sustainability rules of the Bank including the guidance developed on Mining are now widely recognised as international standards.[164] IBP in Sierra Leone's mining is also enhanced through the World Bank's recent funding of a review of all aspects of the mining industry, with special emphasis on the legal frame work, mineral laws and regulations.[165] Also the Communities and Small-Scale Mining (CASM) secretariat located at the World Bank, provides technical assistance to PDA, to support various programmatic costs.[166]

[158]Cemmats Consultants (supra n.41)

[159]Sep. Op. of Judge Weeramantry (supra chapter 3, p. 108, n.161)

[160]Koenen-Grant J.,(supra n. 111); the homes constructed by the company are reported to be more 'superior' to the previous dwellings of the affected persons.

[161]See OPIC and MIGA (supra n. 122); note also, the 20 Million euros EU loan to SRL under the Sysmin agreement.

[162]This work has revealed for instance how much influence MIGA withholding of its guarantee from KHL had on domestic official implementation (see supra ns. 85 & 86)

[163]See generally Shihata I.F.I The World Bank in a Changing World, Martinus Nijhoff Publishers 1991, Boston, Massachusetts, 1991.

[164]Note that most of the guidelines, policies, operational directives, and other publications of the World Bank (including the IFC) have been adopted under Sysmin, and is directly applicable to the regulation of SRL (see supra chapter 5, p.151, n.45)

[165]See Wright L., "Sierra Leone" in Mining Annual Review, 2002, p.1.

[166]PDA is a civil society group concerned with implementing the CDF and reclamation of mined-out lands. (See PAC-NMJD (supra n. 45) p.11

Even so, procedures of these international institutions are not beyond scrutiny. The World Bank for instance, has been criticised for limiting transparency and inclusiveness in decision-making and for 'often [falling] short of [its] own best practice guidelines'.[167] In practice, 'the political importance of a deal [could mean] due diligence rushed, corners cut, sponsors hurried and effectiveness and impact compromised'.[168] These loan financing, guaranteeing and insuring organisations have in the past, also not done well on post project approval monitoring, though this has been recently addressed by the institution of the IFC's monitoring arm, the CAO.[169] This improved show of accountability could help to influence the practice of companies whose projects they finance or guarantee. But, it will be more sustainable if international lending institutions place equal emphasis on company violations of statutory prohibitions as they place on documentation of environmental and social impacts. By doing so, they will enhance company compliance with national legal requirements (including sectoral laws) as the basis upon which sustainable development can be truly localised, and CR effectively implemented, monitored and measured.

A final and important aspect of instilling IBP within CR relates to the extent of transnational enforcement of environmental law (both national and international) through national legal systems, especially by courts in developed countries where companies are incorporated or headquartered.[170] This is considered important considering the largely multinational and transnational nature of most of the companies holding various mineral rights in the country.[171] Two very important areas of emphasis have been advocated on this subject: First, that national law should be enabled to allow for transboundary access to justice and public interest litigation in environmental cases; and second, that national courts must be open to use by foreign plaintiffs seeking redress against multinational companies.[172] International law can play a useful role in facilitating these objectives by

[167]CAO Report (supra n. 84) pp. 25, 28 &32; see also "The EIR Central findings" at <http://www.bicusa.org/>

[168]Ibid

[169]CAO < http://worldbank.org>

[170]For examples of the series of efforts made in effecting transnational enforcement of environmental laws see supra chapter 2, p.67 n. 155. Implementation by enforcement through Sierra Leones Courts (where mining is occurring) is addressed subsequently under 'Legalisation'.

[171]See supra n. 121 above for examples

[172]See the Draft 'Hague Convention on Jurisdiction and Foreign Judgments in Civil and Commercial Matters' negotiated under Hague Conference on Private International Law (HCCH). It seeks to strengthen the global enforcement of private judgments and injunctive relief in commercial litigation. Nearly all civil and commercial litigation is included. Parties (currently 49 members) agree to enforce nearly all of the member country judgments and injunctive orders, subject only to public policy exception and treaty exclusions on certain anti-trust claims. There are also no restrictions on the types of national laws to be enforced, or requirements for harmonisation of substantive national laws (only rules regarding jurisdiction and enforcement of laws are to be harmonised). <http://www.cptech.org> see also ILC Report of the 2001 HCCH on the Draft Convention on Jurisdiction and Foreign Judgments in Civil and Commercial Matters<http://www.cptech.org>

laying down obligations for States to secure access to effective remedies under domestic administrative and civil law in transnational environmental disputes (as a matter of national law, not intra-state liability) at the international level.[173] More specifically, it has been recommended that such rules should cover the liability of private Actors *vis-à-vis* private claimants, as well as public authorities;[174] the latter's liability is to be applicable where they are not exercising public authority powers.[175]

Also, series of cases have been litigated in recent years that have developed the law with respect to access to justice for overseas victims of MNCs and multinational accountability, with some legal successes that especially deny MNCs the defence of *'forum non conveniens'*.[176] These legal developments have become the most important weapon for plaintiff attorneys challenging foreign investment by U.S. corporations.[177] Elsewhere these developments on international enforcements in national courts have helped enhance CR in social and environmental issues and already produced a powerful deterrent against such corporate abuses.[178]

---

[173]See ILA- CEEL: *Transnational Enforcement of Environmental* (second report) *Law* Berlin Conference (2004) available at http://www.ila-hq.org/; Amongst the principles identified as 'global' and relevant for such international environmental jurisdiction are principle of '*actor sequitur forum rei*', and the principle of liability of MNCs for the acts or defaults of their subsidiaries in environmental matters. The defendants' forum is defined as 'habitual residence' (for natural persons) or its statutory seat, incorporation, formation, central administration or principal place of business (legal persons). The report also suggests ways of affixing direct liability on the parent corporations and several means of recompense that States could make available to victims, especially of transboundary harm.

[174]Note that the Minerals Acts (and sectoral legislations) make public authorities the primary actors for ensuring compliance with environmental law obligations including recovery of cost for cleaning of pollution, reclamation or rehabilitation of land by companies, through civil and criminal enforcement proceedings 'before any court of competent Jurisdiction'. This leaves wide the choice of jurisdiction and could be relevant for international enforcements

[175]See ILA- CEEL (supra n.173). Three legal challenges have been noted as enabling MNCs to avoid responsibility for their overseas operations; these are: The principle that a claim brought in a multinational's home court can be halted on the grounds that the local 'host court' is a more appropriate venue (doctrine of *'forum non conveniens'*); The 'corporate veil' barrier which generally shields a parent company shareholder from the wrongdoing of its subsidiaries; and the obstacles to access to justice in local courts for people in developing countries. (see Leigh Day & Co. Solicitors, "Corporate Responsibility: the legal responsibility of multinational companies" at <http://www.leighday.co.uk/doc>
  The OECD Guidelines on MNEs, the 'ILO Tripartite Declaration of Principles concerning MNEs' and 'UN International framework for multinational accountability have all emphasised MNCs accountability for their activities especially human rights.

[176]See *Shalke Willem Lubbe et al v Cape PLC*, (Judgment of House of Lords delivered on 20 July 2000); this case was brought by more than 3,000 South African asbestos victims, for compensation against the parent company of a multinational in its home court in England. The House of Lords ruled allowing claims to proceed in England if a claimant could establish that there was no funding available to obtain legal and expert representation in his/her local courts. Also in *Wiwa v. Royal Dutch Petroleum Co., et al.*, 226 F.3d 88 (2nd Cir. 2000), Royal Dutch Shell, its London subsidiary, and the former head of its Nigerian subsidiary were sued in respect of human rights violation in the Ogoni region of Nigeria during the 1990s. In 1998, the district court found personal jurisdiction over the corporate defendants in New York, but dismissed the case on grounds of *forum non conveniens*. On appeal, the Second Circuit affirmed the trial court's ruling on personal jurisdiction, but reversed the trial court's ruling on forum non conveniens grounds. Note that this case was brought under the *1789 Alien Torts Claim Act*, a statute which enables the US courts to exercise extra-territorial jurisdiction over specified claims, including particular categories of human rights violation. (See generally Belgore Y., "Forum non conveniens in England and USA for litigation against oil multinationals" in *Oil gas and Energy Law Intelligence* Volume I, issue # 01 - January 2003; USA-Engage, "The Alien Tort Provision: Correcting the Abuse of an Early Federalist Statute" at http://www.usaengage.org/legislative/2003/; Meeran R, "Access to courts for corporate accountability: Recent Developments" at http://www.minesandcommunities.org/company)

[177]USA-Engage *ibid*

[178]See Meeran (supra n.168)

7:3 Legalisation: Consolidating Sustainable Development Within the National Legal system

The importance of 'legalisation' for implementation of sustainable development in mining cannot be over-emphasised. Previous chapters have exposed relevant principles of the concept in national legislation. But the process of consolidating sustainability objectives as a legal process goes beyond their representation in existing national legislation to include new enactments, importation of international environmental laws, judicial, adjudicatory or deliberative processes and enforcement of legal rules.[179] The goal in each case should be aimed at grounding environmental protection, and natural resources management objectives within the legal system. It is assumed that the outcome of any such legal effort would have implications for Sierra Leone's mining environments.

7:3:1 National Laws

(i) Review of Legislation

Most of the laws deemed relevant for ensuring sustainability in mining operations have already been discussed including the extent of their implementation.[180] As at time of writing, there has been no new environmental legislation or a substantial alteration of the environmental provisions in the mining, environmental and sectoral legislation. In short, the country has not sought to implement the objectives of the concept either through further legislation or modifications through by-laws. It is therefore important to reflect on the caution, that without the articulation and incorporation of sustainable development principles into legislative regimes, it is less likely that that all the policy commitments of government to sustainability will be implemented.[181]

In respect of the selected existing legislation, discussed earlier, while it is true that some measure of sustainability objectives are being implemented through their provisions, most of these laws are largely out-dated and too under-resourced to be implemented satisfactorily. Questions still remain over their sufficiency or efficiency in directing sustainability, especially in terms of clarity and consistency of provisions and the determination of

---

[179]This paradigm is derived from my submissions on the legal character of sustainable development; Note that 'deliberative' processes as a legal function may result in agreements, Voluntary Initiatives, or other regulatory measure. (See supra chapter 2, p.57).

[180]See supra chapters 5 & 6 respectively; note that emphasis will not be placed on sectoral legislations in this analysis.

[181]See Boer B. (supra chapter 2, p. 64, n.133).

responsibility and liability. A few examples are giving of more problematic areas hereunder.

First, some legal complications are engendered by the selective ratification of mining agreements, a situation that affects the legal efficiency of other acts. For instance, having secured a place within the body of laws of Sierra Leone, the SRA is expressed as valid notwithstanding 'anything contained in any law';[182] while provisions in the KPML guarantees KHL exclusion from any future regulatory changes occasioned by new legislation, administrative rule or practice within the national legal framework.[183] These expressions, legally enabled by the fact of ratification, do not only place the agreements in direct conflict with their parent legislation and the EPA, but also afford them reason to avoid current and future environmental dictates - municipal and international –not contemplated in them. There is therefore need to amend the respective agreements to recognise their relationship with the EPA and its authority on environmental issues, or alternatively tailor other environmentally oriented regulations and procedures outside the mining laws to overcome present and future limitations placed on their applicability to them.

On the issue of clarity, one could find difficulty ascertaining the correct legal situation of environmental obligations in existing laws due to inconsistencies, especially where laws regulating similar concerns create different obligations. For instance, the EPA prohibits the undertaken of all mining projects without first obtaining 'a valid licence', 'notwithstanding the provisions of any other law'.[184] The Minerals Act provides for the conduct of EIA only in respect of mining leases, but not for artisanal and small-scale mining.[185] The SRA does not provide for conduct of EIA, or even mention the term,[186] while the KPML provides for EIA, but limits the application of these to standards prevailing at signing of the agreement.[187] The petroleum act and its model agreement do not provide for EIA and are excluded from the jurisdiction and provisions of the EPA. The conflicts and inconsistency engendered by these provisions is glaring and unhelpful to any meaningful implementation of legal rules. As noted by Wälde, inefficient rules are likely to result in wastage and lower environmental quality than can be achieved.[188]

---

[182]SRA (supra chapter 5, p.134, n. 42 &43)

[183]KPML (supra chapter 5, p.141, ns.86 & 87)

[184]The EPA, (supra n.24) s. 14(1-2); see also first schedule.

[185]The Minerals Act, (supra chapter 5, p.127 n .6) s. 92.

[186]Note that the company's obligation in this respect is to submit final report on its environmental programs; (SRA (supra chapter 5, p.134, n.39)) clause 10(k)-(i)

[187]KPLM (supra chapter 5, p. 139, n.69) Clause 11:4:1 and schedule 8, para. 2, respectively

[188]Wälde (supra n. 111) p. 149

The wording of section 21 of the Minerals Act creates similar complication. By this provision, where the 'doing of any act' is regulated or prohibited by a 'written law', no provision in the Minerals Act should be construed as authorizing a mineral right-holder to do that act, otherwise than in accordance with the 'written law'. This provision may create scope for the imposition and enforcement of environmental objectives that are part of the body of written laws of the country. But it could equally be used as a shield to defend preference for lax or ambiguous environmental provisions in other laws, and may serve to exclude mining companies from liability under the predominantly unwritten common law and customary laws of the country.

In the light of the forgoing, there is urgent need to update these provisions, with a view of harmonising them, while also noting parallel provisions of instruments in other sectors. The effort will help clarify legal obligations, enhance proper co-ordination of laws, promote enforcement, effect legal coherency and consistency and afford a rational basis for according wider enforcements rights and access to justice,[189] and consequently, breed sustainable laws for sustainable development.

(ii) Enforcements

Other than instances of administrative procedures, the rating on enforcement of environmental provisions to regulate mining is negligible. One fundamental reason for this lies in the way some of the laws translate liability and responsibility. First, much of the legislation discussed so far are long on empowering the responsible authorities to institute legal proceedings for breaches, but are not sufficiently specific on environmental protection,[190] and are short on imputing responsibility for effective management of particular resources or environmental degradation. Under the circumstances therefore, it becomes difficult to achieve best environmental results through enforcement of the legislation.

Similarly, none of the selected legislations try to induce environmentally sound behaviour through modern innovative means like economic incentives or environmental agreements, which could aid progressive

---

[189]Stallworthy M., "Environmental Liability and Statutory Authority" in *JEL* Vol. 15/ 1, 2003, p.4

[190]Note that the legislations are generally hinged either on conditions, or seek to achieve the environmental objectives by controlling, and restricting certain activities.

enforcement of sustainability objectives and address the gaps in prescriptive rules.[191] Recent practice however, shows the GOSL concluding environmental agreements for environmental management of one of its major forests. This could have enormous implications for sustainable utilisation of the related natural resource in mining.[192] Otherwise, heavy reliance is still being placed on penal sanctions (fines and/or imprisonment), which are either inadequate for any given damage resulting from breach, or too minimal to serve as effective deterrents for offenders or violators, especially those in the mining business who are more likely to have the ability to pay.

Enforcement is also deterred by conflicting provisions in respect of liability, especially in relation to quantum of fines for pollution. Implementation by enforcement is further daunted by legal and administrative procedural complications, and the lack of standards by which breach can be defined.[193] The dominance of these shortcomings has a direct relationship with the persistent non-compliance of companies and officials alike with fulfilling or enforcing environmental obligations and responsibilities, and has engendered implementation failures at various levels.[194] It might aid implementation efforts if, as suggested by Brown-Weiss, a mechanism is elaborated for accountability for relevant actors.[195]

A final difficulty in enforcement relates to the broad title of the environmental legislation, as 'EPA', which assumes it as an all embracing legislation for environmental protection, but affording less protection to individuals that interact with the environment.[196] The representation seems dubious, since the legislation does not cover every environmental aspect.[197] It specifically fails to afford comprehensive or effective protective legal redress machinery for individuals and their environment. Individuals or groups do not acquire enforcement rights under it either to challenge

---

[191]'Environmental Agreement' has been described as an agreement between national, provincial and/or local authorities and a group of companies regarding the reduction of adverse environmental consequences from production processes, energy use or products and which could involve participation of NGOs and other third parties. (For detailed discourse on categories of Environmental Agreements, see Bailey P.M.; "The Creation and Enforcements of Environmental Agreements" in *European Environmental Law Review* Vol. 8/6, June 1999; 171)

[192]CSSL, in collaboration with the Royal Society for the Protection of Birds (RSPB has embarked on a three-year pilot project to explore the feasibility of managing 75,000 hectares of the Gola forests for conservation, in cooperation with local communities and government. If the pilot project is successful, the partners will embark on a scheme to conserve these forests forever. This will include *inter alia* monitoring and protecting the forest and its special wildlife and restoring degraded forests; (see CSSL, (supra n.106)

[193]Note that sustainability could best be achieved at the national level, through clear and effective laws coupled with uncomplicated procedures for enforcements; (see MMSD (supra n. 131) executive summary)

[194]Note Wolfrum's observations on the vicious circle between, implementation, enforcement and compliance; (Wolfrum R., (supra chapter 2, p.68, ns.156 &157))

[195] Brown Weiss (supra chapter 2, p.68. n.161)

[196]Note that the formal definition of the 'environment' in the EPA recognises this interrelationships; (see EPA (supra n. 24) interpretations)

[197]Generally, the act is more administrative and institutional with a main objective to provide for coordination of activities likely to have an impact on the environment

environmental decisions, mining agreements or seek redress by it for environmental protection.[198]

(iii) Judicial Processes

Perhaps the area most impacted by this 'blocking of access to justice' consequent upon the forgoing enforcement difficulties is the role of the judiciary. They have been affirmed as crucial partners for promoting compliance with the implementation and enforcement of international and national environmental law;[199] and more particularly in the balancing of environmental and developmental considerations.[200] Almost all the relevant laws analysed in this work provide for some form of judicial redress in case of breach of one form or the other, with the prescribed medication of fine or imprisonment.[201] These provisions unequivocally create a role for the country's judiciary in environmental decision-making.

But before one could determine the effectiveness of this role it is important to clarify the extent of judicial responsibility in these matters. The judiciary is generally responsible 'to mould emerging principles of law with a view to giving these a sense of coherence and direction, while always acting within the frame work of legislation and law...'[202] And on the specific issue of environmental obligations, they are expected to achieve the principles of sustainable development, 'even with limited black-letter legal weapons', to provide a means for enforcing basic environmental standards or to provide the substantive basis for protection of the environment.[203] The judiciary also has a role in promoting CR, and more importantly to invoke the extraordinary jurisdiction of the Supreme Court in environmental matters.[204] However the specific role of the judiciary in a particular case may either be

[198]Note that provision is made under the Constitution for any person to challenge legal dictates or administrative decisions or actions in the Supreme Court, when they are deemed inconsistent with or in contravention of provisions of the constitution. So individuals could use it to question mining in protected areas (as a public interest good for conservation of natural resources).The Court may make a declaration in respect thereof including directions and orders to give effect to it; (The Constitution (supra n.26) s.127 (1)-(4)).

[199]"The Johannesburg Principles on the Role of Law and sustainable development" adopted at the Global Judges symposium, Johannesburg, South Africa, 18-20 august 2002, p.1 (available at <www.unep.org/dpdl/symposium>

[200]"Regional Symposium on the Role of the Judiciary in Promoting the Rule of Law in the Area of Sustainable Development" Convened by UNEP in Partnership with South Asia Co-operative Environmental Programme (SACEP)) Colombo Sri-Lanka 4-6 July 1997 (UNEP/SACEP Symposium). See also, Kurukulasuriya L., "Role of Judiciary in Promoting Sustainable Development" in EPL, 28/1 (1998), p. 27

[201]In all cases other than in the public health act, it is the responsible authority who can bring such action; Note also that only the respective mining agreements lack provisions for judicial redress in any case of breach.

[202]Kurukulasuriya (supra n.200) p.28 Note that this should be accomplished without trespassing on the legislative and executive branches of government'

[203]Carnwath L.J (supra chapter 2, p.66, n.151) p.317-318; they can accomplish this using 'judicial ingenuity' for example in adapting constitutional guarantees, like 'the right to life'.

[204]Kurukulasuriya, (supra n.202)

supervisory, determined by the regulatory competence of individual countries; or by using ingenious articulations to fill in 'the gap', where administrative systems are relatively underdeveloped.[205]

Judged from these perspectives, Sierra Leone's judiciary has little to boast of in enforcing environmental principles through relevant legislation, whether against mining companies or responsible officials; or in securing the publics' interest through the 'ingenious gap-filling' techniques; or in aid of instilling a 'sense of coherence and direction' in the laws.[206] But while the negligible intervention of could generally be blamed on other enforcement problems, the judiciary cannot escape criticism for not having invoked its extraordinary jurisdiction in furtherance of environmental objectives, such as invoking sustainability principles in tortuous actions. Finally it is however important to stress that, the judiciary's competence, capacity or willingness to achieve the above objectives could be enhanced by further interests or professional development in environmental and development issues of judges and barristers, law enforcement and administrative officials and the public. Even more crucial, is the need to remove cost of court proceedings as an obstacle, create a right in public interest litigations, and enhance state machinery for local inquiry or the creation of new environmental tribunals.[207]

---

[205]Carnwath (supra n.203); More specifically, see supra chapter 3, p.113, ns.187-189. Note that the Indian Judiciary represents an expressive example for implementing principles of sustainable development in regulation of development activities. For instance, in *Rural Litigation and Entitlement Kendra v. State of U.P.*, (Dehradun quarries case) (1985) 2 SCC 431, it stopped mining operations, noting that any 'hardship' caused to the developers is 'a price that has to be paid for protecting and safe-guarding the right of the people to live in healthy environment...'(see also *M.C. Mehta v. Union of India*, (Stone Crushers Case) WP 4677/1985; *M.C. Mehta v. Union of India*, (Doon Valley case) WP 4677/1985; *M.C. Mehta v. Union of India*, (Taj Trapezium Case) (1997) 2 SCC 353; *MC Mehta v. Kamal Nath* (1987) SCC p.482); and in *Narmada Bachao Andolan v. Union of India* (2000) 10 SCC 664, it allowed construction of a dam, subject to rehabilitation, aforestation and compensation conditions.

In *Vellore Citizens Welfare Forum vs. Union of India*, WP 914/1991 (1996.08.28) (Tamil Nadu Tanneries case) (1996) 5 SCC 647, it accepted the "Precautionary" and "Polluter-pays" principles as part of the environmental law of India, interpreting the "Polluter Pays Principle" to mean the absolute liability for cost to compensate victims of pollution and for reversing damage to ecology; (see also *M.C Mehta v. Kamal Nath* (2000) 6 SCC 213). In applying the precautionary principle, in *A.P. Pollution Control Board v. Prof. M.V Nayudu*, (1999), 2 SCC 718, it placed the burden of proof on those 'attempting to alter the status quo', and is to be discharged by showing the absence of a 'reasonable ecological or medical concern', failing which, the presumption should operate in favour of environmental protection.

In *State of Himachal Pradesh v. Ganesh Wood Products*, (1995) 6 SCC 363, the court invalidated forest based industry, recognising the principle of intergenerational equity as being central to conservation of forests; (see also *ICELA v. Union of India*, (CRZ Notification Case) (1996) 5 SCC 281; *M.C Mehta v. Kamal Nath* (1997) 1 SCC 388).

[206]Enforcements under Common law tortuous principles of private nuisance and *Rylands v Fletcher* (1868) LR 3 HL 330 is still the approach. Principles set in old English cases like *Bliss v Hall* (1838) 4 Bing NC 183; *Sturges v Bridgman* (1879) 11 Ch D 852; *Read v Lyons & Co. Ltd.* [1945] KB 216 at p.236.), *St Helen's Smelting Company V.Tipping (1865) 11 H.L.C 642*, have been adopted in Sierra Leone cases (see *Mason v Pearce* (1964-1966) ALR SL.438). These principles entail some general obligations that could afford protection of competing interests in resource utilisation. For textual exposition on the subject, see: -Bell & Macgillavray: *Environmental Law* 5th Edition, chapter 10; Cooke & Oughton: *Common Law of Obligations*, 3rd Edn. 2000 chapter 29; see also articles by- Gearty C*., "The Place of Private Nuisance in Modern Law of Torts", (1989) 48 *Cambridge Law Journal*, pp.214-242; Steele J., "Private Law and the Environment: Nuisance in context" (1995) 15 *Legal Studies* pp.236-259; and Rodgers C.P. "Liability for the Release of GMOs in the Environment- Exploring the Boundaries of Nuisance", *C.L.J* Vol. 62 (Part 2) July 2003, pp. 371.

[207]See Carnwath (supra n.203) p.318; Lord Woolf, in "Are the Judiciary Environmentally Myopic?" in *JEL* 1992 Vol.4, No.1, p.1, advocates for 'a multi- faceted, multi-skilled body which would combine the services provided by existing Courts, Tribunals and Inspectors in the environmental

(iv) Adjudicatory or Deliberative Processes

Considering the intricate and complex issues often surrounding environmental concerns and the procedural technicalities of judicial enforcement, adjudicative and deliberative processes are deemed very important (as quasi legal efforts) for implementing principles of sustainable development.[208] But other than the mining agreements, which provide for arbitration (in case of breach of environmental obligations), and negotiations (in respect of compensation), the legislation are more command and control based. However, the value of adjudicatory and deliberative mechanisms is gradually being appreciated especially in resolving environmental and social disputes resulting from mining operations, especially those relating to resettlement, transparency and benefits-sharing with the local communities. While there are instances of government intervention seeking dialogue with local communities, NGOs and civil society groups have been very successful in implementing this aspect of sustainability. They even secured one environmental agreement with a mining company in one case on behalf of local people displaced by mining operations,[209] while in another case commitments were secured to return part of the mining proceeds to the communities.[210] The values of such efforts do not only speak for immediate redress to environment concerns, but also of new and further obligations by companies with some legal relevance. Above all, it affords the local communities actual participation in the decision-making process.

7:3:2 International Laws

It is recognised that the first method for implementing sustainability within domestic legal systems is by introducing or importing international laws that promote sustainable development, make them effective through municipal initiatives of ratification and or implementation.[211] The Biodiversity and Wetlands Conventions are among such international laws, which are considered directly relevant to mining. Sierra Leone is a party to both environmental conventions and has imported them by ratification.[212] However, they have not been legally planted within the legal system by the required implementing legislation, and therefore are not directly

---

[208]See supra chapter 2, p.57

[209]See supra n. 109

[210]See supra n. 108

[211]See Agenda 21 and ILA Report of the 66th Conference (supra chapter 2, p.64, ns. 136 &137)

[212]Both conventions respectively ratified in 1994

applicable.[213] But this fact alone does not completely exclude or limit the application of these conventions to contribute to sustainable mining in Sierra Leone. In my view, several reasons support their applicability. Firstly, most of the relevant sustainability principles of these conventions are already incorporated into the NEP, the NEAP and government policies.[214] Second, it will be recalled that the mining agreements directly invoke the 'applicable' international law and standards to govern them. This fact buttressed by their ratification, opens the possibility of, imputing or interpreting the conventions standards into environmental obligations under the relevant agreements, especially where the provisions are clear about their objectives. Further, as will be observed subsequently, Convention objectives are being implemented through programmes and projects and national committees have been established to support these efforts.[215] These facts, (less legislation) justify the applicability of the biodiversity and Wetlands conventions in Sierra Leone to regulate mining. Even more compelling is the fact that the legal character of sustainable development canvassed in this study, does not only rest on creating obligations through command and control instruments that can bind people's actions, but also includes result-orientated efforts and initiatives in environmental protection. To this end, it is important to briefly analyse these conventions to prove the relevance of their objectives to mining laws in sierra Leone and to reveal their application, in spite of the lack of implementing legislation.

(i) The Convention on Biological Diversity[216]

CBD aims at the conservation of biological diversity, the sustainable use of its components and the fair and equitable sharing of the benefits arising from the utilisation of genetic resources.[217] This underlying principle make CBD applicable to all processes and activities that are likely to have significant

---

[213]The Constitution (supra n. 26) s.40; entrenches a dualistic legal system, where treaty obligations only acquire domestic enforceability by virtue of some specific legislative act.

[214]See supra chapter 2 p.67 on implementation by 'localisation'

[215]Note the suggestion that conventions can be implemented through administrative rules (or actions) adopted under rulemaking authority originally granted for quite different purposes. (See Morrison Fred L., "The Relationship of International, Regional, And National Environmental Law" in *International, Regional and National Environmental Law*, Morrison & Wolfrum (eds) 2000 Kluwer International, Hague/London/Boston 2000, p. 131. CBD entails principles upon which states can act without waiting for additional international instruments to protect biodiversity; (see Koester Veit., "The Five Global Biodiversity-Related Conventions: A Stocktaking", in Reciel 11 (1), 2002, p.96).

[216]"Convention on Biological Diversity" UN Doc. UNEP/Bio.Div/N7-INC.5/4; also in 31 *ILM* 818 (1992) (hereinafter CBD); the analyses will not cover aspects of the CBD relating to genetic resources or the Biosafety Protocol, though the study appreciates their relevance *inter alia* for, trade, technology transfer and human health.

[217]*Ibid.* Article 2 of the convention defines 'biological diversity as: 'the variability among living organisms from all sources including, *inter alia* terrestrial, marine and other aquatic ecosystems and the ecological complexes of which they are part; this includes diversity within species, between species and of ecosystems'.

impacts on the conservation of biodiversity and thus, aims to avoid or regulate such impacts.[218] Mining does happen to be one such activity, that impacts on biodiversity and which can be regulated by implementation of the Convention, especially through its conservation-biased provisions,[219] and emphasis on the sustainable utilisation and 'non-compatible use' of components of biodiversity.[220] The principle of 'sustainable use' is transformed under the CBD into a legally binding obligation, and acquires a new purpose that 'allows a variety of flexible approaches, (such as monitoring of use and flexible management strategies) so long as their goal is achieved'.[221] There is thus little doubt that the conservation and sustainable utilisation objectives of the CBD could direct sustainable mining, and the convention seeks to guide states (through obligations) on how to achieve this outcome.

(a) Analyses of Relevant Convention Obligations and Implementation

Under the CBD, states must '...develop national strategies, plans or programmes for the conservation and sustainable use of biological diversity or adapt for this purpose existing strategies, plan or programmes...' They must further 'integrate the conservation and sustainable use of biological diversity into relevant sectoral or cross-sectoral plans, programmes and policies'.[222] In fulfillment of this requirement, Sierra Leone has in place a National Biodiversity Plan (NBP).[223] However, within certain limits, the NBP could not be said to represent the comprehensive biodiversity strategy called for under the convention.[224] Nonetheless, giving that most of the recommendations in the Plan reflect the tenants of the CBD, and the convention itself accepts as an alternative, the adaptation of existing plans for this purpose, the structure of the NBP could serve as useful basis for

[218]Wolfrum R. "The Protection and Management Of Biological Diversity" in *International, Regional and National Environmental Law*, Morrison & Wolfrum (Eds.) 2000 Kluwer International, Hague/London/Boston 2000, p.357

[219]For emphasis on the CBD conservation biases, including use economic incentives to achieve conservation goals, see: - Herkenrath P., (supra n.68) p.29; Jacquemont & Caparros "The Convention Of Biological Diversity and the Climate Change Convention 10 Years After Rio: Towards a Synergy of the Two Systems", in *Reciel* Vol.11 (2), 2002, p. 169; McGraw D., "The CBD: Key Characteristics and Implications for Implementation" in *Reciel* Vol.11 No.1 2002 p. 23.

Wolfrum *(ibid)* p.371; and Boyle A., "The Convention on Biological Diversity" in *The Environment After Rio: International Law and Economics*, (1994), Campiglio et.al (Eds.), London/Dordrecht: Graham and Trotman/Martinus Nijhoff, p.115

[220]Birnie and Boyle, *International Law and the Environment*, 2nd edition, Oxford, 2002, p. 576

[221]*Ibid*

[222]The CBD, supra n. 216) Articles 6(a) &(b) respectively

[223]NEAP/SL (supra n.9) pp 56-61; generally, the NBP includes a biodiversity- specific country study and includes references to existing biological resources and efforts made at their conservation.

[224]*Ibid* The NBP itself recommends the formulation of a National Biodiversity Strategy and Action Plan which would develop the national policy, program, and strategy for the conservation and sustainable use of biological diversity to meet the objectives of the Convention (pp. 56-61)

efforts to regulate mining through its implementation.[225] Also, most of the plans and programmes recommended in the NBP have already been identified in sectoral policies.[226]

The next obligation goes beyond statements of policies and plans, to require physical identification of components of biological diversities important for conservation. Categories of activities that are likely to have significant adverse impacts on the conservation and sustainable use of biodiversity must also be identified and the effects monitored; and some form of data on the components must be maintained.[227] In this regard, the NBP clearly identifies various components of biodiversity in the country, ranging from ecosystem and habitats,[228] to plant, animal and micro-organism species populations.[229] Also, 'mining' is effectively identified amongst categories of activities that threaten or impact the conservation and sustainable use objectives, because of the substantial deforestation it causes.[230] As one author puts it, this 'stocktaking' of biological diversity and the existing effort for its conservation, already marks a major part of the implementation of the convention.[231]

Similarly, Article 8 of the CBD sets several proactive obligations that are necessary to realize the conservation objectives of the convention. The pertinent ones relate to the establishment of protected areas for conservation purposes; regulation and management of biological resources within and outside such areas; promotion of environmentally sound and sustainable development in areas adjacent to protected areas; protection of ecosystem and natural habitats; rehabilitation and restoration of degraded ecosystems and to maintain legislation or regulatory provisions for protection of threatened species.[232] These provisions represent the more precautionary approach canvassed at Rio. Sierra Leone has made some effort in this area to the extent that there has been notified or proposed several protected and

---

[225] *Ibid* The specific programmes for action recommended in the NBP will include *inter alia*, promotion of environmentally sound and sustainable development of biosphere reserves; establishment of in-situ conservation of habitats of threatened and endangered species and of plants *and* wildlife for improved management; promote the rehabilitation and restoration of damaged ecosystems; the establishment of ex-situ sites and Gene Banks; Wildlife inventories and National Parks.

[226] For Programme related initiatives see Prof. Cole N.H.A., (supra n.102)

[227] The CBD, (supra n. 216) article 7(a)-(d)

[228] Such as forests, woodlands, savannah and grassland; Other ecosystems proposed are Mangrove (provides habitat to diversity of fauna) and lake ecosystems (Lakes Makpe, Magbesi identified as waterfowl and waders habitats respectively (see CSSL, 1993 supra n.63) See generally, PRSP Environmental Report (supra n. 33) pp.39-47

[229] NEAP/SL (supra n.9) p.56; more than 2,000 plant species have been identified in the Gola Forests and at least 74 endemic plant species nationwide. Other reports identified 761 species of mammals and birds (Citing the World Conservation Monitoring Centre 1992 and the IUCN 1992).

[230] Ibid p.58 The NBP also describes the biological losses that result, from the socio-economic impacts on biodiversity.

[231] Herkenrath P., (supra n.68), p. 31

[232] The CBD (supra n.216) article 8(a), (c), (e)(f)&(k)

conservation areas.[233] Also, provision is made under the WCA and the Forestry act,[234] for the regulation and management of these resources, even including listed categories of protected animals and threatened species.[235] Efforts are also being made to rehabilitate degraded mined out lands.[236]

However, most protected areas are not sufficiently managed and land use that is contrary to the conservation objectives of the convention can often take place, through licences and permit systems.[237] In other respects, so called Protected Areas and forests (including nature reserves) exists as what has been essentially described as 'paper-parks',[238] symbolising their existence mainly on paper, but non-functional in practice. This problem is not unconnected with the fact that protected area planning is not integrated within a wider land use planning scheme, which could enhance such efforts. Finally, parties also have the obligation to prepare environmental assessments of proposed projects which are likely to have significant adverse effects on biological diversity, with a view to avoiding or minimising these impacts; including consideration of environmental consequences of government sponsored policies and programmes.[239] This obligation is principally regulated under the EIA mechanism set up in the EPA.[240]

Thus far, the analysis has revealed the main objectives of the CBD as generally compatible with national trends for conservation and resources management and therefore its legal validity for regulating mining, including its implementing capacity cannot be denied. Perhaps its most far-reaching obligation especially in relation to mining is that requiring states to rehabilitate and restore degraded ecosystems. However, the CBD has been criticized for employing qualifications such as 'as far as possible and as appropriate' and 'in accordance with particular conditions and capabilities', as weakening of the obligations it seeks to create. But while many will derive from this qualification an indication of economic capability,[241] in my view,

---

[233]PRSP Environmental Report (supra n.34) pp.39-47 Examples include National Parks- Outamba-Kilimi, Loma Mountain, Lakes Sonfon, Makpe and Magbesi; SNR- Kuru, Kangari &Tingi Hills, Port Loko and Bo research reserves, Kagboro creek etc; nature reserves- Wemago (Gola East) and Mogbai (Gola North); and Games Reserves - Tiwai Island and 'Mamunta-Mayosso.

[234]See generally supra Chapter 6.

[235]The WCA (supra chapter 6, p.162, n. 61) particularly s. 29(1) & (2) including the second and third schedules. For a more updated version of Biodiversity and Protected Areas in Sierra Leone see Earth trends: Country Profile at < http://earthtrends.wri.org/ >

[236]See supra ns. 101ff.

[237]See Garnett (supra n. 51)

[238]Herkenrath P., (supra n.68) p. 33

[239]The CBD (supra n.216) article 14

[240]See generally discourse on the EIA Procedure (supra chapter 6, pp. 160-162; more particularly, note the factors to be addressed in the Environmental Statement (EPA (supra n. 24) third schedule.

[241]See Wolfrum R., (supra n.218) p. 359

the very basis of the qualifications makes possible the implementation of the conventions objectives within already existing policies plans, regulatory controls and legislations. It makes for improved perspective on how to secure the rest of nature from mining in the interest of generations, canvasses attention to the mismanagement of natural resources, and defines a general direction for informing processes that will conserve biological diversity.[242]

(ii) The Ramsar Convention[243]

Like the CBD, which recognises the intrinsic value of nature as the basis for conservation, Ramsar recognises 'the fundamental ecological functions of wetlands as regulators of water regimes and as habitats supporting a characteristic flora and fauna, especially waterfowl'.[244] It therefore 'seeks to stem the progressive encroachment on, and loss of wetlands' through activities like mining.[245] Ramsar thus sets some main obligations on states as the mechanisms by which this protection could be achieved.[246]

First, States must designate at least one wetland to be included in the list of 'wetlands of international importance', which once listed, must be preserved and protected.[247] This obligation is ensured by the fact that the designation is made a condition for membership into the convention. Accordingly, Ramsar came into force for Sierra Leone on 13th of April 2000, by the designation and listing of one Wetland site (of international importance) with a surface area of 295,000 hectares.[248] But the protection mechanism envisaged under Ramsar goes beyond such designation and listing.

Parties must formulate and implement their planning so as to promote the conservation of wetlands included in the list, and as far as possible, the 'wise

[242]See McGraw D., (supra n.219) p.18 (citing Chayes & Chayes)

[243]The Convention on Wetlands of International Importance Especially as Waterfowl Habitat (Ramsar), 2nd February, 1971, reprinted in 11 ILM 1972, 963; (reprinted with amendments in *Sourcebook on Environmental Law* (2nd edition), (Sunkin et.al. eds), 2002, Cavendish, London/Sydney. pp 625-9

[244]*Ibid.* Preamble.

[245]*Ibid* Note that alluvial diamond and gold mining in Sierra Leone depends on wetlands like the Sewa and Male River basins while Rutile mining needs at least an artificial wetland to be effective. (See Alieu E.K., (Director of Forests) "Economic Importance of wetlands", MAFFS, Sierra Leone at http://www.ramsar.org/mtg_sierraleone). For threats to wetlands from mining (see Siaffa D.D (CSSL) "Major Threats to the Wetlands of Sierra Leone and How Their Impact Could be Contained"; also at http://www.ramsar.org/mtg_sierraleone .

[246]For an overview on Ramsar see Guruswamy & Hendricks International *Environmental Law In a Nutshell*, West Publishing, 1997, p.118ff; and Alejandro Iza "Developments Under the Ramsar Convention: Allocation of Water for River and Wetland Ecosystems in Environmental Policy and Law", *Reciel* Vol.13, (1) 2004. p.40-ff

[247]Ramsar (supra n. 243) article 2(4); the article also states the criteria for listing and de-listing of wetlands. De-listing or restricting a site specification must be compensated with another site of the same or similar potential (article 4(2)).

[248]"The Annotated Ramsar List of wetlands of International Importance: Sierra Leone" <http://www.ramsar.org/ profiles_sierraleone.htm> The designated site "Sierra Leone River Estuary"; is an Estuary near Freetown Peninsula, dominated by mangrove systems, with lowland coastal plains to the north. (Visit site for detailed specifications).

use' of unlisted wetlands within their territories.[249] This scope of protection that is generally afforded to other unlisted wetlands is very vital for controlling mining activities. States must protect them (including listed ones) through the concept of conservation and 'sustainable use of wetlands ...in a way that is compatible with maintaining the natural properties of the ecosystem'.[250] Also, laws, practices and institutions, must be reviewed or amended to ensure that the wise use guidelines are applied.[251] Thus, under these provisions conservation acquires different implications that could pose strong challenges to mineral resource developments, especially because conservation also require the preservation of their habitats, of related species as well as the non-living elements on which they depend.[252]

But in spite of the impressive number of wetlands in Sierra Leone,[253] wetlands are still not under any legal national protection status;[254] and a number of projects (including mining) are reportedly being implemented in or within close proximity of various wetlands, which tends to upset or disturb the balance of that ecosystem.[255] Also, rehabilitation fees paid by mining companies to government are reportedly not easily accessible for rehabilitation purposes.[256]

A National Wetlands Committee has also been formed since 2001, with the view of formulating national wetland policies and possibly, to address all problems and activities related to wetlands within a national context.[257] If the principles of the convention are to be effectively applied to control mining, much needs to be done in the area of planned strategies, data collection, surveys, monitoring of the wetlands and their resources and involving the local communities in implementation of any such conservation agenda.

However, Ramsar has been strongly criticised for its failure to provide for a standard regulatory regime for provision of water for the aquatic

---

[249]Ramsar (supra n.243) article 4

[250]*Ibid.* Article 3(1) and article 6(3) Note that the above quote is a redefinition of the concept of 'wise use' in Art.3. (see also Recommendation 3.3, on 'wise use of wetlands; Third meeting of the COP(Regina 27 May -5 June 1987 at <http://www.ramsar.org/key_rec_3.3.htm>

[251]See Resolution VII.7 Guidelines for Reviewing Laws and Institutions to Promote the Conservation and Wise Use of wetlands, seventh meeting of the COP (San Jose10-18 may, 1999) at < http://www.ramsar.org/key_res_vii.07e.htm >

[252]Birnie & Boyle (supra n.220) p.465; They suggest that Ramsar is the first wildlife convention to be concerned solely with the protection of habitat.

[253]Alieu E.K., (supra n.245)

[254]Siaffa D.D (supra n.245)

[255]Conteh A.F (Assistant Director of Forests), "Wetlands and National Development: The Pros and Cons of Development Projects in Third world Countries", MAFFS, Freetown.

[256]D.D Siaffa (supra n. 245)

[257]Fofanah A.S., (supra n.102)

ecosystems.[258] This observation has far-reaching implications for its implementation in the regulation of mining activities. Accordingly, there is need for provisions that ensure the management of water resources at river basin level; and such provisions to clarifying the status of basic human right to water and to establish quantitative and qualitative objectives of aquatic ecosystems.[259] Notwithstanding its shortcomings, Ramsar has been credited for representing 'a rather modern approach to the solution of environmental problems, including both nature conservation and preservation of the cultural environment'.[260]

7:4 Institutionalisation: Strengthening Institutional Structures to Adapt Sustainability Goals

7:4:1 The Environmental Department

States are required to develop, re-organise and integrate their environment and economic institutions as the bottom line for actual implementation of all its elements and principles.[261] GOSL has effected such institutional reorganisation by creating the ED as the formal coordinating body for national and international environmental matters at the national level. The ED is also the administrative machinery that would oversee environmental aspects of development activities like mining.[262] In general, the ED is responsible for formulation of national environmental policies, goals, strategies and regulations, co-ordinate and monitors national environmental policies; and co-operate with other ministries and organizations on all matters relating to environmental protection and management.[263] Also, the minister of MLHCPE has specific responsibility to implement international environmental conventions and protocols acceded to by Sierra Leone.[264]

The NEPB has responsibility to adopt standards, guidelines and regulations, and to promote the integration of environmental considerations in all aspects of social and economic planning.[265] It also has a duty to investigate any activity, occurrence or transaction that it considers likely to have or result in

---

[258] Alejandro (supra n.246) p.46; Note that some of the threats causing rapid deterioration of wetlands includes degradation of watershed, soil erosion, siltation, diversion of water supplies and pollution;(see Sands P. *Principles of International Environmental Law*, 1995 Vol. 1, Manchester University Press, p. 404

[259] Alejandro, *Ibid*.

[260] Koester Veit (supra n.215) p.96

[261] WCED (supra n.5) p.310

[262] EPA (supra n. 24) s. 11 & 12 (1); The ED is housed within the, MLHCPE

[263] *Ibid*. s. 12(a)-(m))

[264] *Ibid*. s. 9(1) (a)-(f) and 9(2)

[265] *Ibid*. s. 2; the NEB is composed of a Director and twelve other members.

harmful consequences to the environment and to advice on measures necessary to prevent or minimise such consequences.[266] In terms of policy planning, the ED is supervised by the NEB, the NEC[267] and the States Lands Committee.[268] The institutional framework also contemplates relationship with MoM (and other sectors), by maintaining their environmental management functions and activities, and provides for coordination and monitoring of such activities and the setting of standards to manage mining impacts.

From a general perspective, efforts are being made to implement some of the forgoing institutional functions. For example, where EIA is deemed necessary, and the MoM forwards applications to the ED, the process does, to a certain extent take a co-ordinated and integrated approach involving a number of institutional stakeholders, through notification.[269] Also, the DoE has regular representation on Boards and meetings of various sectors, including MoM.[270] But in other respects, there is 'a virtual disconnect' between the ED and stakeholders of other environmental sectors.[271]

7:4:2 Institutional Weaknesses

The institutional framework of the ED, including implementation of its specified functions has been challenged at several levels. Paramount amongst the criticisms is its structural capacity to effectively regulate development activities including mining. Firstly the location of the ED within the MLHCPE has considerable impact on its authority and efficiency in the implementation of its functions.[272] Apart from concerns over the 'lethargy' and 'inertia' of government bureaucracy, the constitution of the ED as an arm of the MLHCPE, (which itself undertakes development activities like housing), presents less incentive for other development originating sectors as Mines to submit to its authority for coordinating and monitoring

---

[266]*Ibid.* s.4(e) ,(f) and 4(d)

[267]The NEC is also a policy making body which advises the Head of State on major environmental issues, with membership including ministers of Lands, Housing and the environment (chairman), Mineral Resources, Forestry, Tourism, Energy and Power, Health, Foreign Affairs, Justice, Marine Resources and the Inspector General of police.

[268]Note also a Technical sub-committees (of Departmental heads including mines) and an Environmental Task Force (of University scientist), has been set up to ensure inter-ministerial and inter-sectoral coordination of economic activities, and to study specific occurrences of major environmental problems respectively (see *The NEAP/SL* (supra n. 9) p. 40)

[269]Sellu A. (supra n. 40)

[270]For example the chairman of the NEB has a seat on the MAB

[271]PRSP Environmental Report (supra n. 34) p.2)

[272]Note that the Permanent Secretary is the administrative head of all divisions in the MLHCPE, including the ED and supervises all their activities and logistics.

their activities.[273] This may be responsible for what has been characterised as laxity on the part of sectors in complying with environmental requirements, vague linkages with other ministries and lack of commitments to agreements on the distribution of roles.[274]

There is thus urgent need for a reorientation of the ED as an independent and autonomous agency preferably a private one.[275] Such an agency must not be subject to political control, and must be imbibed with more power and authority to call to question all environmentally adverse development activities, including government projects.[276] It must also have responsibility to establish policy, laws and standards, while allowing sectors to undertake management and enforcement. Above all there must be reserved in such agency, a right to compel relevant sectors to performance.[277]

Other instances of institutional weakness in control of mining activities exist in the areas of the precautionary objectives, such as environmental auditing, co-ordination, co-operation, information, reporting and monitoring. Under the institutional arrangements these are overlapping functions of the ED shared between the Minister and the NEB, and in some respects with other sectors. This division of responsibilities tends to be complex, especially for administration and enforcement purposes and creates scope for inaction and blame shifting, at the expense of the environment. In fact, co-operation with 'traditional departments,'[278] is reported to be only 'on face value', with no real cooperation in terms of exchange of information or consultation. Cognisance is usually, taken of the ED monitoring authority only when environmental issues are raised by international organisations.[279] It is therefore imperative to clearly identify and define the linkages and relationships between various regimes that should exercise regulatory controls and effect closer harmonisation between them for implementation efficiency.[280]

Perhaps the most fundamental institutional weakness relates to the inability or failure to formulate or adopt standards (or by-laws) for environmental

---

[273]PRSP Environmental Report (supra n. 34) p.27

[274]Ibid.

[275]The PRSP Environmental Report recommends the creation of an autonomous agency (by parliamentary act), staffed by a multidisciplinary team of experts, each with a directorate, and located under the office of the Vice President. It however omits any reference to legal expertise among its stated category of 'multidisciplinary team of experts' (Ibid. pp. 99 -102).

[276]Under present legislation, the capacity of the NEB is inherently advisory, with powers to make only recommendations to the Minister in almost all matters.

[277]For example, a national environmental agency could be established under a framework law that will allocate responsibilities among government sectors.

[278]The term distinguishes the recent creature of Environmental institutions by this term, and by analogy to impute a lesser authority.

[279]Kamara S. (Environmental Officer), MLHCPE, Freetown.

[280]The issuance of codes and practice guidelines will be helpful.

regulation in the country.[281] Standards are invaluable, especially for ascertaining the extent of environmental damage and irreversible limits that mining operations can impose on nature. It is difficult to see how the NEPB could effectively implement its EIA functions for example, when protective provisions relating to licences, monitoring, of environmental auditing, insurance schemes, should be based one way or another, on some sort of national environmental standards as provided for by the EPA. In a practical case of determining environmental fees for instance, the standard is determined not according to the potential of impact of the related mining activity, but by 'the outlay of the capital investment in the operation per annum'.[282] Standards therefore need to be set (or adopted) for the maximum impact allowed, including efforts to determine naturally set limits on the basis of quantifiable and measurable factors as indicators of sustainability.[283] The lack of standards has led to pollution of rivers, streams, lakes and underground water resources in mining operations. Policies and legal provisions prohibiting pollution of water are meaningless in the absence of quantifiable and qualified standards for appreciable water quality, of acceptable risks and water use value. An effort in this direction is therefore vital as it will not only encourage mining companies to treat and conserve water, but will also enable industrial water use to be priced at its true marginal economic, social and environmental cost in line with the polluter-pays principle.[284]

The problems with implementing institutional environmental functions to regulate mining also have closer relation with functional, as opposed to structural capacity, or "lethargy". There is considerable lack of human resources, necessary expertise, or support structure with which to pursue effective implementation. The department is reportedly hugely understaffed. The entire ED has only 8 personnel including the DoE.[285] Only one officer is positioned in each of the four regions without any supporting staff.[286] It is

[281]'Environmental standards' have been described as the result of a multidimensional process analysis, evaluation, balancing and decision-making, and ultimately the result of pan-social discourses and political decisions, which must recognise that socio-cultural factors cannot replace the basic conditions and limits set down by nature. (see GCEA Report (supra n.18) p. 97)

[282]Proposals for development of standards, regulations, national environmental documentation centre and information system, were shelved because of lack of funds.(Bah S.A (supra n. 77))

[283]GCEA Report (supra n.18) p.97.Note also that IPVS in the environmental arena could be adopted (ISO 1400) (See Roht-Arriaza N., "Private Voluntary Standard Setting, the International Organisation for Standardisation, and International Law making" in YB Int Env L, Vol.6, OUP, 1995 pp 107-145.); she argues that adopting IPVS has distinct advantages especially where public resources available for standard setting for public agreements are woefully inadequate.

[284]Note that this will also aid and enable the effective implementation of the Pollution provisions under the PHA and Water Acts already discussed in chapter 6.

[285]Confirmed by the PRSP Environmental report (supra n.34) p.5

[286]Bah S.A (supra n.77) Note that Environmental Officers are responsible for monitoring of conditioned EIA projects.

difficult to rationalise that monitoring and auditing functions can be effectively implemented amidst lack of logistics such as vehicles, 'mobile testing units' and even comfortable offices and stationery to write up reports.[287] Such situations provide seedbed for influencing environmental officials to relax environmental conditions by holding out other incentives to them.

Finally, the institutional problems are indeed very real but are not insurmountable. What is required in my view is a strong political will and commitment of the government (including those with environmental responsibilities) to address environmental concerns. Where this exists, the necessary logistics for institutional functioning will be prioritised, the institutional authority will be strengthened, cooperation and coordination will be enhanced, standards will be developed and the environmental results for mine regulation will be improved within sustainability.

Conclusion

This chapter was set out to evaluate the extent to which environment and development concerns have been integrated as a national strategy, to assess the efficiency of the manner and methods of implementation of the various principles identified in the relevant legislations and to ascertain any linkages between the adverse effects of mining in Sierra Leone and the implementation methods. These objectives have been fulfilled through a thorough scrutiny of all aspects of the implementation methods under categories of 'localisation', 'legalisation' and 'institutionalisation'.

Policy analysis revealed much of the integration objectives. National policies on every environmental sector, and particularly the mining sector, supported the concept of development that is environmentally and/or socially sustainable, thus effectively localising the concept as a national strategy. The findings on the efficiency of implementation of the principles identified in the relevant legislations including other aspects of the legal character of sustainable development reveal some pluses and minuses. On the strong points, legislation dictates are being implemented to some extent to regulate mining (EIA, development funds, licences and fees). There is in place a national institutional framework to coordinate environment and development issues and objectives of relevant international conventions are being adapted within existing laws, plans and policies in some measure.

However deficiencies do exist in all fields. Discretion still dominates

---

[287] *Ibid.*

decision-making processes, even with regard to implementation of legal prescriptions. Participatory rights especially the access to justice component for individuals and groups is nil. Corporate Responsibility is only recently been acknowledged in mining policy but leaves a lot to be desired in realty. Use of innovative mechanisms (such as performance agreements and anti-pollution incentives) to regulate mining is uncommon both as evidence of government usage or voluntary initiative of mining companies. Implementation was also proved severely impacted by legal inefficiencies relating to conflicts, inconsistencies and disharmony between existing laws especially on questions of liability and responsibility. Also exposed is the lack of guidelines, procedures and standards for enforcement. Further revealed is the almost redundant capacity of judicial role in implementation and enforcements of sustainability objectives despite their prominence in legislations; and the negligible employment of adjudicatory and deliberative methods to enhance legal processes. A final compliment to the forgoing shortcomings on implementation is the evident institutional incapacity - structural, legal and functional - such as would handicap any implementation efforts.

Premised on the forgoing implementation deficiencies and inadequacies, mining faces little challenge on the ground, though the principles canvassed by the concept of sustainable development remain unaltered within legal and policy dictates. The mechanisms (localisation, legalisation and institutionalisation) designed for implementing the relevant principles of sustainable development in international law at the national level have been justified to the extent that they have represented the lenses through which inefficiencies can be detected at all levels of state structure. It will therefore be difficult not to assume a direct link between the atrocities of mining in Sierra Leone and the implementation aspects of sustainability principles at the national level.

8   GENERAL CONCLUSION

The purpose of this book has been to show that the concept of sustainable development in international law is very valuable for ensuring sound legal and policy guidance on how development activities can be made socially and environmentally sustainable. Chapter 1 presented a background overview of how concerns with public and private sector agendas to reap economic benefits from mining in Sierra Leone, overshadowed adverse social and environmental consequences of mining. It emphasised the need for a reorientation of such activities in the concept of sustainable development in international law. Chapter 2 proves that despite definitional controversies, the concept does have direct relevance and primary purpose in promoting environmental protection (as opposed to economic development), in the exploitation and utilisation of natural resources, especially for economic purposes. This book further shows how the goal of sustainable development is made attainable through the robust legal character of the concept, which enables its relevant principles to be applied to policy, legal rules and processes with flexibility and practicability that attunes with regulating development activities at the national level.

This work has further demonstrated in chapter 3, how sustainability can be achieved at the domestic level through some relevant elements and principles of the concept - Environmental Protection, Integration, Inter and Intra-generational Equity, Sustainable Utilisation, Polluter-Pays and Precaution, EIA and Public Participation - which jointly and severally, define the social and environmental parameters within which development activities should generally be conducted. It has also illustrated how these principles effect to impose certain restraints and responsibilities on developers and those who regulate them, to implore consideration for the natural and social environment within which development activities take place. Chapter 4 justified and illustrated the applicability of the concept of sustainable development (through its relevant principles) to mining generally.

In chapters 5 and 6, this work proves the value of sustainable development for providing effective legal and policy guidance for environmental protection in conduct of development activities, by examining as case study, the legal aspects of environmental regulation of mining in Sierra Leone. The study identified relevant principles of sustainable development in a cross section of laws and agreements of that country. It demonstrates that environmental and social sustainability can be directed, promoted and/or achieved through the formulation, interpretation and application of the relevant sustainability principles that were uncovered within the selected legal mandates.

The book further proved in chapter 7, the value of sustainable development for regulating development activities particularly mining, by examining the methods of national implementation of principles of sustainable development identified in legal mandates and policies. The implementation aspects for ensuring compliance and promoting environmental and social sustainability in mineral resource development activities were found to be inadequate. Implementation difficulties, deficiencies and inadequacies were identified, which accord mining activities little challenge on the ground, though the relevant principles of sustainable development in international law as represented throughout this thesis, remain unaltered within legal mandates and policies. It puts into sharp focus the international concern with national implementation of the principles of the concept as the corner stone for sustainability of development activities, and the emphasis on state and corporate action in promoting it.[1]

What emerges from the entire work is a recognition that the concept of sustainable development and its elements are not devoid of purpose, but do hold solid valuable recipe by which economic activities can be regulated for environmental and social sustainability. But that, the representation of these value-oriented principles within legal mandates and policies alone cannot direct sustainability without effective implementation, compliance and enforcement of rules including the promulgation and adoption of standards, viable structures and institutions (administrative, legal and financial) that should drive them. Giving the severe implementation difficulties uncovered by this study, it will be difficult not to assume a direct link between the environmental atrocities of mining in Sierra Leone as illustrated in chapter 1, and the implementation aspects of sustainability principles at the national level.

Thus, the unavoidable conclusion arrived at by this thesis is that the values of sustainable development and its relevant principles for promoting or

---

[1]See Stockholm Declaration; UN GA Resolution 44/228 on UNCED (GA Res. 44/228, 1989; the Rio Declaration; Agenda 21, WSSD Johannesburg Declaration and POI.

achieving environmentally sound mining are real, effective and workable. However, these principles have to be made to work through proper implementation, compliance and enforcement strategies and efforts, if they are to achieve their primary objective of making economic exploitation and utilisation of natural resources environmentally and socially sound undertakings. Specifically, Sierra Leone has to adopt precautionary values of standard setting as the basis for proper regulation of development activities for environmental protection. This conclusion justifies sustainable development as a process and goal-based objective,[2] that can be made real and tangible within laws, (legislative and judicial), rules, agreements and policies including deliberative processes, but one that is only attainable through effective implementation, compliance and enforcement.

---

[2]See Higgins R.; *Problems and Process: International Law and How We Use It*, Clarendon Press, Oxford 1994, p.2. According to her, international law is best seen as a process rather than just rules. See also, Fitzmaurice, Lowe and De Sadeleer on the legal character of sustainable development (supra chapter 2, pp. 55-56, ns 79-84).

BIBLIOGRAPHY

1. Alejandro Iza "Developments under the Ramsar Convention: Allocation of Water for River and Wetland Ecosystems in Environmental policy and law", Reciel Vol.13, 1 (2004)

2. Alieu E.K. "Economic Importance of wetlands", MAFFS, Sierra Leone at <http://www.ramsar.org/mtg_sierraleone>

3. Akiwumi F. A., "Roots of Conflict: Water, World View and sustainability in a West African Environment at <http://www.ucowr.siu.edu/proc/W4D.pdf>.

4. AMCO- Robertson Mineral Services in *SL Diamond Policy Study*; (DFID) January, 2002

5. Armstrong Kit, "The Green Challenge: Managing Environmental Issues in Natural Resources Projects in Developing Countries" 42 *Rocky Mountain Mineral Law Institute* 1996

6. Auty R.M and Mikesell R.F., *Sustainable Development in Mineral Economies* OUP, Oxford 1998

7. Auty R. *Sustaining Development in Mineral Economies: The Resource Curse Thesis*. London and New York: Routledge, 1993

8. Auty R.M., *Patterns of Development- Resources, Policy and Economic Growth*, Edward Arnold Publishers, London, NY, Melbourne Auckland 1995

9. Bailey P.M.; "The Creation and Enforcements of Environmental Agreements" in *European Environmental Law Review* Vol. 8/6, June 1999

10. Bank Information Center, USA- "Civil Society Groups in Sierra Leone Voice Concerns about Proposed MIGA Project" available at <http://www.bicusa.org/bicusa/issues/africa/1363.php>

11. Bartlett R., 'Ecological Reason in Administration: EIA and Administrative Theory' in *Managing Leviathan – Environmental Politics and the Administrative State* Paehllee and Torgerson Eds. London, Belhaven 1990

12. Bastida E., "Integrating Sustainability into Mining laws: The Experience of some Latin American Countries" in *International Law and Sustainable Development, Principles and Practice*, Schrijver & Weiss (Eds.) Martinus Nijhoff Publishers Leiden/Boston 2004

13. Beckerman W., In Defence of Economic Growth, Jonathan Cape Publishers Limited, 1974

14. Beckerman W., "Sustainable Development: Is it a Useful Concept?" in *Environmental Values* 3, The White Horse Press, Cambridge, U.K.1994

15. Beckerman W., Small is Stupid- Blowing the Whistle on the Greens, Duckworth Publishers, U.K. 1996

16. Belgore Y., "Forum non conveniens in England and USA for litigation against oil multinationals" in *Oil gas and Energy Law Intelligence* Volume I, issue # 01 - January 2003

17. Bhattacharya, J., "Sustainable Development of Natural Resources: Implications for Mining and Minerals" in *Mineral Resource Engineering,* Vol.9, No.4 (2000)

18. Bellini M., "IUCN Mining Policy" in EPL, 26/6 (1999)

19. Bendu P.E., "Mining Sector Reactivation: Real Help and/or Real Impact" in *Enviroscope* Vol. 5 No.3 August 2002

20. Bergen Ministerial Declaration on Sustainable Development, 20 EPL (1990)

21. Berlin II Guidelines for Mining and Sustainable Development UN, 2002 available at http://www.mineralresourcesforum.org/Berlin/index.htm (also in 10 *Journal of Natural Resources and Energy Law* (1992)).

22. Bilderbeek S., (Ed.) *Biodiversity and International Law* (Netherlands National Committee for the IUCN) IOS Press, Amsterdam, Oxford 1992

23. Birnie and Boyle, *International Law and the Environment*, (2nd Edition) Oxford University Press, 2002

24. Boer B., "Implementation of International Sustainability Imperatives at the National Level" in *Sustainable Development and Good Governance,* Ginther, Denters & De Waart (Eds.) Martinus Nijhoff Publishers Dordrecht/Boston/London, 1995

25. Boyle A., "Codification of International Environmental Law and the International Law Commission: Injurious Consequences Revisited" in *International Law and Sustainable Development*, OUP Oxford, 1999

26. Boyle A., "The Convention on Biological Diversity" in *The Environment After Rio: International Law and Economics,* (1994), Campiglio et.al (Eds.), Graham and Trotman/Martinus Nijhoff, London/Dordrecht 1994

27. Boyle A., "Globalising Environmental Liability: the Interplay of National and International Law" *Journal of Environmental Law*, Vol.17, 2005

28. Boyle and Freestone (Eds.) *International Law and Sustainable Development* OUP, Oxford, 1999

29. Brandi Meredith "From Rio to Johannesburg: Toward Sustainable Development" in *Human Rights Law, Newsletter* (IBA Section on Legal Practice) No.7 October 2004

30. Brown Weiss E., "Environmental Equity – The Imperative for the 21st Century" in *Sustainable Development and International Law*; Lang, W. (Ed), Graham and Trotman/Martinus Nijhoff, London/ Dordrecht/Boston, 1995

31. Brown Weiss E., "Understanding Compliance with Soft Law" in *Commitment and Compliance The Role of Non-binding Norms in the International Legal System*, Shelton D. (Ed.), OUP, New York, 2000

32. Brown Weiss E., *In Fairness to Future Generations: International Law, Common Patrimony & Intergenerational Equity*, Falk R. (ed.) the UN University, Japan / Transnational Publishers Dobbs Ferry, New York, 1988

33. Brown-Weiss "The Planetary Trust: Consequences and Intergenerational Equity", *Ecology Law Quarterly*, 11 1984

34. Brima A., "Problems in the Mining Sector", DSPWP (DFID), March 2003

35. Brownlie I., "Legal Status of Natural Resources in International Law", 162 *Recueil des Cours* 245 1979

36. Brownlie I., Principles of International Law (fifth Edn.), OUP 2002

37. Brunner, "Of Sense and Sensibility: Reflections on International Liability Regimes as Tools for Environmental Protection," 53 ICLQ 351 2004

38. Brundtland G.H., "Our Common Future and Ten Years after Rio: How Far have we Come and Where Should We Be Going" in *Earth Summit 2002: A New Deal*, Dodds F. (Ed.) Earthscan, London, 2000

39. BSL, Economic Trends in *Mining Annual Review*, 1989

40. BSL, *Annual Report and Statement of Account*, (1980s) BSL Freetown

41. Burhenne W. (Ed) *International Environmental Law- Multilateral Treaties* 1992

42. Bureau of African Affairs: "Sierra Leone Business Mining" Africasat.com <www.sierraleone.org.SL/pages /business>

43. Caldwell L.K., *International Environmental Policy* (2nd Edition), Duke University Press, Durham London 1990

44. Campins-Eritja M. & Gupta J., "The Role of "Sustainability Labeling" in the International Law of Sustainable Development" in *International Law and Sustainable Development*, Schrijver & Weiss (Eds.) Schrijver N. & Weiss F., (Eds.) Martinus Nijhoff Publishers Leiden/Boston 2004

45. Carnwath (Lord Justice) "Judicial Protection of the Environment at Home and Abroad" in *Journal of environmental Law* Vol. 16, No.3 2004 pp.315-327

46. Chandler M., "The Biodiversity Convention: Selected Issues of Interest

to the International Lawyer" in Colorado *Journal of International Environmental Law Policy*, vol.4 (1993)

47. Charney J., "Compliance with International Soft Law" in *Commitment and Compliance: the Role of Non-binding Norms in the International Legal System*, Shelton D., (Ed) OUP New York, 2000

48. Charney J., "Transnational Corporations and Developing Public International Law" in *Duke Law Journal* 748, 1983

49. Charnovitz S., "The World Trade Organisation and the Environment" in 8 *Yearbook of International Environmental Law* 98, 1998

50. Churchill Robin & Scott Joanne*, "The Mox Plant Litigation: The First-Half" in ICLQ vol. 53, July 2004

51. CIA: The World Fact Book-Sierra Leone, 2002, at http://www.umsl.edu/services/govdocs/wofact99/267.htm.

52. Cleeve E.A., *Multinational Enterprises in Development: Mining Industry in Sierra Leone*, Avebury Publishers U.K

53. Cohen M., "A New menu For the Hard-Rock Café: International mining Ventures and Environmental Cooperation in Developing Countries" in 15 *Sanford Environmental law Journal* 130 1996

54. Cook & Kothai (Eds.) *Participation: The New Tyranny?* Zed Books, London, New York 2001

55. Cooke and Oughton, *Common Law of Obligations*, Butterworths, 2000

56. Cooper J., *Public Legal Services: A Comparative Study of Policy. Politics and Practice*, Sweet & Maxwell, 1983

57. Cooper J. & Trubek L. (Eds.), *Educating for Justice: Social Values and Legal Education*, Ashgate, 1997

58. Codjoe, V.S., Land as a factor of Inequality in Kenema District; B.A Dissertation (unpublished) 1986 Fourah Bay College, USL.

59. Cole N.H.A.; "Profile of Community Biodiversity Action Network (CBAN), Sierra Leone, CBAN-SL, Freetown, Sierra Leone

60. Conteh A.F (Assistant Director of Forests), "Wetlands and National Development: The Pros and Cons of Development Projects in Third world Countries", MAFFS, Freetown.

61. Cordonier Segger M., & Khalfan A., *Sustainable Development Law, Principles, Practice and Prospects*, OUP, Oxford New York, 2004

62. Cordonier Segger M., "Sustainability & Corporate Accountability Regimes: Implementing the Johannesburg Summit Agenda" in *Receil* Vol. 12 Issue 3, 2003

63. Cordonier Segger *et. al.* "Prospects for Principles of International

Sustainable Development Law after WSSD: Common but Differentiated Responsibilities, Precaution and Participation" in *Receil* 12 (1) 2003

64. CCSL: *Wild Life and Nature Reserves in Sierra Leone*, (GTZ funded) 1993, Freetown

65. Date-Bah S.K., "Rights of Indigenous People in Relation to Natural Resource Development: An African Perspective" 16 *Journal of Energy and Natural Resources Law* (1998)

66. D'Amato A., "Do We Owe a Duty to Future Generations to Preserve the Global Environment?" in 84 AJIL 190, (1990)

67. De Sadeleer N., *Environmental Principles-From Political Slogans to Legal Rules;* OUP, Oxford 2002

68. De Shalit A., *Why Posterity Matters- Environmental Policies and Future Generations,* Routledge, 1995

69. De Waart P., "Sustainable Development through a Socially Responsible Trade and Investment Regime" in *International Law and Sustainable Development, Principles and Practice*, Schrijver & Weiss (Eds.) Martinus Nijhoff Publishers Leiden/ Boston 2004

70. Diaz A., Permanent Sovereignty Over Natural Resources, 24 *EPL*, 1994

71. Dowdeswell, E., "Sustainable Development: The Contribution of International Law" in *Sustainable Development and International Law;* Lang W. (Eds), Graham & Trotman/ Martinus Nijhoff, London/ Dordrecht/ Boston 1995

72. Drummond & Masden: *The Condition of Sustainability*, Routledge, London/ New York, 1999

73. Dzidzornu D. M; "Environmental Protection in Africa; A Panorama of the Law and Practice" in *Journal of Energy and Natural Resources Law,* Vol. 22 No. 2, May 2004

74. Earthtrends: Biodiversity and Protected Areas: Sierra Leone available at , http://www.earthtrends.wri.org/>

75. Ebbesson J., "The Notion Of Public Participation In International Environmental Law" in *Yb Int Env L 98, 1997*

76. Ebbesson J., "Innovative Elements and Expected Effectiveness of the 1991 EIA Convention" 19 *EIA Review* 47, 1999

77. El Serafy, S. "The Proper Calculation of Income from Depletable Natural Resources: in *Environmental Accounting for Sustainable Development*, Yusuf J. Ahmad, Salah El Serafy, and Ernst Lutz, (Eds.), World Bank, Washington, DC 1989

78. El Serafy S. and Lutz E., "Environmental and Resource Accounting: An

Overview" in *Environmental Accounting for Sustainable Development* (Yusuf, Ahmad, El Serafy and Lutz (Eds.) (1989). The World Bank, Washington, DC, 1989

79. Eliot J. A., *Introduction to Sustainable Development* (2nd Ed.), Routledge London 2001

80. Emole C.E., "Regulation of Oil and Gas pollution in Nigeria in EPL 28/2 1998

81. ESCAP & UNEP: *Mineral Resources Development and the Environment* 1992

82. Ewing, Hutt & Petersen, "Corporate Environmental Disclosures: Old Complaints, New Expectations" in *Business Law International*, Vol. 5 No 3, Section of Business Law (IBA) Publication, September, 2004

83. Franck T.M., *Fairness in International Law and Institutions*, OUP, New York Oxford 1997

84. Freestone D., "International Fisheries Law since Rio: The Continued Rise of the Precautionary Principle", in *International Law and Sustainable Development*, Boyle & Freestone (Eds.) OUP, Oxford, 2001

85. French D.," The Role of the State and International Organisations in Reconciling Sustainable Development and Globalisation" in *International Law and Sustainable Development:* Schrijver N. & Weiss F., (Eds.) Koninklijke Brill NV. The Netherlands 2004

86. Friends of the Earth (US): "Review For Sierra Rutile Limited", July 20 1997 at <http://www.moles.org/ProjectUnderground/ drillbits/970821/97082102.html>

87. FIELD: "Report of Consultation on Sustainable Development" in Reciel Vol.2 No. 4, 1993

88. Fitzmaurice M., *International Protection of the Environment;* (Hague Academy of International Law), Martinus Nijhoff Publishers, Hague/ Boston/ London 2002

89. Fitzmaurice M., "International Law as a Special Field", 25 *NYIL* 181, 1994

90. Fitzmaurice M., "Dispute Concerning Access to Information under Article 9 of the OSPAR Convention (Ireland v United Kingdom and Northern Ireland) in *International Journal of Marine and Coastal Law* Vol.18 2003

91. Fijalkowski A., and Fitzmaurice M., (Eds.) *The Right of a Child to a Clean Environment,* (programme on International Rights of the Child) 2000

92. Gaines S.E., "International Trade, Environmental Protection and

Development as a Sustainable Development Triangle" *Receil* Vol. 11. Issue 3, (2002)

93. Gearty C*, "The Place of Private Nuisance in Modern Law of Torts", 48 *Cambridge Law Journal* 1989

94. Ghai D. and Vivian J. (Eds.) *Grassroots Environmental Action: Peoples Participation in Sustainable Development*, Routledge, London, 1992

95. Ginther, Denters & De Waart (Eds.) *Sustainable Development and Good Governance*, Martinus Nijhoff Publishers, Dordrecht/Boston/London, 1995

96. Gray* K.R, "International Environmental Impact Assessment: Potential for a Multilateral Environmental Agreement" in *Colorado Journal of International Environmental Law & Policy*, Vol.11, No.1, 2000

97. Goode R., "Interests in Securities held with an Intermediary" in *From Government to Governance: 2003 Hague Conference on Contemporary Issues of International Law*, TMC Asser Press, The Hague 2004,

98. Gordon K. "The OECD Guidelines and Other Corporate Responsibility instruments: A comparison" December 2001 at http://www.oecd.org/dataoecd/

99. Gower B., "What Do We Owe Future Generation"; in *The Environment in Questions - Ethics & Global Issues*, Cooper D & Palmer J. (Eds.) Routledge, London 1992

100. Goldin & Winters, " Economic Policies for Sustainable Development" in *The Economics of Sustainable Development*, (Centre For Economic Policy Research) Goldin & Winters (Eds.) 1995, Cambridge University Press, Cambridge, U.K 1995

101. Gilbert S., (De Beers Group London): "World Class Mining Majors and Their Role in the Future of the Diamond Industry in Sierra Leone", DSPWP, (DFID) Freetown, March, 2003

102. Guruswamy & Hendricks *International Environmental Law in a Nutshell*, West Publishing, 1997

103. Gillespie A., *International Environmental Law, Policy and Ethics*, OUP, Oxford, 2002

104. Handl G., "Human Rights and Protection of the Environment" in *Economic, Social and Cultural Rights* Eide/Krause/Rosas (Eds) 2001

105. Handl G. "Environmental Security and Global Change: The Challenge to International Law in *1Yearbook of International Environmental Law 3*, 1990

106. Handl G., "Controlling Implementation of and compliance with

International Environmental Commitments: the Rocky Road from Rio", 5 *Colorado Journal of Internatonal Environmental Law and Policy* 327 1994

107. Handl et. al. (Eds.), *Yearbook of International Environmental Law*, Vol. 3 1992 Graham & Trotman/, London/Dordrecht/ Boston 1992

108. Hanemann P., *Economics and the Preservation of Biodiversity*, Wilson, E.O (Ed.) National Academy Press, Washington 1988

109. Harwood Richard "Environmental Impact Assessment: What's Next?" in *Journal of Environmental and Planning Law*, September 2004

110. Herkenrath P., "The Implementation of the Convention on Biological Diversity-A Non-Governmental perspective ten years on" in *Reciel* 11 (1) 2002

111. Hassan P., "Toward an International Covenant on the Environment and Development" in *Proceedings of the American Society for International Law*, Vol. 87, 1993

112. Hassan P., "The IUCN Draft International Covenant on Environment and Development: Background and Prospects" in *Essays in Honour of W.E Burhenne*, 1994

113. Hartwick, J.M. and Olewiler, N.D., *The Economics of Natural Resource Use*, (Second Edition), Addison-Wesley Educational Publishers Inc., Reading Massachusetts, 1998

114. Harwood R., "Environmental Impact Assessment: What's Next?" in *Journal of Environmental and Planning Law*, September 2004

115. Hey, E., "The Precautionary concept in Environmental Policy and Law: Institutionalizing Caution" in *Georgetown Environmental Law Review* IV, (1992)

116. Holmes, "Sustainable Development: Most Effective Way to Put Principles into Practice" Geneva, 28 July 2004 WBCSD, available at <http://www.wbcsd.ch/plugins/DocSearch/details>

117. Higgins R., *Problems and Process: International Law and How We Use It* Clarendon Press, Oxford 1994

118. Hsu B.F.C* "Constitutional Protection of Sustainable Environment in the Hong Kong Special Administrative Region" in *Journal of Environmental Law* Vol. 16, No 2, 2004

119. Hughes D. *et.al.*, *Environmental Law* (Fourth Edn.) Butterworths, Lexis Nexis U.K 2002

120. Hurrell A. and Kingsbury B., (Eds.) *The International Politics of the Environment*, OUP, Oxford 1992

121. IBA: *Environmental Liability* (Section On Business Law) Graham &

Trotman, London/ Dordrecht/ Boston, 1991

122. IIED/WBCSD, Breaking New Ground: Mining, Minerals and sustainable Development The Report of the Mining Minerals and sustainable Development Project , Earthscan London/ Sterling, VA, 2002

123. ILA: Sixty-Sixth Conference (Buenos Aires) 1994 (First Report) Crawford & Williams (Eds.), London 1994

124. ILA: Sixty-Seventh Conference (Helsinki) 1996, (Second Report), London 1996

125. ILA: Sixty-Eight Conference (Taipei) 1998, (Draft Third Report) London 1998

126. ILA: Sixty-Ninth Conference (London) 2000, (Fourth Report), London 2000

127. ILA: Seventieth Conference (New Delhi) (Fifth & Final Report), London 2002

128. ILA- CEEL: *Transnational Enforcement of Environmental Law* (second Report) Berlin Conference (2004) available at http://www.ila- hq.org/

129. ILA: "New Delhi Declaration of Principles of International Law Relating to Sustainable Development", ILA Resolution 3/2002 of 6th April 2002 (available as UN Doc. A/57/329; also at http://www.ila- hq.org/

130. "ILC Draft Articles on Prevention of Transboundary Environmental Harm from Hazardous Activities" in *Report of the ILC*, 53rd Sess., UN GAOR, 56th Sess., Supp. No. 10, at 370- 436, UN Doc.56/10 2001

131. ILC: "Report of the 2001 HCCH on the Draft Convention on Jurisdiction and Foreign Judgments in Civil and Commercial Matters"<http://www.cptech.org>

132. ILC: "Draft Principles on Environmental Liability" in *JEL*, 17, 2005

133. IUCN *World Conservation Strategy*, Switzerland 1980, also at <http://www.unep/wwf/iucn.nr>

134. IUCN, *A Guide to the Convention of Biological Diversity* 2 1997

135. IUCN, WWF, WRI *Conserving the Worlds Biodiversity* IUCN Gland 1990

136. IUCN/UNEP/WWF (1991) *Caring for the Earth: A Strategy for Sustainable Living*; Munro & Holdgate (Eds.) Gland, Switzerland, (1991)

137. IUCN & ICEL (1995) *Draft International Covenant on Environment and Development* (EPL Paper No. 31 1995), IUCN Gland, Switzerland, Cambridge, 1995 U.K

138. IUCN/WCPA "Position Statement on Mining and Associated Activities in relation to Protected Areas" in *EPL* Vol.29 No. 6, 1999

139. "IUCN Guidelines for Protected Area Management Categories- Part 11" in *EPL* Vol. 29, No. 6, 1999

140. Institute of Mining and Metallurgy: *Mining in Latin America Challenges in the Mining Industry* 1994

141. Jacobs, M. *The Green Economy: Environment, Sustainable Development and the Politics of the Future*, Pluto Press, London/Boulder/Colorado 1991

142. Jacobs, M. "Sustainable Development as a Contested Concept" in *Fairness and Futurity*, Dobson A. (Ed) OUP Inc. New York 1999

143. Jacquemont F. & Caparros A., "The Convention of Biological Diversity and the Climate Change Convention 10 Years after Rio: Towards a Synergy of the Two Systems", in *Reciel* Vol.11 (2), 2002

144. Johannesburg Principles on the Role of Law and sustainable development adopted at the Global judges symposium, Johannesburg, South Africa, 18-20 August 2002, available at www.unep.org/dpdl/symposium

145. Johnson O.E., *Economic Analysis and the structure of Land Rights in Sierra Leone* Dissertation (PhD), University of California., L.A 1970

146. Kachiwu M.K; "Diamonds and Civil Conflict in Africa- the Conflicts in Central Africa and West Africa: Law and Practice" in *Journal of Energy and Natural Resources Law*, Vol. 22 No. 2, May, 2004

147. Kameri-Mbote P. & Cullet P., "Biological diversity Management in Africa: Legal and Policy Perspectives in the Run-up to WSSD" in *Reciel* 11 (1) 2002

148. Kamara-Boie O., (DDM) "Mineral Rights, Ownership, Access and Exploitation", DSPWP (DFID), Freetown March 2003

149. Keilli A., "Environmental and Sustainable Development Challenges for Sierra Leone's Mining Industry" DPSWP (DFID), Freetown, March 2003

150. Kennedy W.V., "Environmental Impact Assessment in North America, and Western Europe: What has Worked Where, How, and Why" – *International Environmental Reporter* 11 April 13, 1988.

151. Kettlewell U., "The Answer to Global Pollution: A Critical Examination of The Problems and potential of the Polluter-Pays Principle" in *Colorado Journal of International Environmental Law and Policy*, vol. 3 No.2 1992

152. Kingsbury B. "Operational Policies of International Institutions as Part of the Law-Making Process: The World Bank and Indigenous Peoples" in *The Reality of International Law*, (Essays in honour of Ian Brownlie) Goodwin-Gill & Talmon (Eds.) Oxford, Clarendon, 1999

153. Kwiatkowska, B., "The Southern Bluefin Tuna (New Zealand v Japan;

Australia v Japan) Cases" in *The International Journal of Marine and Coastal Law* Vol.15, No.1, Kluwer Law International, 2000

154. Kwiatkowska B., "The Ireland v United Kingdom (Mox Plant) Case: Applying the Doctrine of Parallelism", 18 *International Journal of Marine and Coastal Law*, 2003

155. Koester Veit., "The Five Global Biodiversity-Related Conventions: A Stocktaking", in *Reciel* 11 (1), 2002

156. Knox J.H, in "The Myth and Reality of Transboundary EIA" *AJIL* Vol. 96:291 2002

157. Kurukulasuriya L., "Role of Judiciary in Promoting Sustainable Development" in *EPL* 28/1 1998

158. Lang W., "How to Manage Sustainable Development", in *Sustainable Development and Good Governance*, Ginther *et al* (Eds.) Martinus Nijhoff Publishers, Dordrecht/Boston/London, 1995

159. Lang, W.(Ed) *Sustainable Development and International Law;*, Graham & Trotman/ Martinus Nijhoff, , London/Dordrecht/ Boston 1995

160. Layard A., "The Legal Framework of Sustainable Development" in Layard, Davondl & Batty (Eds.) *Planning for a Sustainable Future*, Spon Press, London, 2001

161. Lefevere R., *Transboundary Environmental Interference and The origin Of State Liability*, Kluwer Law International, The Hague/London/Boston 1996

162. Leigh Day & Co. Solicitors: "Corporate Responsibility: The legal responsibility of Multinational companies" at http:// www.leighday.co.uk/doc

163. Liobl G., "Environmental Protection & Sustainable Development", in *United Nations Law and Practice* (Cede/ Sucharipa (Eds.) 2000

164. La Vina Antonio G.M. "The Right to a Sound Environment in the Philippines: The Significance of the Minors Opasa Case", *Receil* Vol. 3 No. 4 1994

165. Lindner W.H "Sustainable Development: Its Social Political and Economic Implications", in *Environmental Liability*, Graham & Trotman, London/ Dordrecht/ Boston (IBA Series) 1991

166. Lomé Peace Accord between the GOSL and the RUF of Sierra Leone, 7th July 1999 also at <www.usip.org/library/pa/sl>

167. Lowenfeld A.F "National Jurisdiction and the Multinational Enterprise," in: *International Litigation and the Quest for Reasonableness*, Oxford, Clarendon 1996

168. Lowe, V. "Sustainable Development and Unsustainable Arguments" in *International Law and Sustainable Development*, Boyle & Freestone (Eds.), OUP, Oxford, 1999

169. Lucas Bergkamp, Hunton & Williams, (Brussels) "Corporate Governance and Social Responsibility: A New Sustainability Paradigm" in *European Environmental Law Review*, May 2002

170. Malanczuk P., "Sustainable Development: Some Critical Thoughts in Light of The Rio Conference in *Sustainable Development and Good Governance*, Ginther, Denters & De Waart (Eds.) Martinus Nijhoff Publishers, Dordrecht/Boston/London, 1995

171. McGraw D. "The CBD-Key Characteristics and Implications for Implementation" in *Reciel* Vol.11 No.1 2002

172. Meeran R, "Access to courts for corporate accountability: Recent Developments" available at http://www.minesandcommunities.org/company

173. Middleton N., and O'Keefe P., *Disaster and Development: The Politics of Humanitarian Aid, Pluto* Press, London 1998

174. Middleton N. & O'Keefe P: *Redefining Sustainable Development*, Pluto Press London 2001

175. Minnitt R.C.A, "Ensuring the Mining Sectors Contribution to Sustainable Economic Development:" in *The Challenge of Sustainable Development for the Minerals and Metals Industry*, Witwatersrand, South Africa July 2001

176. Miller Marian A.L, *The Third World in Global Environmental Politics*, Buckingham, Open University Press, 1995

177. Mommer B., *Global Oil and the Nation State*, OUP, Oxford 2002

178. Monroe & Lammers (Eds.), *Environmental Protection and Sustainable Development: Legal Principles and Recommendations*; (Expert Group on Environmental Law of the WCED) Graham and Trotman/Martinus/Nijhoff Publishers, London/Dordrecht/Boston 1996

179. Monshipouri M., Welch C.E. & Kennedy E.T., "Multinational Corporations and the Ethics of Global Responsibility: Problems and Possibilities", in *Human Rights Quarterly*, Vol.25 No.4, November 2003

180. Morrison Fred L., "The Relationship of International, Regional, and National Environmental Law" in *International, Regional and National Environmental Law*, Morrison & Wolfrum (Eds.) 2000 Kluwer International, Hague/London/Boston 2000

181. Morrison & Wolfrum (Eds.) *International, Regional and National*

Environmental Law, Kluwer Law International, The Hague/London/ Boston 2000

182. Mulinchksy P., *Multinational Corporations and the Law*, Blackwell, Oxford 2003

183. Mulinchksy P. "Corporations in International Litigation: Problems of Jurisdiction and the United Kingdom Asbestos Cases," in *ICLQ* 1 50(1) 2001

184. Mullerat Ramón (OBE) "The Still Vague and Imprecise Notion of Corporate Social Responsibility" in *International Business Lawyer*, Vol. 32 No. 5 October 2004

185. Naess A., *Ecology, Community and Life Style*, Cambridge University Press, Cambridge, 1989

186. Nollkaemper, "What You Risk Reveals What You Value and Other Dilemmas Encountered in the Legal Assault on Risk" in *The Precautionary Principle and International Law: The Challenge of Implementation* Freestone and Hey (Eds.), Kluwer Law International, The Hague/ London, 1996

187. Nickson A., The Export of Bauxite from Sierra Leone (1979) (a study Commissioned for the Central Planning Unit), Ministry of Development, and Economic Planning, Freetown

188. Novoa V.L., "Sustainable Development and Its Relationship with Mining and Law" (Special Institute on Mineral Development in Latin America) 7-1 Rocky Mountain Mineral Law Foundation Ed. 1997

189. National Biodiversity Strategies and Action Plans and National Reports under the CBD; See the Biodiversity support Programme at <http://www.undp.org/bpsp> and also http://www.gefweb.org

190. Nieuwenhuys E., "Global Development through International Investment Law: Lessons Learned From the MAI" in *International Law and Sustainable Development, Principles and Practice*, Schrijver & Weiss (Eds.) Martinus Nijhoff Publishers Leiden/Boston 2004

191. Okidi, C. "Incorporation of General Principles of Environmental Law in National Law with Examples from Malawi" in *EPL* 27/ 4 1997

192. O'Flaherty Michael* "Sierra Leone's Peace Process: The Role of Human Rights Community" in *Human Rights Quarterly*, Vol.26, No.1 February 2004.

193. Pallmearts M., International Environmental Law From Stockholm to Rio: Back to the Future?" *Reciel* Vol.1, No.3 1992

194. Pallmearts M., "International Law and Sustainable Development: Any Progress in Johannesburg? In *Reciel* Vol.12 Issue 1 2003

195. Pauwelyn J., "How to Win a World Trade Organisation Dispute Based on Non-World Trade Organisation Law?" in *Journal of World Trade* 37(6) 2003

196. Pauwelyn J., *Conflict of Norms in Public International: How WTO Law Relates to Other Rules of International Law*, Cambridge University Press, Cambridge, 2003

197. Pearce, D., "An Economic approach to saving the Tropical Forests", in *Economic Policy towards the Environment;* Helm D. (Ed), (Blackwell, Oxford 1992) 239

198. Pearce D.W., Markandya A & Barbier E., *Blueprint for Green Economy*, Earthscan, London 2000

199. Pearce D.W. and Barbier E.B *Sustainable Development: Economics and the Environment in the Third World* Earthscan London 1990

200. Pearce D.W. & Turner K., *The Economics Of Natural Resources And The Environment*, Harvester Weatsheaf Publishers, New York/London/ Toronto/ Sydney Tokyo/ Singapore, 1990

201. Porter J.A., Santana L.S., & Culbertson KD; "Reconciliation of Mining with the Concept of Sustainable Development, Miners Gerais, Brazil", in *Mining Latin America: Challenges in the Mining Industry* (The Institute of Mining and Metallurgy Eds.)

202. Porras I., "The Rio Declaration A New Basis for International Cooperation" in *Receil* Vol. 1 No.3 1992

203. Picolotti R. and Taillant D. (Eds.) *Linking Human Rights and Environment*, Tucson Arizona, University of Arizona Press, 2003

204. Picolotti R., "Agenda 21 and Human Rights" in *Linking Human Rights and Environment*, Picolotti and Taillant (Eds.) Tucson, Arizona, University of Arizona Press, 2003

205. Pinto M., "The Legal context: Concepts, principles standards and Institutions" in *International Economic Law with a Human Face*, Weiss F., *et al.* (Eds.) Kluwer Law International, The Hague 1998

206. PAC & NMJM *Diamond Annual Review*, February 2005 – (Diamonds and Human Security Project,) Gberie, Ahmimed & Smillie (Eds.) Partnership Africa-Canada & Network Movement for Justice and Development (Sierra Leone) Feb 2005

207. PAC- NMJD *Diamond Industry Annual Review Sierra Leone*, Gberie, Isaac & Smillie (Eds.) 2004, Freetown

208. Prince and Nelson, "Developing an Environmental Model: Piecing Together the Growing Diversity of International Environmental

Standards and Agendas Affecting Mining Companies", 7 Colorado *Journal of International Environmental Law & Policy*, 247 1996

209. Pring, Otto & Naito, "Trends in International Environmental Law Affecting the Minerals Industry" in *Journal of Energy and Natural Resources Law*, 17, 1999

210. Pring & Noe, "The Emerging International Law of Public Participation Affecting Global Mining, Energy and Resource Development", in *Human Rights in Natural Resources Development*, Zilman, Lucas & Pring (Eds) OUP 2002

211. Pring G .W (Rock) "International Law and Mineral Resources" in *Mining Environment and Development*, (UNCTAD Publication) available at <http://www.natural-resources.org/minerals/CD/docs/unctad/pring.doc >

212. Provost René, "International Criminal Environmental Law" in *The Reality of International Law*, (Essays in honour of Ian Brownlie) Goodwin-Gill & Talmon (Eds.) Oxford, Clarendon, 1999

213. Quarrie J. (Ed), *Earth Summit '92*, UNCED, Rio De Janeiro, The Regency Press Corporation, London, 1992

214. Qureshi A.H (Ed), *Perspectives in International Economic Law*, Kluwer Law International, London/ The Hague/ New York, 2002

215. Rajamani L., "From Stockholm to Johannesburg: The Anatomy of Dissonance in the International Environmental Dialogue" *Receil* Vol.12 Issue 1, 2003

216. Revesz, Sands & Stewart (Eds.) *Environmental Law, The Economy and Sustainable Development: The United States, The European Union and The International Community*, Cambridge University Press, 2000

217. Rest A*, "Implementation of Rio Targets-Preliminary Efforts in State Practice" in *EPL* Vol. 25 No.6 1995

218. Redgewell C., "Life, the Universe and Everything: A Critic of Anthropocentric Rights" in *Human Rights Approaches to Environmental Protection* Boyle & Anderson (Eds.) Claredon Press, Oxford 1998

219. Redgewell C., "Environmental protection in the Antarctica: the 1991 Protocol" in 43 *ICLQ*, 599, 1994

220. Redclift M., Sustainable Development: Exploring the Contradictions, Routledge London 1984

221. Renner D., "Mining Companies Are Socially Responsible" *Africa News*, 14 September 2004

222. Roht-Arriaza N., "Private Voluntary Standard Setting: the International

Organisation for Standardisation, and International Law making" in *YbIEL*, Vol.6, OUP 1995

223. Rotston H., "Valuing Wetlands", in *Environmental Ethics*, 7, 1985

224. Rehbinder E., "Environmental Agreements - A New Instrument of Environmental policy", in *EPL*, Vol. 27 No.4, 1997

225. Renner-Thomas A.R. D., *A Dual System of Land Tenure: the Sierra Leone Experience*, PhD Thesis (Laws Board of Studies) 1984 Ext.

226. "Report of the Expert Group meeting on identification of Principles of International Law for Sustainable Development", Geneva Switzerland, 26-28 Sept 95, and Background paper 3 for the CSD Fourth Session, 1996

227. "Report of the German Council of Environmental Advisors; "In pursuit of Sustainable Environmentally Sound Development" in *EPL*, vol.25/3 1995

228. Rigby S & Diab R, "Environmental Sustainability and the Development Facilitation Act in South Africa", *Journal of Environmental Law*, Vol. 15. No. 1 2003

229. Rodgers C.P., "Liability for the Release of GMOs in the Environment-Exploring the Boundaries of Nuisance", *C.L.J Vol. 62 (Part 2)* July 2003

230. Sadler B., *Environmental Assessment in a Changing World: Evaluating Practice to Improve Performance 25* 1996

231. Sachs W. (Ed), *The Development Dictionary*: Zed Books London 1992

232. Stallworthy M., "Environmental Liability and Statutory Authority" in *Journal of Environmental Law* Vol. 15 No.1 2003

233. Steele J., "Private Law and the Environment: Nuisance in context" (1995) 15 *Legal Studies* pp.236-259

234. Sands P., *Principles of International Environmental Law* (Second edition), Cambridge University Press, Cambridge 2003

235. Sands P. (Ed), *Greening International Law* Earthscan London 1993

236. Sands P., "International Law and Sustainable development" in *Environmental Law, The Economy and Sustainable Development* Revesz, Sands & Stewart (Eds.) Cambridge University Press 2000

237. Sands P., "UNCED and the Development of International Environmental Law", *YbIEL* Vol. 3 (1992), Handl *et al.* (Eds), Graham &Trotman/ Martinus Nijhoff, London/Dordrecht/ Boston 1992

238. Sands P., International Law in The Field Of Sustainable Development: Emerging Legal Principles" in *Sustainable Development and International Law,* Lang W. (Ed.) Graham &Trotman/ Martinus Nijhoff, London/ Dordrecht/ Boston 1995

239. Sands P., "International Courts and the Application of the Concept of 'Sustainable Development'" in *Max Planck Yearbook of United Nations Law*, Vol.3. (1999) 398; also in *Law and Development: Facing Complexities in the 21st Century* - Hatchard & Perry-Kasseris (Eds.), London Cavendish, 2003

240. Sunkin et.al (Eds.), *Sourcebook on Environmental Law* (2nd Edition), Cavendish, London/Sydney 2002

241. Schabas W.A., "The Relationship between Truth Commissions and International Courts: the Case of Sierra Leone" in *HRQ*, Vol. 25, No.4 November 2003

242. Schoenbaum T.J., "International Trade and Protection of the Environment: The Continuing Search for Reconciliation" *AJIL*. Vol. 91 1997

243. Schrijver N., *Sovereignty over Natural Resources*, Cambridge University Press, Cambridge 1997

244. Schrijver N. & Weiss F.,(Eds.), *International Law and Sustainable Development, Principles and Practice* Martinus Nijhoff Publishers Leiden/ Boston 2004

245. Shelton D., "Human Rights, Environmental Rights and the Right to the Environment" in *28 Stanford Journal of International Law*, 103, 1991

246. Shihata I.F.I., *The World Bank in a Changing World*, Martinus Nijhoff Publishers, Boston, Massachusetts 1991

247. Sipkins S., "Sierra Leone Mining and the Environment", (1995) available at www.american.edu/projects/mandala/Ted/leone.htm

248. Siaffa D.D. (CSSL) "Major Threats to the Wetlands of Sierra Leone and How Their Impact Could be Contained" at http://www.ramsar.org/ mtg_sierraleone

249. Slinn P., "Differing Approaches to the Relationship between International Law and Development" *in Law and Development: Facing Complexities in the 21st Century*- (Essay in honour of Peter Slinn) Hatchard & Perry-Kasseris (Eds.), London Cavendish, 2003

250. Slinn P. E., The Northern Rhodesia Mineral Right Issue, 1922-1964; Thesis (PhD) University of London 1974

251. Smith, S. L., "Ecologically Sustainable Development: Integrating Economics, Ecology, and Law", 31 *Willamette Law Review*, 1995

252. Spooner D., *Mining and Regional Development*, OUP 1981

253. Stuart Bell & Donald Macgillavray; *Environmental law: The Law and Policy Relating to the Protection of the Environment* (5Th Edn), Blackstone

Press Ltd 2000,

254. Sierra Leone: *Reports of the Mine's Department*, 1939/44 at the CIMRD UK

255. Sierra Leone: *National Environmental Action Plan*, Vol.1 & 2, MLHCPE, February 1995

256. Sierra Leone: "The National Environmental Policy: (NEP)" in *Sierra Leone: National Environmental Action Plan* Vol. 1(1995), MLHCPE, 1995

257. Sierra Leone: "Peace Agreement between the Government of Sierra Leone and the RUF of Sierra Leone", Lomé, 7 July 1999, available at <www.usip.org/library/pa/sl>

258. Sierra Leone: *Environmental Impact Assessment Procedures*, MLHCPE: July, 1999

259. Sierra Leone: *Diamond Policy Study*; (DFID Sponsored) January, 2002

260. Sierra Leone: *Details of New Policy Measures Relating to Small Scale and Artisanal Mining and marketing of Precious Minerals*, Ministry of Mines Freetown, 2002

261. Sierra Leone: *Mineral Potential of sierra Leone*, Geological Survey Division, Ministry of Mines, Freetown, December 2002

262. Sierra Leone: *Ready For Business*, Magazine, February 2003

263. Sierra Leone: *Core Mineral Policy*, Ministry of Mineral Resources, September, 2003; also at <http:www.minmines-sl.org/>

264. Sierra Leone *Promotion of Investment Code for Sierra Leone* (Final Draft), Ministry of Trade and Industry, February 2003

265. Sierra Leone: "Industrial Mining Rights in Sierra Leone" (Status 2004) available at http://www.daco-sl.org/encyclopedia2004/

266. Sierra Leone: *Draft Water Sector Review for the PRSP*, MDEP/SL May, 2004 also at http://www.daco-sl.org/encyclopedia2004/

267. Sierra Leone: *Report of Workshop on Policy Support Planning for Mining Sector* (January 28th and 29th, 2004) Ministry of Mines Freetown, 2004

268. Sierra Leone: *Report on Poverty and the Environment (Environmental Contribution to the PRSP)* MDEP, (Bomah & Bassir) Freetown, April 2004

269. Sierra Leone: *The Energy Policy For Sierra Leone* (Draft), (A UNECA Sponsored Study undertaken by Cemmats Group Ltd.) Ministry of Energy and Power May 2004

270. Sierra Rutile Limited: *Environmental and Community Development Plan* ,Rep. No. 92040, Creamer and Warner, July 1990

271. Sierra Rutile Limited: *Implementation of the Environmental and Community*

Development Programme, January 1992

272. Sierra Rutile Limited: *Environmental and Social Impact Assessment*, Knight-Piésold Consultants, October 2001

273. Silveira M.P., "The Rio Process: Marriage of Environment and Development" in *Sustainable Development and International Law*; Lang, W. (Ed), Graham & Trotman/ Martinus Nijhoff, , London/Dordrecht/ Boston 1995

274. Simon Gilbert (De Beers Group London): "World Class Mining Majors and Their Role in the Future of the Diamond Industry in Sierra Leone": Paper Presented at Diamond Sector Policy Workshop, Freetown; March, 2003;

275. Suebedi S.P., " Sustainable Development Perspective In International Economic Law" in *Perspectives in International Economic Law*, Asif H. Qureshi (Ed), Kluwer Law International, London/ The Hague/ New York, 2002

276. Synder and Slinn (Eds.), *International Law and Development: Comparative Perspectives*, Abingdon Professional Books 1987

277. Swarray-Dean M., "Private Sector Development in Sierra Leone" at http://www.dse.de/ef/publicbads/deen.htm

278. Szuniewicz et. al (Eds.) *Exploitation of Natural Resources in the 21st Century* (International Energy Resource law and Policy), Kluwer Law International, The Hague, Netherlands

279. Tani Pratt L.J., "The Contribution of the Diamond Industry to the Economy of Sierra Leone"; DSPWP, (DFID) Freetown March 2003

280. Thorsen Skadegaard Sune and Oury James "Corporate Social Responsibility and Lawyers" in *Human Rights Law, Newsletter* (IBA Section on Legal Practice) No.7 October 2004

281. UN/CSD - "Industry and Sustainable Development Meeting" in *Environmental Policy and Law*, 28/2 1998

282. UN Integrated Regional Information Networks: "Sierra Leone: Diamonds Shine Brighter, But Remain Dull", February 24, 2005 http:// allafrica.com/stories/200502240813.html

283. *UNEP's Guidelines on Offshore Mining and Drilling* 1982

284. UNEP: *Capacity Building for Sustainable Development: An overview of UNEP Environmental Capacity Development Initiatives*, UNEP Publications, December 2002 ISBN: 92-807-2266-2.

285. UNEP *Overview of Land-based Sources and Activities Affecting the Marine, Coastal and Associated Freshwater Environment in the West and Central*

African Region (UNEP/ GPA Co-ordination Office & West and Central Africa Action Plan, Regional Coordinating Unit) 1999 ISBN: 92-807-1800-3

286. UNEP *Global Environment Outlook 2000: UNEP's Millennium Report on the Environment* 338, London, Earthscan Publications Ltd, 1999

287. UNEP Water Strategy and Policy-(Draft); Statement of Key and Emerging Issues related to Water in *Environmental Policy and Law*, Vol.29 1999

288. UNEP: *Sustainability and the United Nations Environment Programme. Buried Treasure – Uncovering the Business Case for Corporate Sustainability*, London 2001

289. UNEP New Way Forward: *Environmental Law and Sustainable Development* Kurukulasuriya L (Eds.) 1995

290. UNEP/SACEP "The Role of the Judiciary in Promoting the Rule of Law in the Area of Sustainable Development" Regional Symposium Convened by UNEP in Partnership with South Asia Co-operative Environmental Programme (SACEP)) Colombo Sri-Lanka 4-6 July, 1997

291. UNCTAD *World Investment Report: Foreign Direct Investment and The challenge of Investment* UN, New York & Geneva, 1999

292. UNCTAD *World Investment Report 2001: Promoting Linkages*, UN: Geneva/New York, 2001.

293. UNESC: "Basic problem of improving capacity of developing countries and economies in transition to capture the maximum economic and social benefits of their potential for mineral production" UNESC Committee on Natural Resources, Fourth Session 10-19 March 1998; E/ C.7/1998/1 available at <http://srcho.un.org/ >

294. UNFPA: *Report on The State of the World Population: Footprints and Milestones* UNPF-UNFPA 2001 available at <www.unfpa.org>

295. UNRFNRE "Revitalization Plan": *Achieving Sustainable Development of Mineral Resources in Harmony with the Environment* (Brochure) 1995

296. USA-Engage, "The Alien Tort Provision: Correcting the Abuse of an Early Federalist Statute" at <http://www.usaengage.org/ legislative/2003>

297. USAID (OTI) "Sierra Leone Conflict Diamonds", (Progress Report on Diamond Policy Development Programme), March 30, 2001 also at <www.usaid.gov/hum-response/oti >

298. Usman N.L "Environmental regulation in the Nigerian Mining Industry: Past Present and Future" in *Journal of Energy and Natural*

Resources Law Vol. 19 No. 1, 2001.

299. Wälde T., "Environmental Policies towards Mining in Developing Countries", in *Journal of Energy and Natural Resources Law* Vol. 10 No. 4 1992

300. Wälde T., "Natural Resources and Sustainable Development: From "Good Intentions" to "Good Consequences"" in *International Law and Sustainable Development, Principles and Practice* Schrijver & Weiss (Eds.) Martinus Nijhoff Publishers Leiden/Boston 2004

301. Wälde T., "Sustainable Development and the Energy Charter Treaty: between Psuedo-action and the Management of Environmental Investment Risk" in *International Economic Law with a Human Face*, Weiss F., et al. (Eds.) Kluwer Law International, The Hague 1998

302. Walker & Howard; "Finding the Way Forwards: How Voluntary Action Move Mining towards Sustainable Development" (ERM, IIED WBCSD) London, 2002.

303. Westin R., "Intergenerational Equity and Third World Mining" in *University of Pennsylvania Journal of International Business Law* Vol.13, No.1, 1992

304. Weiss F., et al. (Eds.) *International Economic Law with a Human Face* Kluwer Law International, The Hague 1998

305. Wolfrum R., *Means of Ensuring Compliance with and enforcement of International Environmental Law*, Academy of International Law (off print from Recueil des cours, Vol. 272 (1998), Martinus Nijhoff Publishers, The Hague/Boston/ London 1999

306. Wolfrum R., "International Environmental Law: Purposes, Principles and Means of Ensuring Compliance" in *International, Regional and National Environmental Law*, Morrison and Wolfrum (Eds.) Kluwer law International, The Hague/London/Boston, 2000

307. Woolf (Lord Justice) "Are the Judiciary Environmentally Myopic?" in JEL 1992 Vol.4, No.1

308. Wright L., Sierra Leone, in *Mining Annual Review* 2002: London, United Kingdom, Mining Journal Ltd. CD-ROM.

309. World Bank: *The World Development Report* 1992, OUP, Oxford New York

310. World Bank: *World Development Report* 1989, OUP 1989.

311. World Bank: *World Development Report* 2003, *Sustainable Development in a dynamic World-Transforming Institutions Growth and Quality of life*, OUP, Oxford New York 2003

312. World Bank Operational Manual (OP) 4.01 (1991), at <www.worldbank.org>

313. World Bank: IFC: Environmental Assessment Operational Policy 4.01, October, 1998 at <www.worldbank.org>

314. World Bank Environment Department: *The Impact of Environmental Assessment: A Review of World Bank Experience,* World Bank, Washington DC. 1997

315. World Bank: *Mainstreaming the Environment: The World Bank Group and the Environment Since the Rio Earth Summit,* Fiscal 1995, The World Bank, Washington DC 1995

316. World Bank Document: Economic Recovery and Rehabilitation Credit for Sierra Leone Government 2003

317. World Bank: "Environmental Health and Safety Guidelines for Mining and Milling open Pit" 1995 available at <http://www/worldbank.org/html/fpd/ technet/decade/assess.htm>

318. World Bank: Environmental Assessment of Mining Projects *Draft: Environmental Assessment Sourcebook Update* (Feb. 1997), also at http://www/worldbank.org/html/fpd/ technet/decade/assess.htm;

319. World Bank: "Policy on Involuntary Resettlement" (OD4.30), June 1990;

"Policy on Management of Cultural Property" (OP11.03), September 1996;

"Policy on Natural Habitats" (OP4.04) November 1998;

"Policy on Safety of Dams" (OP4.10), September 1991;

"Environmental Health and Safety Guidelines for Port and

Harbour Facilities" 1998; all available at <http://www/worldbank.orgb/>

320. World Bank: *Pollution Prevention and Abatement Handbook,* Washington DC, 1998

321. World Commission on Environment and Development (Brundtland Report) *Our Common Future,* OUP, Oxford, 1987

322. Wurie A C., "The Role of the Geological Surveys In Sierra Leone", Diamond Sector Policy Workshop Paper, March, 2003 Freetown

Ximena F., "International Law-making in the Field of Sustainable development: The Unequal Competition between Development and Environment" *International Law and Sustainable Development, Principles and Practice* Schrijver & Weiss (Eds.) Martinus Nijhoff Publishers Leiden/Boston 2004

LIST OF CASES

1. *Advisory Opinions on the legality of the use by a State of Nuclear Weapons in Armed Conflicts, ICJ Reports,* 1996, 66

2. *United States- Import Prohibition of Certain Shrimp and Shrimp Products* (WT/DS58) Report of the Appellate Body in WTO DSR 1998: Vol. VII, Cambridge 1998

3. *European Communities Measures Concerning Meat and Meat Products (Hormones Case);* (Complaint by the United States (WT/DS26) and Canada (WT/DS48)); Report Of the Appellate Body; WTO DSR Vol.1, Cambridge 1998

4. *Lopez-Ostra Case in Human Rights Law Journal,* Vol.15, No. 11-12

5. *Minors Opasa et al V. Sect. of the Environment & Natural Resources Fulgencio Factoras,* GR. No. 101083, 30 July 1993 Reprinted in 33 ILM 173; 1994

6. *Southern Bluefin Tuna Cases, (Australia v. Japan; New Zealand v. Japan),* Provisional Measures Order of 27th August 1999 at <http:// www.itlos.org/ case documents/1999/ document en 123.doc>

7. *The MOX Plant Case (Ireland v. United Kingdom),* 2001 ITLOS 2 (3 Dec.2001) (Request for Provisional Measures Order of 3rd December 2001) Reprinted in 41 ILM 405, 2002 also at <http://www.worldlii.org/ int/cases/ITLOS/2001/2.html>

8. *The MOX Plant Case (Ireland v. United Kingdom),* Order No.3, 2003 (Suspension of proceedings on Jurisdiction and Merits and request for further Provisional Measures) at <www.itlos.org>

9. *Gabcikovo - Nagymaros Project (Hungary v. Slovakia)* 1997, *ICJ Reports* 15 September 1997, GL No. 92

10. *Read V Lyons & Co. Ltd* ([1945] KB 216

11. *St Helen's Smelting Company V.Tipping* (1865)11 H.L.C 642.

12. *Rylands V. Fletcher* (1868), LR 3 HL 330

13. *Mason V Pearce* (1964-1966) ALR SL 438

14. *Schalk Willem Burger Lubbe et. al. v Cape PLC,* (House of Lords Session 1999-2000) available at <http://wwwhrothgar.co.uk/webCases/hol/ reports >

15. *Wiwa v. Royal Dutch Petroleum Co., et al.,* 226 F.3d 88 (2nd Cir. 2000)

16. *The Chañaral Case* (Pedro Flores Y Otros v. Corporacion Del Cobre,

Codelco, Division Salvador. Recurso De Proteccion Copiapo) Supreme Court of Chile ROL.12.753.FS. 641 1988 available at ESCAP Virtual Conference, <http://www.unescap.org/drpad/vc/document/compendium/ch1.htm>

17. *The Huasco Case* available at<http://www.natural-esources.org/minerals/CD/docs/unctad/pring.doc>

18. *The Ok Tedi Copper-Gold Mine Case*, available at <http://dte.gn.apc.org/cstd1.htm>

19. Vellore Citizens Welfare Forum vs. Union of India, WP 914/1991 (1996.08.28) (Tamil Nadu Tanneries case) (1996) 5 SCC 647

20. Rural Litigation and Entitlement Kendra v. State of U.P., (Dehradun quarries case) (1985) 2 SCC 431

21. A.P. Pollution Control Board v. Prof. M.V Nayudu, (1999), 2 SCC 718

22. State of Himachal Pradesh v. Ganesh Wood Products, (1995) 6 SCC 363

23. Indian Council for Enviro-Legal Action (ICELA) v. Union of India, (CRZ Notification Case) (1996) 5 SCC 281

24. M.C. Mehta v. Union of India, (Delhi Land Use Case: Stone Crushers) WP 4677/1985 (1992.05.15) available at <http://www.elaw.org/resources/text>

25. M.C. Mehta v. Union of India, (Delhi Land Use Case: Badkhal Lake and Surajkund) WP 4677/1985 (1996.10.11) <http://www.elaw.org/resources/text>

26. M.C. Mehta v. Union of India,(Taj Trapezium Case) (1997)2 SCC 353

27. M.C Mehta v. Kamal Nath (2000) 6 SCC 213

28. M.C Mehta v. Kamal Nath (1997) 4 SCC 463

29. M.C Mehta v. Kamal Nath (1987) 1 SCC 388

30. Narmada Bachao Andolan v. Union of India (2000) 10 SCC 664

LIST OF TREATIES AND INTERNATIONAL INSTRUMENTS

1940
Convention on Nature Protection and Wildlife Preservation in the Western Hemisphere (Washington), 161 *UNTS* 193

1948
Universal Declaration of Human Rights, 10 Dec.1948, *UNGA Res.* 217 A (III)

1959
Antarctic Treaty (Washington) 402 *UNTS* 71

1966
International Covenant on Economic and Social and Cultural Rights 993 UNTS 3; 6 *ILM* 1967, 368
International Covenant on Civil and Political Rights, 993 *UNTS* 171; 6 ILM 1967, 360

1968
African Convention on the Conservation of Nature and Natural Resources (Algiers), 1001 *UNTS* 4

1969
US/NEPA (1969) 40 *C.F.R1500.1 -1517.7* (and also *42 U.S.C* ss. 4321- 4370, 2000)

1962
UN GA Resolution 1831(XVII) on 'Economic Development and Conservation of Nature' *UNYB* (1962)

1971
Convention on Wetlands of International Importance (Ramsar), 996 *UNTS* 245; 11 *ILM* (1972) 963

1972
Declaration of the United Nations Conference on the Human Environment (Stockholm), UN Doc A/CONF 48/14 Rev.1; 11 *ILM* 1416 (1972)

OECD Council Recommendation on Guiding Principles Concerning the International Economic Aspects of Environmental Policies, *OECD Council Recommendation C(72) 128 (1972)* ;< http://www.oecd.org/ >

1973

The EC First Programme of Action on the Environment (1973) (*O.J. (112) 1 (1973)*

Convention on the International trade in Endangered Species of Wild Flora and Fauna (Washington, 993 UNTS 243; 12 ILM 1085 (1973)

1974
UN Charter of Economic Rights and Duties of States (1974), GA Res. 3281 (XXIX) 12 Dec.1974

1976
OECD Guidelines For Multinational Enterprises, 21 June 1976 available at <http://www.oecd.org/>

1978
UNEP Principles on Conservation and Harmonious Utilisation of Natural resources Shared by Two or More states, 17 ILM (1978) 1094

1980
"Historical Responsibility of States for the Preservation of Nature for Present and Future Generations" UN Doc. A. /RES/35/8 (1980) 30 Oct)

1982
The Nairobi Declaration, 18 May 1982, UNEP Report. 37 UN GAOR

United Nations Convention on the Law of the Sea *21 ILM* (1982)1261

World Charter for Nature 1983) UNGA Res. 37/7(Annex), UN Doc A/37/51, (1982); *22 I.L.M. 455* (1983)

1985
ASEAN Agreement on the Conservation of Nature and Natural Resources (Kuala Lumpur) 15 EPL (1985); also at http://sedac.ciesin.org/entri/texts/asean.natural.resources.1985.html
EC Directive on EIA, Directive 85/337 (1985) O.J. L175/ 40, amended by Directive 97/11/ EC (1997) *O.J.73/5*; (also at http://europa.eu.int/eur-/ex/en/index.html>)

1987
UNEP Guidelines on Goals and Principles for Environmental Impact Assessment (1987) UN DOC UNEP/Z/SER A/9 (1987)

UN/ECE Convention on Access to Information, Public Participation in Decision-Making and Access to Justice in Environmental Matters (Aarhus) UN Doc. ECE/ CEP/ 43 (1998) at <http://www.unece.org/env/pp/ treatytext.htm>

Recommendation 3.3 on 'wise use of wetlands; Third meeting of the COP (Regina 27 May -5 June 1987) at < http://www.ramsar.org/ key_rec_3.3.htm>

1988
Convention on the Regulation of Antarctic Mineral Resource Activities (Wellington) *27 ILM* (1988) 868

Convention on Jurisdiction and the Enforcement of Judgments in Civil and Commercial Matters (done at Lugano on 16 September 1988 (88/592/EEC), (1988) OJ L 319/9

1990
EEC Directive on Access to Environmental Information, Council Directive 90/313/1990, *O.J. c158/56*

EEC Directive on Access to Environmental Information, Council Directive 90/313/1990, *O.J. c158/56*

"Ministerial Declaration on Sustainable Development" (Bergen Conference) *EPL20 (1990)*

Bergen Conference: "Ministerial Declaration on Sustainable Development", *Environmental Policy & the Law*, 20 (1990), 104

UN Code of Conduct of Transnational Corporations (Draft) (1990) UN Doc.E/1990/94 of 12 June 1990
1991
Protocol to the Antarctic Treaty on Environmental Protection *30 ILM* (1991) 1461

Convention on Environmental Impact Assessment in the Trans-boundary Context (Espoo Convention) *30 ILM* (1991) 802; also at <www.unece.org/ env/eia>

1992
Declaration of the UN Conference on Environment and Development UN

Doc A/CONF 151/26 Rev.1), (*Report of the UNCED*) (1992); *ILM 874*, 1992

Helsinki Convention on the Protection of the Baltic Sea Area (1992) *3 YBIEL* (Article 3(2))

Maastricht Treaty on European Union, (1992) 31 *ILM* 247

Convention on Biological Diversity UN Doc 31 *ILM* 818 (1992); also in UNEP/Bio.Div/N7-INC.5/4

United Nations Framework Convention on Climate Change (1992) 31 *ILM* 851

Agenda 21(1992) (approved by the UNCED at Rio de Janeiro) UN Doc A/ CONF. 151/26 (Vols.1-111) reprinted in *Earth Summit '92, United Nations Conference on Environment and Development Rio De Janeiro*, Quarrie J. (Ed), The Regency Press Corporation, London, (1992)

Non-Legally Binding Authoritative Statement of Principles for a Global Consensus on the Management, Conservation and Sustainable Development of All types of Forests (Forest principles) UN Doc. A/Conf 151/26 (vol. III) (1992), 31, ILM 881(1992); 3 *YbIEL* (1992) 830

UNECE Convention on the Transboundary effects of Industrial accidents (Helsinki) 17 March 1992 31 *ILM* 1330 (1992)

Convention on the Protection and Use of Transboundary Watercourses and International Lakes (Helsinki) 31 *ILM* 1312

OECD Declaration and Decisions on International Investment and Multinational Enterprises (Paris) 1992 both available at< http:// www.oecd.org/ >

1993
Convention on Civil Liability for Damage Resulting from Activities Dangerous to the Environment (Lugano) 21 June 1993 (nif) 32 *ILM* 1228 (1993)

Convention on the Protection of the Marine Environment of the North East Atlantic (The OSPAR Convention) 1992, 32 *ILM*, 1069 (1993) (also in *International Environmental Law-Multilateral Treaties* W.Burhenne, (Ed.) 1992 71

Revised Treaty of the Economic Community of West African States (ECOWAS), 1993, article 29, reprinted at (1996) 8 *Afr.J.I.C.L* 189

The Ministerial Declaration on the Protection of the Black Sea, (1993) in 23 *EPL* 235

The North American Agreement on Environmental Cooperation (Can.-Mex-US), *32 ILM 1480* (1993); 4 *YbIEL* (1993), 831; also at <http://www.cec.org/pubs-info-resources/law-treat-agree/>
1995: UN Agreement Relating to the Conservation and Management of Straddling Fish Stocks, 34 *ILM* 1542; 6 *YbIEL* 841

1997
Convention on Civil Liability for Oil Pollution Damage Resulting from Exploration for the Exploitation of Seabed Mineral Resources (London)

UN Convention on Non-Navigational Uses of International Watercourses, *32 ILM* (1997), 700; 27 *EPL* (1997), 233

Programme for the Further Implementation of Agenda 21, UN GAOR, 19th Spec. Sess. Annex, Agenda item 8. UN DOC. A/S – 1929 (1997)

Report of the Secretary General, UN Commission on Sustainable Development, (Rio Declaration on Environment and Development: Application and Implementation) 5th Session, UN DOC. E/CN.17/1997/8 (1997)

1998
UN/ECE Convention on Access to information, Public Participation in Decision-Making and Access to Justice in Environmental Matters (Aarhus) UN Doc. ECE/ CEP/ 43 (1998); 38 ILM (1999) 517 also at <http://www.unece.org/env/pp/treatytext.htm>

Wellington Convention on the Regulation of Antarctic Mineral Resource Activities (nif)(Article 8)

ILO Declaration on the Fundamental Principles and Rights at Work 18 June 1998 available at <httpwww.ilo.org>

1999
Resolution Vll.7 Guidelines for Reviewing Laws and Institutions to Promote

the Conservation and Wise Use of wetlands, seventh meeting of the COP (San Jose10-18 may, 1999) at <http://www.ramsar.org/key_res_vii.07e.htm

2001
"ILC Draft Convention on Prevention of Transboundary Environmental Harm from Hazardous Activities" in *Report of the ILC* (2001) 53rd Sess., UN GAOR, A/56/10; (56th Sess., Supp. No. 10, at 370- 436, UN Doc.56/10) 2001

Council Regulation (EC) No. 44/2001 on Jurisdiction and the Recognition and Enforcement of Judgments in Civil and Commercial Matters, (2001) *OJ* L12/1,(latest *consolidated* version in (1998) *OJ* C 27/1)

2002
Plan of Implementation of the WSSD" Report of the WSSD Johannesburg, South Africa, 26 Aug – 4 Sept 2002); UN Doc. A/CONF .199/20 Resolution 2, (Annex at 7-77) also available at <http://www johannesburgsummit.org/ html/documents/summit-docs.html>

Johannesburg Declaration on Sustainable Development, Report of the WSSD Johannesburg, South Africa 26 Aug – 4 Sept 2002), UN Doc A/CONF, 199/20 Resolution 1,(Annex at 1-5) also available at <http://www johannesburgsummit.org/ html/documents/summit-docs.html>

2004
Draft "Hague Convention on Jurisdiction and Foreign Judgments in Civil and Commercial Matters" (negotiated under Hague Conference on Private International Law (HCCH)) available at http://www.cptech.org

United States Foreign Assistance Act (22 U.S.C. § 1291)

United States Alien Tort Claims Act (ATCA) 28 U.S.C.S. § 1350 (Revised 2004)-

LIST OF NATIONAL INSTRUMENTS

1. The Constitution of Sierra Leone (1991), Act No. 6 of 1991,

2. The Mines and Minerals Act (1994), Act No. 5 of 1994

3. The Sierra Rutile Agreement 1989 (Ratification) Act, 1989 (Act No.8) of 1989;

4. The Sierra Rutile Agreement (Ratification) Act (2002), Act No. 4 of 2002

5. Loan Agreement between SRL and the GOSL, dated 2nd August 2004 (Sysmin Agreement)

6. The Bauxite Mineral Prospecting and Mining Agreement Decree 1992

7. The Koidu Kimberlite Project Mining Lease (modification and ratification) Act (2002)

8. The Petroleum Exploration and Production Act (2001), Act No. 11 of 2001

9. The Model Petroleum Agreement of Sierra Leone

10. Penalties (Amendments) of Specified Fines Act (1993) Act No. 9 of 1993

11. The Forestry Act, (1988), Act No. 7 of 1988

12. The Wild Life Conservation Act (1972), Act No. 27 of 1972

13. Provinces Land Act Cap 122, Laws of Sierra Leone

14. Town and Country Planning Act (1946) Cap.81 Act No. 19 of 1946

15. Town and Country Planning (Amendment) Act, (2001), Act No. 3 of 2001

16. Town and Country Planning Act (Amendment) Decree, 1967

17. Statutory Nuisances (Summary Punishment) Act, of 1968

18. Water (Control and Supply) Act (1963) Act No. 16 of 1963

19. Guma Valley Water Act (1961) Act No. 3 of 1961

20. Public Health Act (1960) Act No. 23 of 1960

21. The Forestry Order in Council Cap 189, 1414

22. The Forestry Amendment Order 1981

23. The Forestry (Forest Protection Order in Council) Reserve Orders P.N No. 25 of December 1982

24. Gafele Forest Reserve Order P.N No. 26 of 1982

25. Woa Forest Reserves Order (Kenema district) P.N No. 26 of 1982

26. Tajayei Forest Reserve Order (Kenema District) P.N No. 27 of 1982

27. Mansayei Forest Reserve Order (Kono District) P.N No. 28 of 1982

28. Sierra Leone: Gazette No.100, of 10 March 1995; and Gazette No.43 of 30th July, 1998

29. Sierra Leone: "Assignment of Responsibilities to Ministers" in *The Sierra Leone Gazette*, Vol. CXXXIII, No.47 of 30th July 2002;

30. Mining Lease Agreement between the GOSL and Branch Energy Ltd. Dated 22nd July 1995

31. Mining Lease Agreement between the GOSL and SRL, dated 20th November, 2001